# Critical Issues in Educational Leadership Series
Joseph Murphy, Series Editor

Who Governs Our Schools?
Changing Roles and Responsibilities
DAVID T. CONLEY

School Districts and Instructional Renewal
AMY M. HIGHTOWER, MICHAEL S. KNAPP,
JULIE A. MARSH, AND MILBREY W. MCLAUGHLIN, EDS.

Effort and Excellence in Urban Classrooms:
Expecting—and Getting—Success with All Students
DICK CORBETT, BRUCE WILSON, AND BELINDA WILLIAMS

Developing Educational Leaders: A Working Model:
The Learning Community in Action
CYNTHIA J. NORRIS, BRUCE G. BARNETT,
MARGARET R. BASOM, AND DIANE M. YERKES

Understanding and Assessing the Charter School Movement
JOSEPH MURPHY AND CATHERINE DUNN SHIFFMAN

School Choice in Urban America:
Magnet Schools and the Pursuit of Equity
CLAIRE SMREKAR AND ELLEN GOLDRING

Lessons from High-Performing Hispanic Schools:
Creating Learning Communities
PEDRO REYES, JAY D. SCRIBNER, AND
ALICIA PAREDES SCRIBNER, EDS.

Schools for Sale: Why Free Market Policies
Won't Improve America's Schools, and What Will
ERNEST R. HOUSE

Reclaiming Educational Administration as a Caring Profession
LYNN G. BECK

D1531333

# *Who Governs Our Schools?*

## Changing Roles and Responsibilities

### DAVID T. CONLEY

Teachers College, Columbia University
New York and London

Published by Teachers College Press, 1234 Amsterdam Avenue, New York, NY 10027

*Library of Congress Cataloging-in-Publication Data*

Conley, David T., 1948–
    Who governs our schools? : changing roles and responsibilities / David T. Conley.
       p. cm. — (Critical issues in educational leadership series)
    Includes bibliographical references and index.
    ISBN 0-8077-4332-1 (pbk.) — ISBN 0-8077-4333-X (cloth)
    1. School management and organization—United States.  2. Education and state—United States.  3. Educational change—United States.  I. Title.  II. Series.

  LB2805.C6313 2003
  379.73—dc21                                                          2002038429

ISBN 0-8077-4332-1 (paper)
ISBN 0-8077-4333-X (cloth)

Printed on acid-free paper

Manufactured in the United States of America

10  09  08  07  06  05  04  03      8  7  6  5  4  3  2  1

For Judy, who believes a book is best appreciated when it's finished.

# CONTENTS

*1* SIZING UP THE CHANGING LANDSCAPE OF EDUCATIONAL GOVERNANCE    1
The Rapidly Increasing Federal Influence    2
States Take More Control over Education Policy    3
Other Factors That Shape the State's New Role in Education Policy    6
Implications for State–District Relationships    11
How Will Educators and Local Boards of Education Be Affected?    13
Understanding Who Is in Control of American Education    14

2 THE EVOLUTION OF EDUCATIONAL GOVERNANCE AND THE FEDERAL ROLE    16
Education as a System to Achieve Social Goals:
    Federal Involvement in Education    20
Where Is the Federal Role Heading?    26
Why Has This Increased Federal Role Been Sustainable?    33
The New Federal–State Relationship    34
Will Federal Influence Decrease at Some Future Point?    36

3 POWER TO THE STATES: WHY AND HOW STATES ARE
MORE ACTIVELY SHAPING EDUCATION POLICY    **38**
Increased State Responsibility for Funding and Its
    Relationship with Education Reform    38
Education Reform in the 1980s    42
The State Role in Education Reform in the 1990s    45
Statewide Systemic Reform    53
Beyond the Coleman Report: School Effects on Student Learning    55
New State Expectations for Educational Leaders    58
Linking Funding and Performance: The Next Step    59

4 THE COMPETING FORCES SHAPING GOVERNANCE AND POLICY    **64**
Five Forces Behind State Reforms    65
Nongovernmental Influences on Education Policy,
    Practice, and Governance    75
Education Under Siege?    83

5  WHY IS IT SO DIFFICULT TO IMPLEMENT STATE POLICY
   AT THE SCHOOL LEVEL?                                               84
   The Interplay Between State and Local Levels in Policy Implementation   84
   How Schools Process Reforms                                        88
   Compliance-Oriented Implementation vs.
      Goal-Oriented Implementation                                   91
   Organizational Challenges to Reform Implementation                92
   Rethinking Governance as a First Step Toward
      State–Local Partnerships                                       98

6  ALIGNING POLICY LEVERS                                            103
   Pluses, Minuses, and Limitations of Alignment                     104
   What Are the Levers for System Alignment?                         111
   K–16 Alignment: What Is It and What Does It Look Like?            117
   Alignment: More Energy, Better Results?                           125

7  CHANGES IN ROLES AT THE STATE LEVEL                               126
   The Changing Role and Structure of State Policy Mechanisms        126
   The New Role of State Boards of Education                         130
   The Contradictory Goals of State Education Agencies               132
   Transforming Departments of Education                             134
   The Role of Commissions and Extra-Governmental Agencies           138
   What's Next for the State Level of Governance?                    143

8  CHANGES IN ROLES AT THE DISTRICT LEVEL                            144
   Local Boards of Education                                         144
   Superintendents and Central Offices                               153

9  CHANGES IN ROLES AT THE SCHOOL LEVEL                              159
   Principals                                                        159
   Teachers                                                          163
   The Reluctant Partners                                            177

10 WHAT CHALLENGES AND POSSIBILITIES LIE AHEAD?                      178
   Taking Stock: Where Are We? Where Are We Heading?                 178
   What Are the Longer-Term Implications of Current Trends?          183
   Aligning Governance with Key Values, Goals, and Purposes          188
   Outlines of a New Governance System                               192
   The Pressing Need to Create New Governance Models                 198

REFERENCES                                                           201
INDEX                                                                227
ABOUT THE AUTHOR                                                     239

# *Who Governs Our Schools?*

## Changing Roles and Responsibilities

# Chapter 1

# SIZING UP THE CHANGING LANDSCAPE OF EDUCATIONAL GOVERNANCE

A revolution is taking place. It's not easy to see, and those experiencing it have yet to fathom its full depth and impact. That revolution is the reshaping of power and authority relationships at all levels of the educational governance and policy system. Although this revolution began perhaps 30 years ago, its pace and intensity accelerated during the 1990s. During this time, almost every state has been evolving from a "local control" model of governance and finance, where districts generate and control a significant portion of their operating revenues and instructional programs locally, to a state system of finance, specified standards and content knowledge, and statewide tests and assessments. During this period, the state and federal role in education policy has become increasingly activist, and, when viewed from the local perspective, intrusive.

Nearly every state legislature has assumed more control over school funding and education policy (Hirth, 1996). State assessment systems and accountability systems are being created in nearly every state to provide data on performance and to compare schools (Goertz & Duffy, 2001). In some states these efforts are subtle; in other states they drive education policy (Olson, 1999). Some states have even begun to link funding with expected student learning (Conley, 1999).

Evidence suggests that these policies are beginning to exert influence on the curriculum being taught in schools (Cohen & Hill, 2001; Firestone, Mayrowetz, & Fairman, 1998; Fuhrman, 2001; Jones, Jones, Hardin, Chapman, Yarbrough, & Davis, 1999). Although the effect to date has been modest in many states, the strength and frequency of linkages between standards and assessments, and various rewards and sanctions, in particular, are increasing. As of late 1999, 48 states had statewide academic standards; 39 mandated tests aligned with their standards; 19 required high school exit exams, and eight others were planning to do so (Education Week, 2002).

## THE RAPIDLY INCREASING FEDERAL INFLUENCE

Standards and assessments have moved to stage center in the national arena as well. In fact, national education policy is being crafted around the assumption that standards and assessments are in place in all states and that they are valid measures of student learning and valid tools for comparing states and nations. Such comparisons have become ever more commonplace since Secretary William Bennett began his "Wall Charts" in the 1980s. The nature of the comparisons has become increasingly sophisticated and they have been drawn from more measures over time.

For example, the National Assessment of Educational Progress (NAEP), which was instituted in the 1970s as a way to gauge effects of Great Society education programs, has become an increasingly influential data source documenting the state of American education. The media are beginning to report NAEP results with increasing frequency and to compare their home states with others that participate in NAEP. The Elementary and Secondary Education Act (ESEA) reauthorization of 2001, known as the No Child Left Behind Act of 2001, requires every state to use NAEP scores in reading and math every other year to provide a point of comparison with results of the state's own tests.

International comparisons of curriculum and student performance across national borders have become more sophisticated and increasingly credible. The influence on policy of measures such as the Third International Mathematics and Science Study (TIMSS) has become substantial. A cursory examination of the media coverage TIMSS received in comparison to that accorded the First and Second International Mathematics and Science Studies shows how the audience for these reports has shifted from statisticians and academics to policy makers and the general public. The effects of TIMSS at the state level have been significant as well. Numerous states launched reviews of their math programs, influenced at least in part by their state score and by the TIMSS critique of mathematics teaching in the United States. TIMSS seeks to change state and local education practice, not just report results. Its stated goal is "to identify differences in curriculum and the organization of instruction that may lead to changes in how school systems all over the world organize instruction" (Third International Mathematics and Science Study, 1995).

This type of direct influence on curriculum and instruction emanating from the national level is a new phenomenon. The primary focus of federal education policy during the second half of the 20th century was enhanced equity of educational opportunity via desegregation and equal-rights legislation, like Title IX and the Individuals with Disabilities Education Act (IDEA). Federal legislation focused on large-scale compensatory assistance for students most in need, primarily through ESEA. The federal courts supported this trend as they upheld key provisions of Title IX and IDEA.

These interventions were really part of a larger set of changes in national policies for which the schools were simply the vehicle of implementation. The federal goal was not specifically to reshape education practices or power relationships. In fact, one of the reasons that desegregation was achieved so gradually and with such limited and disappointing effects on the achievement of racial minorities was that the fundamental legitimacy, power, and autonomy of local school districts to design education programs were never seriously questioned. Courts were more prescriptive than was Congress in terms of mandating specific education programs at the local level. State governments, however, remained reluctant to interject themselves into the functioning of local districts.

Current federal education policy has diverse, ambitious goals that pay lip service to local control but have a series of confusing and often contradictory effects on the functioning of schools. However, the cumulative effect of these policies is to insert the federal government into local schools in an ever-widening circle—formally and directly, informally and indirectly—in ways that exert influence over education practices. When combined with state policies that also seek to appropriate the local policy agenda, the available "policy space" within which local schools operate is significantly restricted.

## STATES TAKE MORE CONTROL
## OVER EDUCATION POLICY

The single most important underlying factor in understanding the flow of power from the local to the state level is the transformation in education funding that began in the early 1970s and continues to the present (Odden & Wohlstetter, 1992). Substantive challenges to state funding systems were launched in the early 1970s, a time when equality of opportunity was a key social concern. Differences in resources available to districts that had been racially segregated helped serve as a driver in some lawsuits to establish equitable funding systems. Others were propelled by urban–suburban–rural inequities. The courts were frequently more responsive to equity arguments than were state legislatures. Their decisions spurred governors and legislatures to act, often resulting in the appointment of blue-ribbon commissions charged with making recommendations for fundamental redesign of state finance systems. Few, if any, of these panels recommended changes in governance structures or relationships, and, in fact, finance reform seldom was accompanied by any explicit changes in the roles and responsibilities of the state or of local districts. These suits were so successful in achieving their goals that by the end of the 1970s the contribution of local districts had dropped from 52% to 43%, while the state's contribution to education funding rose from 39% to 47% (Odden & Picus, 2000), a trend that continued throughout the 1980s and, with brief interruption, the 1990s.

## States Begin to Search for a New Relationship with Local Districts

Throughout this period, few explicit changes were made in the governance system. School districts were expected to process state reforms and respond accordingly. While districts gladly accepted increases in funding, they proved less amenable to the accompanying demands embedded in state reform policies. Districts proved more capable of implementing reforms that had dollars specifically targeted to them, could be enacted by adding on programs and staff, and had clear legal consequences to ignoring them. Those that required policy changes, such as new teacher evaluation or career ladder programs, generally were implemented, but with less effect. Reforms whose impacts were more difficult to measure and that required changes in classroom practices, such as new curriculum tied to state assessments, seemed to be most problematic to put into place.

In other words, local districts were largely able to preserve their cultures and structures throughout a period of intense policy activity at the state level and in the courts. Legislatures' increasing influence over local education was occurring without any specific acknowledgment of this phenomenon by state or local policy makers. Legislatures and governors often were unwilling to come to grips with this changing role or preferred not to create tension between the state and local levels by emphasizing the state's new position of dominance.

The evidence suggests that the reforms of the 1980s did have effects, generally in the area of "intensification"—making schools do more of what they already were doing, rather than getting them to do things differently (Grossman, Kirst, & Schmidt-Posner, 1986). The initial exercise of state authority to reform local school practices was played out within the arena of existing practices, assumptions, and relationships. Subsequent reforms began to move outside that arena.

In fact, many states began to implement reforms that devolved power directly to schools. The mid-1980s saw the first attempts by legislatures to change the structural relationship between schools, districts, and the state (Prasch, 1984). This first generation of structural change was based on the transfer of more responsibility to school sites (Guthrie, 1986). The states' initial attempts to resolve their new authority for education by delegating decision making and authority to schools did not yield hoped-for improvements or changes in education. This left states searching for new ways to control education policy and practices.

## States Take Charge in the 1990s

The same forces that drove control of education policy toward the state level in the 1970s and 1980s continued and intensified in the 1990s. Courts continued to overturn school finance systems as inequitable and inadequate. Legislatures continued to mount large-scale reform programs with linkages to funding. Accountability expectations continued to increase. And for the first time, legislatures seemed less reluctant to wade more deeply into the affairs of local districts and to seek ways to ensure that reform goals were achieved.

"Systemic reform" (Fuhrman, 1994) and "coherent policy" (Fuhrman, 1993b) became familiar vocabulary in meetings sponsored by national policy groups such as the Education Commission of the States. The states were going to create programs of reform that addressed all the various interconnected issues necessary to change and ostensibly improve their schools. These programs were to go beyond the piecemeal reforms of the 1980s and provide educators with clear messages about what they needed to do and how they were to be judged successful. The reforms would ensure that all aspects of the educational system were aligned to guarantee that desired goals were achieved. Policy areas like teacher education and licensure, teacher evaluation and dismissal, academic standards and assessments, funding and accountability measures would be linked to create incentives and sanctions that would motivate educators to design effective education programs that met state goals while still retaining local control.

At the same time, the 1990s witnessed the first real wave of disillusionment by legislatures with public education and the initiation of a search for alternatives. The strength of this sentiment varied dramatically from state to state, as did individual motivations and state policy responses. In some cases, legislators used the failed reforms of the 1980s as proof that schools would not change and that the system needed to be abandoned. In other cases, legislators sought to build upon the reforms of the previous decade and to seek new ways to make schools accountable, effective, and efficient. Legislatures developed programs such as charter schools, vouchers, open enrollment, postsecondary options, and others that enabled select groups or categories of individuals to avoid the public schools if they so chose. Legislatures did this without directly addressing governance relationships between the state and school districts. Educators in school districts felt under siege without necessarily comprehending the tectonic shifts in governance that were enabling these state initiatives.

## OTHER FACTORS THAT SHAPE THE STATE'S
## NEW ROLE IN EDUCATION POLICY

A number of factors combine to create momentum for a sustained state focus on education reform. These include a general belief by the public at large that schools need to change; the loss of institutional memory and the tendency to tackle complex issues with simple solutions fueled by term limits in some states; the loss of control of education as a public policy issue that educators suffered over the past 3 decades; the attempts by political parties to capture education as an exploitable political issue and the ensuing increase in partisan education policy; the decrease in the number of small school districts that were not capable of processing complex, demanding state policies; and the emergence of statewide data systems that allow comparisons of schools and districts in ways previously impossible. These and other more idiosyncratic factors combine in states to sustain education reform as a central state policy issue.

### Continuing Public Pressure for Improvement of Schools

The sustained nature of education reform and its continuing position as one of the key policy issues on the national agenda and many state agendas is remarkable. It has been nearly 2 decades since the initial burst of activity around the report *A Nation at Risk* in 1983. Much of this attention led to reforms bred of an optimism that public schools could be dramatically improved via state policy. The limited success of the reforms also has led to increasing impatience by legislators with the pace of educational change and to a public perception that schools generally are not very good.

While most polls conducted throughout the 1990s confirm that people rate schools close to them higher than those more distant (Elam & Rose, 1995; Elam, Rose, & Gallup, 1991; Rose & Gallup, 1999), the broadly held assumption that schools do not work well is fueled by a number of sources, among them, media reports, test scores, and international comparisons; the problems of urban districts in deep distress; public perceptions that teachers' unions protect poor performers; and the subsequent inability of school administrators to remove incompetent teachers. The business community seems to be becoming restive with the pace of change in school systems. Advocates of poor and inner-city students, who previously have focused more often on opportunity to learn than on equality of outcomes, are showing increasing impatience and frustration with the state of urban schools, calling for evidence of improvement in student learning and the closing of the achievement gap that exists between racial and income groups. The net effect is to create an atmosphere in many legislatures where it is permissible and politically profitable to push for increased accountability for schools and for increasingly more radical solutions to the education "problem" when schools don't show improved performance.

## Term Limits

The accelerated turnover of personnel in the 18 state legislatures subject to term limits has led to changes in the way education policy is formulated. Term limits encourage legislators to seek rapid change in schools where results often take years to demonstrate themselves. Shortened institutional memory leads toward a fragmentation of education policy or an emphasis on education-policy-by-anecdote. Fewer legislators have the statewide power base or legitimacy necessary to sponsor legislation that would redefine clearly the governance relationships between state and district. The type of consistency that is necessary to sustain a conscious change in relationships from session to session is more difficult to sustain.

## Appropriation of the Education Agenda by Noneducators

Analyses of interest groups in education before the 1970s indicated that education-related groups were the primary initiators of education policy (Wirt & Kirst, 1989). From the 1970s on, new groups outside education were able to take control of the education issue agenda. Politicians, prominent individuals from outside education and government, and commissions reviewing some aspect of social or economic policy all exerted influence on the shaping of educational issues that made their way onto the policy agenda in states.

Educators found themselves increasingly reacting to the initiatives of these constituencies. Often the voices of educators, particularly lobbyists for educational organizations and interests, were considered the least credible in the hearings and debates surrounding key education policy. A sentiment developed within many legislative committees that educators had had their chance to solve the problem being presented and had failed to do so, and it was now time for others outside of education to offer solutions from a new perspective. The success that teachers' unions had in influencing legislatures to increase education funding during the 1970s and 1980s often became a liability as legislatures swung to more conservative fiscal perspectives. Educators were viewed by many legislators as believing that the only solution to all educational problems was more money, and, generally, more teachers or employees.

## Increasingly Partisan Nature of Education Policy

The Progressive movement at the turn of the twentieth century emphasized nonpartisan governance structures for education. Candidates for local
boards of education were to serve without party affiliation. Professional administrators, like superintendents and principals, were to be selected independent of their political beliefs. State superintendents of public instruction
also were to be elected or appointed on a nonpartisan basis. Legislatures were
to respect this nonpartisan structure and not embroil schools and education
policy in purely partisan politics. In this environment, educators, including
university faculty and administrators, were important generators of policy.
They possessed the legitimacy associated with the label of nonpartisan.

The past 2 decades have seen the emergence of education as a central
political topic in many states as it has become the most important element in
state budgets. Politicians include more specific references to education in their
campaigns. Political parties seek to distinguish their education platforms from
one another. As a result, education policy has moved in the direction of increased partisanship (Sandham, 1999).

Paradoxically, education policy does not lend itself well to the traditional
distinctions between the two political parties. Republicans have found themselves caught in the seemingly contradictory position of supporting local
control and increased state oversight of local districts. Democrats have found
themselves opposing state standards in favor of local decision making. Both
parties find themselves in favor of state intervention into the functioning of
local districts; Republicans for fiscal reasons, Democrats for equity reasons.
Democrats may be found favoring school-to-career programs, which tend
to benefit business, while some Republicans may be adamantly opposed to
them on grounds they represent unwarranted governmental intrusion into
matters best left to families. Republicans may be the sponsors of voucher
and charter school legislation in suburban areas, while Democrats may favor similar measures if they can be tailored to benefit urban students. Bilingual education has made strange bedfellows of conservatives who favor
English-only policies and some immigrants who are not natural constituents
of the Republican party but want their children instructed in English.

Why, then, is education policy becoming more clearly partisan? The
sustained public interest in education over the past 2 decades has made it a
natural political issue, first at the state level, but increasingly at the national
level as well. Polls showed education was the number one issue for voters in
the 2000 elections (Balz & Morin, 2000). Education is an appealing issue
precisely because of the interest it generates among a wide range of voters.

Governors have made education the centerpiece issue in state races,
particularly as more states take control of school finance. They have become

perhaps the most significant new players in education policy (Sandham, 1999). In the past, policy initiatives grew out of the "iron triangle" consisting of the education committee chair and key staffers, department of education staff, and heads of state education organizations (Wirt & Kirst, 2001). With the transfer of fiscal responsibility to the state level, governors' budgets are ever more important tools for shaping schools. This power, combined with the public attention garnered by ongoing education reform, has led many governors to advocate sometimes sweeping programs, often reflecting a particular political philosophy.

One effect of increasing partisanship is to make education policy more controversial as it becomes an arena where competing social agendas vie for dominance. The reaction to education standards in many parts of the country constitutes an example of this phenomenon (Grant, 1997). Additional examples of this phenomenon include "Reading Wars" (Goodman, 1995), which pit whole language against phonics, and school-to-career programs that some view as attempts by government to force youth into the service of business.

Grass-roots opposition to standards arose in many states, seemingly out of nowhere, to object to specific standards, but, more important, to object to the idea in any form (Kannapel, 1995; Pliska & McQuaide, 1994; Rothman, 1992b). Governors, unaccustomed to addressing education policy issues, found themselves having to carve out their positions on education standards, knowing that a great deal politically was riding on their stance. This was a new experience and important precedent for many state chief executives as well as for legislators. In the end, education became more overtly partisan and governors learned how to manage controversial educational policy issues to their political advantage.

## Small-District Consolidation

While not a critical driver, the continuing consolidation of school districts into larger units, particularly in rural areas, provides some additional ability for states to ask more from districts. When a state has numerous small districts with few resources to respond to state mandates, the state is less likely to make demands on districts. But as districts become larger and begin to have more centralized resources or personnel capable of processing new and complex state policies, the state is less restrained in its ability to ask more of districts. Data reporting, school improvement plan development, test score analysis and data disaggregation, and curriculum alignment are all activities much more easily accomplished in a district with a centralized support staff to take on the burden.

Decreasing the number of districts and increasing their size also tends to remove them from contact with their local communities. Local control has less meaning when the board of education meets many miles away and its members are unknown to the community. As districts become larger, the sense that they represent any particular local group is diminished. Less resistance to state control arises because less allegiance to local districts exists.

## More Standardized Data Collection Systems

One of the historical artifacts of local control is nonstandardized reporting of data from schools to the state. Efforts over the past decade have led to standardization in some areas, including such basic demographic information as attendance and dropout rates. But school data have proven notoriously difficult to compare.

This is changing in many states that are on the threshold of understanding school performance in fundamentally new and different ways. Standardized fiscal accounting and reporting systems are leading to expenditure data that can reveal the differences in the ways two schools with comparable student populations allocate their resources. This permits clearer analysis of the effects of instruction.

Assessment systems are becoming more varied and sophisticated, allowing disaggregation of data by student subpopulations, yielding data that can be much more useful in policy formulation. Teacher and school effects can be identified much more distinctly (Pipho, 1998). Each school can be compared not just with others in its district, but with equivalent schools in the state. Local school districts can be held accountable for the performance of their schools. The value-added element of local control can begin to be determined. Public interest groups have organized their own websites with data on school performance, sometimes including comparisons that state education departments have been unwilling to make (Just for the Kids, 2002). Legislatures will have the ability to reach sophisticated conclusions about the relationships between inputs and outputs.

The tendency of legislatures to intervene into the operations of schools will likely increase as this precision increases, although interventions to date have met with decidedly mixed results (Johnston & Sandham, 1999). This will be particularly true if student performance begins to improve as a result of such interventions. Through this combination of relatively sophisticated data and assessment systems, legislatures will attempt to wield fiscal control to improve school performance. They also will be less reticent to mandate instructional techniques and programs.

The most important change that local school boards and superintendents face in their new relationship with the state is that the individual school, not the school district, is now the unit of accountability. States increasingly judge schools on their performance in relation to other schools with comparable student populations, or on improvement from year to year against some established goal (Steffy, 1993). Furthermore, the knowledge and skills students are accountable to master are more explicit, as is the means of assessing these attributes. This information is reported to parents and the community in ways that allow parents and patrons to ascertain the effectiveness of local schools by using common measures of performance and improvement. This information is broadly available publicly via the Internet from companies specializing in analyzing state data and is beginning to influence myriad decisions, within both schools and the larger community. Schools are under increasing pressure to pay attention to data that are in the public domain. Central offices strive to understand their role in this new data-driven environment where the public has the same information as administrators and is aware of real differences among schools and districts.

## IMPLICATIONS FOR STATE–DISTRICT RELATIONSHIPS

When power is transferred in a system, structural changes generally follow. However, a "cognitive lag" can ensue when perceptions of power relations continue to be based on the old model. In many ways, local school districts are beginning to experience both of these phenomena. The effects of the power shifts as well as the lag in perceptions will be felt particularly at the district level because of the strong traditions of local control that exist in American education.

While scholars debate the degree to which the state can control or change its school system (Conley, 1997b; Kirp & Driver, 1995; Tyack, 1974; Tyack & Tobin, 1994), the culture of most school districts remains stubbornly independent from the state. Sarason (1971, 1990) and others (Klecker & Loadman, 1996) have noted the strength and ability of local school cultures to thwart or redirect the best intentions of the state.

The first attempts by states to restructure governance relationships faltered, but states have not given up attempting to manage their school systems. States continue to experiment with the policy tools they have, combining incentives and sanctions, increasing and decreasing regulation. Schools continue to process state policies in ways that allow school cultures to maintain themselves, particularly when the reforms come close to the classroom.

Local school districts exist in principle to serve the goals of the state. Historically, states sought to nurture local control. The states' goals are now shifting. States continue to increase their emphasis on fiscal accountability and enhanced achievement for all students. They have more explicit goals for schools and schooling. How to achieve the proper balance between centralization and decentralization, and how to blend state incentives and sanctions for maximum effect remain elusive objectives in most states.

Many strategies have been attempted by states during the past 20 years to energize or compel school improvement, with only modest success. The next generation of strategies will likely focus more on the outputs of education than on inputs or methods. The existence of a framework for student performance based on standards, along with data on school functioning, creates a new dynamic between the state and schools. In this new dynamic, legislators know more about the performance and effectiveness of schools on a comparative and absolute basis. They can begin to establish or infer cause-and-effect relationships between state policies and student learning outcomes. They are just beginning to learn how to develop and exploit this newly emerging power to their best advantage.

Educators and local school boards that assume that nothing about the relationship between local districts and the state has changed will find themselves increasingly frustrated and bewildered. They will be less able to adapt to new forms of competition or other policies that require the ability to comprehend the state's new power and goals. Education policy is turning a corner, and educators who have lost sight of this occurrence will have difficulty orienting themselves to an increasingly turbulent and demanding environment.

What options does state government have if it chooses to change its relationship with a loosely coupled system of schools (Weick, 1976) that have strong cultures and histories of local control? The range is quite wide, and states have tried almost every available lever to date.

The application of state policies has occurred in an environment in which the sanctity of local control, and its desirability, is a given. Even in situations where states have intervened in school districts to take them over, the goal has been to return local control as soon and as completely as possible. The contradiction underlying this use of state policy levers is that the state is assuming the existence of a governance and power relationship that is rapidly changing, but is not providing much clear direction to schools on what the new relationship between state and schools should be.

State education departments are constrained in their ability to be useful bridging mechanisms by their long histories as monitoring agencies. States turn increasingly to single-topic commissions to guide them in their assumption of power from local districts. Washington State, for example, established the Commission on Student Learning to develop its learning standards and the statewide assessment system to accompany them. The state later created a commission on school accountability charged with developing a system of school accountability, complete with incentives and sanctions. Kentucky's ambitious education reform program was undertaken as a result of the work of the Prichard Committee for Academic Excellence, whose recommendations helped set the stage for legislation that essentially closed down the existing department of education and replaced it with a new one (Steffy, 1992, 1993).

States do have powerful tools to get the attention of schools, and they have been employing them with increasing frequency and impact. Most important among these are accountability systems that include both public reporting of school performance and provisions for rewards and sanctions for schools and even for individual administrators and teachers. These tools tend to tighten somewhat the historically loosely coupled relationship between state, local school districts, and individual schools. Simultaneously, more communication is being generated locally and is traveling up the system to the state policy-making process. This two-way flow of information also helps states move schools in directions that are mutually desirable.

## HOW WILL EDUCATORS AND LOCAL BOARDS OF EDUCATION BE AFFECTED?

Whenever states make significant changes in education policy, the principal's role is likely to be affected. Current policies in areas such as accountability and assessment are resulting in the principal becoming as responsible to the state as to the local superintendent and board of education. States are judging school success and effectiveness by making comparisons among schools hundreds of miles apart. The ability to bring about improvement will be the key skill for principals whose schools are being rated against state expectations even more than local criteria.

Superintendents and their central office staffs will be called upon to facilitate and support improvement on a school-by-school basis, rather than simply to control subordinates and standardize operating procedures. In some senses superintendents will be much more dependent on principals than they are now for job security and professional success. If principals are not successful, superintendents will not appear effective.

Local boards of education will be challenged in many ways. They will find it difficult to understand where their authority ends and the state's begins. They will be accountable, but little will happen to them if their schools fail to improve. They will have to become adept at making the best personnel decisions possible to ensure that the district and its schools have the leadership needed to enable improvement. They will have to learn to allocate resources in ways that enable schools to improve, in place of micromanaging the operations of the district.

Teachers face the most direct effects of this changing policy environment and at the same time are somewhat more insulated from it. Aside from states like Kentucky, California, and North Carolina that have offered bonuses to schools and then to teachers for improved performance, teachers view reform policy, at least initially, as distant from their practice, even when the state is explicit about the changes it desires in classroom teaching (Cohen & Hill, 2001; Conley & Goldman, 1995, 1998; Goldman & Conley, 1997). And yet the behaviors of teachers have the most direct effects on student learning.

Simultaneous with increased state control and heightened accountability, deregulation, charter schools, voucher plans, and other related policy initiatives present a different sort of challenge to educators (Elmore & Fuhrman, 1995; Johnston, 1996b; Ladd, 1996). Educators must compete not only with one another but also with a new class of school that plays by somewhat different rules.

## UNDERSTANDING WHO IS IN CONTROL OF AMERICAN EDUCATION

An emerging body of policy research comprising case studies of states and individual schools, and interview and survey studies of educators' reactions to reform provides a framework for considering in a systematic fashion the issues outlined in this chapter. This research suggests the ways in which educational practices, perceptions, and organizational structures are affected in this new environment.

The remainder of this book draws upon this research base and other sources to explore in greater depth and specificity the concepts and trends introduced in this chapter. These ideas all require greater explication to understand fully their implications for the policy process and for practitioners. Chapter 2 explores the evolution of the federal role, examining how it has expanded, why it is likely not to decrease, and what the new federal–state partnership may look like. Chapter 3 considers the reasons states are more actively engaged in shaping education policy. Increased state control over education funding and the push for greater equality of educational outcomes have led to much more education policy activity by states focused on measurable educational improvement. Chapter 4 examines a range of forces that interact to shape education policy and the governance of public education. America's decentralized education system is subject to influence from many places, including the public at large, the business community, and nongovernmental organizations with significant power and responsibility. Chapter 5 discusses the reasons it is difficult for state policy to be implemented by schools. Since schools and school districts were not organized in the first place to be responsive to state policy, their new role as the engines for state reforms is problematic in many respects. Chapter 6 presents the concept of alignment and weighs its pros and cons. States have many policy levers available to them to get the educational system to line up around state goals, but there are costs associated with pulling those levers. Alignment between high schools and colleges, in particular, is a new area for state policy. Chapters 7, 8, and 9 are oriented toward those who work in educationalal organizations. The effects of increased state and federal control on all the players in the educational governance system, from state to local, are reviewed. These chapters conclude that no role will be the same as it has been historically and that school boards probably should be viewed as the "losers" in terms of power and control. They face the challenge of redefining themselves if they wish to continue to be important elements in the governance of American education. The book concludes with Chapter 10, which sums up many of the arguments presented throughout the previous chapters and suggests the possible directions educational governance may take in this country. It concludes by reiterating the pressing need to adapt current governance models and create new ones in response to the expectations and goals now being applied to public education.

The goal of the book is to enable the reader to understand better the dynamics that have triggered a changing relationship between schools and state. This will allow the reader to be prepared to cope and adapt successfully as the educational governance system evolves.

# Chapter 2

# THE EVOLUTION OF EDUCATIONAL
# GOVERNANCE AND THE FEDERAL ROLE

To understand the governance structure of American education that has evolved since the arrival of Europeans in North America, but especially since the adoption of the Constitution, it is necessary to understand the conception of government and the role of government held at that time. It can be summarized in the following fashion: The powers of a centralized government should be limited, and centralized power eventually leads to loss of liberty and freedom. From this basis American public education evolved over the past 2 centuries.

The governance structure of the American educational system is very much not the norm when viewed in relation to countries around the world. The distinguishing feature of the American system has been the degree of decentralization and the highly limited role of the central government. Most national education systems tend to have a much larger role for the central government (Schmidt & Prawat, 1999). Generally this derives from the fact that the educational system was organized originally by the central government or that a significant portion of funds for the system derive from the central level. In addition, and perhaps more important, most nations have a history of establishing the goals for their educational system centrally.

The history of education in the United States is the history of a locally organized, locally funded, and locally governed enterprise. This occurred in part because as education arose in the colonies, there was no centralized government close at hand to oversee the development of an educational system. Additionally, education in the newly developing colonies often was linked to religious groups, which shunned central intervention into education. American education from the beginning was open to more students (although by no means all) than its British counterpart. Funding was entirely local, as was choice of curriculum, employment of teachers, and organization of school schedules. As the power of states increased, their formal authority to oversee public education was written into their constitutions. Their role tended to be highly circumscribed, however. They had no army of inspectors visiting schools. States had neither the resources nor inclination to monitor local educational practices closely.

The authority for states to govern education is often traced to the tenth amendment to the Constitution, also known as the "enumeration clause," which states: "The powers not delegated to the United States by the Constitution, nor prohibited by it to the States, are reserved to the States respectively, or to the people."

For most of the past 200 years local educational entities have wielded the lion's share of power to determine education policies and practices. The 1647 Act of Massachusetts General Court required all towns to establish schools. This responsibility is stated in the "1648 Lauues and Liberties of Massachusetts" in the following fashion:

> Forasmuch as the good education of children is of singular behoof and benefit to any Common-wealth; and wheras many parents & masters are too indulgent and negligent of their duty in that kinde. It is therfore ordered that the Select men of everie town, in the severall precincts and quarters where they dwell, shall have a vigilant eye over their brethren & neighbours, to see, first that none of them shall suffer so much barbarism in any of their families as not to indeavour to teach by themselves or others, their children & apprentices so much learning as may inable them perfectly to read the english tongue, & knowledge of the Capital Lawes: upon penaltie of twentie shillings for each neglect therin.

The responsibility to educate was upon the family "to teach by themselves or others, their children and apprentices." The goal was a secular one: to ensure everyone could read English and understand the laws of the state. The state had no formal role in the enforcement of these requirements. It was left to local governments to enact them.

Pennsylvania, in its 1682 Frames of Government document, acknowledged the state's responsibility to specify education for all in order to help ensure at least economic survival.

> That all children, within this province, of the age of twelve years, shall be taught some useful trade or skill, to the end none may be idle, but the poor may work to live, and the rich, if they become poor, may not want.

Regional differences toward educational governance did exist, but they generally concerned the degree of local discretion, not a fundamental distinction between state and local control. Even southern states, with their more centralized educational governance systems, still had more local control than most other countries in the world.

The period of time from the founding of the first local schools through the mid-1800s was one of relatively little change in educational governance. Schools were locally run or affiliated with or operated by churches. When the notion of the Common School, as promoted by Massachusetts chief education official, Horace Mann, occurred beginning in the 1840s, its purpose, as its name implies, was to develop common learning and cultural values. Although local control was a central component, the result was not a highly diverse educational system, even though local districts in principle could organize around whatever set of practices they wished and pursue the goals they set, within very broad state guidelines.

Local control in the mid- to late 1800s did serve some of the needs of communities that often had substantial differences in language, culture, and religion. If a strong state system of education had been in place, the temptation inevitably would have been to standardize the values and beliefs that were taught in the schools. The absence of a strong state force allowed local schools to maintain community values and practices, while core values remained remarkably constant across the nation. For example, instruction in the parents' native tongue was not unusual in schools throughout rural areas where concentrations of immigrants with common language heritage were found, but the values being taught tended to be distinctly American.

Local control in the post-Reconstruction era also led to racially segregated schooling as well as to widespread discrimination toward immigrants. The state had no effective means and little motivation to intervene. When states or the federal government did attempt to intervene, local communities simply created separate school systems or private academies. State control did not effectively override local control even in this extreme situation. States and the federal government did not effectively address these inequities at least in part because local control of education was so ingrained into the governance structure and political system.

The Progressive Era of political and social reform, which occurred around the turn of the twentieth century, served to restructure and renew local control by removing education from local partisan politics to a significant degree. The size of school boards was reduced, and fewer members were elected at large. Elections were nonpartisan, board members were volunteers, and a professional superintendent and principals were appointed to run the daily business of the district. Patronage was dramatically limited, and politicians could not reward supporters with jobs in schools. Education reflected the values of board members, who tended to be upper middle class and socially conservative. Professional administrators were also conservative people who were paragons of local values in their demeanor, behavior, and lifestyle as well as in their actions. This was the result that the Progressives had in mind for local educational governance.

Popkewitz (1991) asserts that the primary reason state oversight of local schools was not necessary throughout much of American history was that common values were so strong that schools reflected similar attitudes toward the state without close supervision. Values such as American republicanism, bourgeois thinking, Protestantism, and meritocracy were broadly accepted and rarely questioned. Unfortunately, so was discrimination toward a range of groups including racial minorities, immigrant children, girls, and those with disabilities.

The same messages tended to emanate from government, religion, business, and the professions. These pervasive values could be found in the policies enacted by small school districts in the midwest. They could be found in big-city newspaper editorials, as well as in the lectures of university professors or the programs offered by local women's clubs. These values were so widely held that there was no need for government to intervene into education policy. Most everyone operated within a constrained set of beliefs about the role and purposes of a public education system, which allowed similar policies and structures to be implemented in a wide range of settings.

This consensus began to dissolve in the post-World War II era as issues of racial equality moved to the top of the national policy agenda and as the composition and fiscal needs of urban districts sharply diverged from those of their suburban and rural counterparts. Equity issues could be taken up effectively only at the national level, and the complex problems of urban districts, tied to equity and resource issues, quickly overwhelmed the capacity of local districts and states to generate solutions.

Education funding derived primarily from local property taxes in most states. Districts maintained that taxes levied locally should remain at the local level, and decisions about the use of those monies also should be made locally. These practices led to widespread differences among schools and school districts in terms of the resources available to them and the salaries and programs they could offer. These discrepancies were considered acceptable when education was strictly a matter of local concern.

However, local financing became a *de facto* tool for retaining and reinforcing racial and class inequality. Rich communities had little incentive to see poorer districts get more resources, and poor communities had no realistic way to increase their funds other than raise their property tax burden to unsustainable levels. The locally levied property tax functioned to create and sustain dramatic inequalities among districts, which helped contribute to unequal educational opportunities and outcomes.

The intensity and depth of the structural inequalities that existed in post-war American society demanded action by the only level of government capable of responding to such profound issues. The stage was set for greatly increased federal leadership and initiative in education policy, a mandate the federal government has fulfilled and expanded over the past 35 years.

## EDUCATION AS A SYSTEM TO ACHIEVE SOCIAL GOALS: FEDERAL INVOLVEMENT IN EDUCATION

The public school system has always served to achieve social goals as well as to provide education. As noted earlier, colonies passed laws requiring that students be trained so that they might be gainfully employed. American education was based on the instrumental values of learning and from the beginning included at least some students from a variety of class backgrounds. While certain groups were systematically excluded from education, the American model did not parallel that of Europe where education was still for the elite and primarily was an end in itself.

The federal government's role has always been subordinate to that of the states. This does not mean that the federal role has not been important. Federal intervention to achieve equity goals in particular has served to shape the overall values and goals of the educational system. Federal interest and involvement in education stems from at least four goals: promotion of democracy, assurance of equality of educational opportunity, enhancement of national productivity, and strengthening of national defense (Center on Education Policy, 2000).

### Job Training Goals

Many examples exist to demonstrate that the American educational system has served as a tool to achieve social goals at the national level. One of the earliest was the Smith–Hughes Act, which was enacted in 1917 at a time when American industry needed more skilled workers and when child labor laws effectively restricted the presence of children in the workplace. The Act provided federal support for vocational education "for the purpose of cooperating with the states in paying the salaries of teachers, supervisors, and directors of agricultural subjects, and of teachers of trade and industrial subjects."

The Vocational Education Act of 1963 broadened the scope of federal aid to and direction of vocational and technical education programs. Each state was required to submit a plan to the U.S. Commissioner of Education in order to be eligible for federal funds, which more than quadrupled between 1964 and 1967. The emphasis of this Act was a social goal, enhancing the probability of gainful employment for the maximum number of citizens. Its purpose was not to influence or control education policy at the local level or to improve schooling in some systematic fashion.

## National Security Goals

The 1957 National Defense Education Act represented a significant racheting up of federal involvement in education. The goal of the Act ostensibly was to heighten national security through strengthening of specific education programs, although its developers believed explicitly in an enlarged federal role in education. The Act was designed to produce more engineers, scientists, and people adept at foreign languages. Although the Act did not involve the federal government directly in the operation of schools, it did serve to direct education policy and curriculum at both the postsecondary and K–12 levels by providing loans and fellowships to college students and school teachers interested in specific areas of study that the federal government deemed important to national security. The linkage between national priorities and the educational system was reinforced, and the precedent for a federal education policy was more firmly established.

## Economic Equality Goals

All previous efforts by the federal government to achieve social goals through public education were dwarfed by the Elementary and Secondary Education Act of 1965. This piece of legislation was the single most significant advancement of federal authority in education to that point. The law led to the creation of a federal education bureaucracy and the capture of state education bureaucracies, which were financed to implement federal policy. The goal was to eradicate poverty by focusing federal resources on the poor so that they might utilize education as a stepping-stone to a better life. In practice, the program sought to achieve multiple political goals, including fiscal equalization and mollification of the South as it struggled with school desegregation, although the law did not address these issues directly. Once again, the federal government did not attempt to influence or control education practice or local decision making directly, only to ensure that specific students were provided specific services, the means of provision being left to local discretion.

## Racial Integration Goals

Perhaps the most significant social goal schools have been asked to achieve is racial integration of American society. Schools have been under continuous pressure to desegregate from the late 1950s through the present.

In the 1970s, they became the focal point for gender equity and for the rights of people with disabilities. In short, schools have been the vehicle by which greater social equality has been pursued. Legislation designed to achieve these same goals in the workplace generally paralleled or preceded school equity legislation and, it can be argued, has been more effective in moving society toward equity goals. The more important point in this context is that in no case was the federal goal the systematic or systemic improvement of teaching and learning; it was the achievement of greater equality of opportunity for groups that previously had been the victims of discrimination that limited their chance to participate fully in American society, economically and socially. Federal efforts at system improvement were primarily in service of these equity goals.

## From Goals to Rules

Broad goals of this nature generally cannot be achieved by simply passing legislation and hoping that all the nation's school districts transform themselves in ways that lead to achievement of legislative goals. This was certainly the case with an American educational system deeply rooted in local control traditions. The result of these tensions was ever increasing specification of the federal role. Rules and regulations followed each piece of federal legislation.

The passage in 1975 of Public Law 94-142, the Education for All Handicapped Children Act, represented the culmination of federal rule making for local school districts. The law itself required 23 pages in the U.S. Code, and its goals were very broad—a "free appropriate public education" that met the "unique needs" of all handicapped children. States had to submit detailed plans to qualify for federal assistance. The procedures local districts had to follow were highly specified, including how to identify the handicapped, the types of facilities, personnel and services to be utilized, parental notification and participation requirements, record-keeping methods, and state reporting formats. Never before had local schools been subjected to such detailed federal direction and oversight.

## Roots of Current Federal Policy Goals

The current objectives of federal education policy were shaped in the 1980s. The 1983 report, *A Nation at Risk*, was unprecedented in its blanket critique and condemnation of the American educational system. No previous federal report had challenged the effectiveness of schools, and by implication of school boards and local control, to the degree this report did. The report served as a catalyst for widespread state policy action and local self-examination. States launched into a period of unprecedented legislative activity that sought to improve educational quality. As will be discussed later, the reasons the states felt entitled and obligated to engage in these reforms were complex and multidimensional. However, *A Nation at Risk* is widely credited with igniting state action.

## Economic Productivity as an Underlying Concern

As U.S. economic productivity continued to lag in the 1980s and the nation struggled to compete with resurgent Japanese and European economies, attention turned to the attitudes, skills, and preparation of American workers as one of the causes of the apparent deterioration of American economic superiority. Business groups at the national level, in particular, led the call for better schools (Committee for Economic Development, 1985, 1987), as did other groups with memberships beyond the business community, such as the National Center on Education and the Economy (Commission on the Skills of the American Work Force, 1990). These groups conducted studies and published analyses that pointed out the inadequacies of American education, and the apparent lack of will or ability to improve the system. The reports culminated with the 1991 report of the Secretary's Commission on Achieving Necessary Skills (SCANS), in 1991, a blueprint for what American students should know how to do to be ready for the work world. While reformers rarely pinpointed the decentralized nature of American educational governance as the problem, their critiques clearly implied that a decentralized system was anachronistic, given the view that education would prepare a national workforce for international economic competition.

## Outlines of a New Federal Role Become Clear

These reports formed the backdrop for the 1989 Education Summit in Charlottesville, Virginia, where then-President George Bush convened all the nation's governors. For the first time in history, the governors met with the president to discuss education policy and to consider the creation of national education goals. The importance and magnitude of the decision by a president to convene this meeting and the willingness of governors to attend illustrate how much education policy leadership had already moved out of districts and even individual states. The fact that the president was from the Republican party, which normally opposes the expansion of federal authority into areas traditionally reserved to the state and local levels, demonstrates a changing alignment of assumptions and roles in education policy formulation.

The content of the goals themselves was not as important as the fact that they were developed and endorsed by the meeting participants, the nation's governors, who normally are notoriously suspicious of federal intervention into state policy arenas. While nominally leaving control of goal implementation in the hands of the states, the act of creating goals at a national level opened the door to a much more activist federal role in education policy. The succeeding administration would seize upon that role and expand it far beyond what the initiators of the goals had in mind. The individual driving this ever more ambitious federal role was himself a former governor and one of the key participants in the Charlottesville meeting—then-Arkansas Governor Bill Clinton.

## How Federal Policies Affect Local Practices

While it is true that no national curriculum has been established and attempts at national assessments have been blunted, the scope of federal education policy has been extended dramatically. The national government now feels free to examine educational functioning, effectiveness, and methods. For example, the Comprehensive School Reform Demonstration Program (also known as the Obey-Porter bill) (McQueen, 1998) created a pilot program that required Title I schools that applied for funds to comply with nine specific components, including using instructional practices that had "reliable evidence of effectiveness" and "a theoretical or research foundation" (U.S. Department of Education, 2000).

In the same year that Obey-Porter was passed, Congress also authorized the Reading Excellence Program (Office of Elementary and Secondary Education, 2001), which subsequently was incorporated into the No Child Left Behind Act of 2001. The stated goal was to improve "K–3 instruction in elementary schools that serve the nation's neediest children through the use of scientifically based reading research" (Office of Elementary and Secondary Education, 2001). The two programs offered states more than $400 million annually as enticement to employ reading strategies that met federal standards and criteria.

Federal programs in 2000 covered a broad range with potential effects on many aspects of local education practice. These include Class-Size Reduction, 21st Century Community Learning Centers, Technology Literacy Challenge Fund, Safe and Drug-Free Schools, Public Charter Schools Program, Advanced Placement Incentive Program (AP), Preparing Tomorrow's Teachers to Use Technology Program (Pt3), the Learning Anytime Anywhere Partnerships (LAAP), and New American High Schools.

The ability of the federal government and its bureaucracy to shape the content of a child's educational experience is clearly increasing, and this transfer of power is occurring without much real resistance from state legislatures and governors or local school boards and school administrators.

In fact, much of it is being encouraged because of the funding that accompanies the programs.

A seeming contradiction to this trend was the Education Flexibility Partnership Demonstration Program, commonly referred to as Ed-Flex, a pilot program that allowed 12 states to qualify for waivers from a range of federal rules and regulations (Office of Elementary and Secondary Education, 1998). The program's goal was to reduce the federal presence in states and local districts to encourage greater local innovation, change, and improvement. In practice, Ed-Flex has not resulted in the removal of the most troublesome of federal requirements, and many states proved incapable of creating the plans required by the law. Even when federal policies could be waived, state policies often stood in the way of districts' efforts to gain greater flexibility (Joyner, 1999).

Ed-Flex was not the first time the federal government had promised to decentralize control of its programs to the states only to end up taking greater control as local authorities remained wary that they would have any true latitude to modify federal programs. The 1981 Education Consolidation and Improvement Act (ECIA) promised to devolve elements of the administration of federal programs to the state and local levels and allow states and districts greater flexibility in constructing such programs with federal funds. The ECIA combined funds from a range of previous federal programs into a block grant that was to be targeted to school improvement programs. However, the total amount of the block grants was lower than the programs they replaced, which meant local programs previously dependent on federal funds could only be maintained, not enhanced, while some elements of the ECIA reduced services in nearly all school systems. Certain areas of the country and specific groups of students, namely, poor and minority students, felt a disproportionately negative impact from the implementation of block grants under the ECIA (Verstegen, 1984). Flexibility, under this approach, proved illusory.

Compliance standards and decision-making processes were unclear. State education officials felt they lacked direction from the U.S. Department of Education. In practice, deregulation ended up being minimal. In fact, the lack of specificity resulted in additional centralized decision making as states deferred to the federal government in areas where they were unsure how to proceed. The ECIA served in many respects to devolve responsibility to the states at the same time that it withheld the ability of states to take substantive control over federal programs (Darling-Hammond & Marks, 1983).

A more fundamental problem with waiving federal regulations is that most relate to equity issues and others have strong bases in case law. Waiving these regulations could result in students being treated less equitably or in lawsuits against districts. Regardless of waivers, the federal government retains a strong and influential place in state and local school policy, particularly around a broad and expanding range of issues related to equitable treatment of and opportunities for all students.

## WHERE IS THE FEDERAL ROLE HEADING?

Where is the federal role likely to head in this jigsaw system of national education policy and governance? Every indication is that it will become a much more significant shaper of policies and practices through several leverage points it can exercise over states and local school districts. Kaestle (Goertz & Duffy, 2001) points out that "while the trajectory of federal involvement in education was generally upward from 1958 to 1978, it was always bumpy, contested terrain. And from the late 1970's to the present, each administration has had to reinvent the federal role in education." Each subsequent reinvention has resulted in expanded federal influence and extended federal authority.

### Use of the Bully Pulpit, Data, and the National Media

Over the past 15 years, the use of the presidency and secretary of education position as a "bully pulpit" to highlight key education policy issues has increased dramatically. A truly national media came into being with the rise of radio, but did not take on its current level of influence until the arrival of television. The media and the nation now pay a great deal of attention to utterances from Washington. Before the early 1980s, the problems of public education were periodically the focus of statements by national leaders, for example, during the Sputnik era when American deficiencies in math and science were decried, but the emphasis on education reform that began with the 1983 release of the *Nation at Risk* report has continued until the present, in no small measure due to the attention given these issues by federal officials with their ready access to national media.

What is new is the increasing quantity and quality of data regarding the state of education nationally and in the states. This information lends itself to a steady stream of reports and findings that detail the limitations and drawbacks of the current educational system. Similarly, data-driven international comparisons of student performance have risen to a level of sophistication and visibility far beyond what initially was envisioned for them. This sort of data provide a ready platform for national pronouncements about education policy, to which states must then respond, either through studies, programs, or simple rejection of the conclusions presented.

The net effect is to put states in the position of reacting to initiatives from the national level, thereby making it more challenging for states to mount programs that ignore the areas suggested by the national reports. States that do initiate reforms in response to national policy initiatives may find their programs highlighted nationally and showered with attention (and often funding). This may be true whether or not the methods in question have been thoroughly tested and proven. This represents one more way the federal government influences the formation of state-level education policy.

### Leveraged Federal Dollars

The federal government will continue to have significant influence through its use of leveraged dollars. These are funds that may constitute only a small portion of a school district's or state's education budget but may require significant change in education policies or practices as a condition of receiving the funds.

The best example of this is the original version of Title I of ESEA, which ostensibly targeted funds to schools with large concentrations of students from low-income families. In practice, most schools receive at least some Title I monies. With these funds comes a range of requirements. One of the most significant is that the progress of Title I students must be evaluated in reading and math and that these results must be reported to state education departments. This policy alone has served as the basis for subsequent state actions to identify low-achieving schools and has caused districts to look more closely at the learning of students in those schools. Goertz (2001a) notes that by aligning Title I with state standards-based reform policies, the federal government has in effect embedded in state performance and accountability systems incentives to provide a quality education to poor, low-achieving children. These policies also have led to a bending of the curriculum to test preparation in some schools, a practice now being emulated by more schools in states with high-stakes assessments (Firestone et al., 1998).

### The New Title I: "No Child Left Behind" Extends the Federal Reach

The one piece of legislation that has extended the federal hand most dramatically is the 2001 reauthorization of ESEA, known as the No Child Left Behind Act of 2001. Its requirements for mandatory assessments in grades 3–8 and an additional test in grade 10, 11, or 12 apply to all states that receive federal funds and, by extension, to all schools in those states. While the law's accountability standards and consequences for schools that do not meet adequate achievement levels apply only to schools receiving Title I funds, it will be difficult for states to create one accountability system for Title I schools and an entirely different one for the rest of their schools. In practice, the law will shape accountability provisions nationwide. In one fell swoop, the American educational system became federalized to an unprecedented degree. The ramifications will be felt over the course of the current decade and beyond, if this policy direction is sustained.

The 2001 reauthorization of ESEA, a massive document over 1,100 pages in length, uses federal funds as the lever to require states to adopt policies or to induce them to undertake programs or activities over a truly breathtaking array of policy areas, ranging from rules defining how states that accept the funds must test students to a prohibition against schools banning the Boy Scouts or any "patriotic society" access to schools for after-school meetings (Robelen, 2002a).

The most important and far-reaching elements of the bill are the annual testing provisions, related academic achievement requirements, and consequences for schools that do not meet standards. By the 2005–06 school year, all states must begin administering annual, statewide assessments in reading and mathematics for grades 3–8. States may select and design their own assessments, but the tests must be aligned with state academic standards. By 2007–08, states must implement science assessments to be administered once during elementary, middle, and high school. A sample of fourth and eighth graders in each state must participate in the National Assessment of Educational Progress in reading and math every other year to provide a point of comparison for the state's results on its own tests. Test results must include individual student scores and be reported by race, income, and other categories to measure not just overall trends, but also gaps between, and progress of, various subgroups.

All states must develop a definition of academic proficiency that all students must meet by 2014. States must set a minimum performance threshold based on the lowest-achieving demographic subgroup, or the lowest-achieving schools in the state, whichever is higher. Each state must raise the level of proficiency gradually, but in equal increments over 10 years, leading to 100% proficiency. The minimum threshold must be raised at least once every 3 years. In addition to reading and math assessments, the states must use one other academic indicator; for high schools, that must be graduation rates.

If a school receiving Title I funds fails to make adequate progress for 2 consecutive years, the school will receive technical assistance from the district and must provide public school choice. After a third year of failure to make adequate progress, the school also will be required to offer supplemental educational services chosen by students' parents, including private tutoring. The district must use up to 5% of its Title I money to pay for that option. The district may use an additional 10% of its Title I aid to pay for public school transportation costs or supplemental services. If the school fails to make adequate progress for 4 consecutive years, the district must implement corrective actions, such as replacing certain staff members or adopting a new curriculum. After 5 years of inadequate progress, the school would be identified for reconstitution and be required to set up an alternative governance structure, such as reopening as a charter school or turning its operation over to the state.

Other provisions of the law similarly extend a federal version of education policy that will affect state policies and district procedures. Several examples help illustrate the breadth of the law's requirements for states and schools.

Beginning with the 2002–03 school year, all states must provide annual report cards with a range of information, including statewide student achievement data broken down by subgroup and information on the performance of school districts in making adequate yearly progress. Districts also must provide similar report cards, including district-wide and school-by-school data.

All teachers hired under Title I must be "highly qualified." In general, under the law, "highly qualified" means that a teacher has been certified (including alternative routes to certification) or licensed by a state and has demonstrated a high level of competence in the subjects that he or she teaches. By the end of the 2005–06 school year, every public school teacher must be "highly qualified." Within 3 years of hire, all paraprofessionals paid with Title I money must have completed at least 2 years of college, obtained an associate's or higher degree, or met a rigorous quality standard established at the local level.

The "Reading First" provisions of the law provide help to states and districts in setting up "scientific, research-based" reading programs for children in grades K–3. States may use up to 20% of the money to provide professional development for teachers of grades K–3, among other options. States must distribute at least 80% of the money to districts through a competitive-grant process, giving priority to high-poverty areas. Other provisions seek to help 3- to 5-year-olds prepare to learn to read and enhance reading readiness for children in high-poverty areas and areas where a high number of students are not reading at grade level.

To ensure that teachers are available and trained to help improve student achievement, the law provides funds that can be used for a variety of purposes, such as hiring teachers to limit class sizes, providing professional development, and funding initiatives to retain highly qualified teachers. Funds for technology are provided that also can be used for a variety of purposes, such as improving access to technology and expanding professional development. Districts must use at least 25% of the money for professional development, unless they can show that they already provide such services.

In the governance arena, the law creates "flexibility demonstration projects" for up to 150 districts that may enter into performance agreements with the federal Department of Education, under which they could consolidate all aid from several major ESEA programs, excluding Title I. The department will review their performance annually. Up to seven states may consolidate all state-administration and state-activity funding under several major ESEA programs, including Title I. Funds also are authorized to help states and localities support charter schools.

To make certain that no stone goes unturned or district unaffected, the law authorizes funds for flexible grants to small, rural districts and specifies that schools must provide military recruiters access to students, and that, as a condition of receiving federal aid, all districts must certify that no policy "prevents or otherwise denies participation in constitutionally protected prayer in public schools."

### Title II's Effects on Teacher Education

Title II of the Higher Education Amendments of 1998 leverages the policy impact of federal funds through grants to states to upgrade their teacher education programs. These grants can have significant influence on teacher preparation in part by causing states to examine practices more closely and to gather data, sometimes for the first time, on the effectiveness of these programs, the characteristics of their graduates, and the qualifications of their faculty.

An examination of the state-level Title II grants indicates the federal intent to promote greater alignment between state academic content standards and teacher preparation programs. In this way the federal emphasis on high content standards for students is carried over and integrated into state education systems, thereby strengthening the likelihood the federal initiatives will be implemented in those states that already have adopted a policy direction consistent with federal policy. Few states appear likely to alter their basic education policy to receive a Title II grant, but for those that had complementary policies, the Title II grants serve to accelerate the alignment of state and federal education policy goals.

Goertz (2001a) asserts that "the success of this new generation of federal education policies depends, however, upon the willingness of states and localities to enact policies that reflect federal objectives." Federal policy is at once both an expression of state policies and an expansion of them. Almost everything contained in the sweeping ESEA reauthorization of 2001 has been attempted by some states, and some of the major provisions seek mainly to extend policies already largely in place in most states. This is the nature of the American federal system: to learn from state experimentation as the basis for national policy. Federal education policy has not followed this model until recently because it was concerned with equity issues that local school districts had ignored. Instituting equity policy often put the federal government in conflict with states and school districts. With the shift to educational excellence, national initiatives align more closely with state priorities and draw increasingly from states' experience and their successful practices. For this reason, current extensions of federal power are more readily accepted by the general public and generate less controversy.

## Controlled Experimentation with Alternative Governance Structures

During the previous decade, the federal government for the first time began to provide resources to an alternative form of educational governance—charter schools. While the educational effectiveness of charter schools remains an open question, they are one of the first new governance structures in public education since the community school boards and alternative schools of the 1960s and early 1970s (Manno, Finn, & Vanourek, 2000). Although states were the initiators of charters, and policies vary widely among states, the federal government began in 1998 to provide aid to those who wished to organize charters through provisions in the Charter Schools Expansion Act. The goals for the $95 million in aid offered initially were, in the words of then-President Clinton, to "help foster the development of high-quality charter schools" and "lead to improvements in public education more generally" (Malico, 1999). The actual effect of that amount of aid on charter school development is not the issue. The intervention by the federal government into an arena that has direct effects on the organization and in some cases the viability of local school districts is a significant departure from all previous federal policy.

The federal government's on-again, off-again flirtation with vouchers is another example of a foray into the governance of public schools (Robelen & Walsh, 2002). This particular intervention has stirred great controversy, but the most interesting aspect of the debate is the length of time it has remained on the federal policy agenda. Support of vouchers as a tool for educational improvement represents a complex merging of political philosophies and agendas fraught with contradictions.

Nevertheless, it appears the federal government will continue periodically to encourage or even initiate new governance models for education. Local school districts are unlikely to be able to withstand large-scale federal initiatives to reconceptualize educational governance. The courts, however, have suggested that there are limits to how much public education can be opened up to competition without violating separation of church and state. This line has helped restrain the growth of federal voucher programs. If the line between church and state is redrawn by the courts, the door will be open for further federal activity in this most volatile of arenas. Public educational governance will continue to evolve and diversify if charters and vouchers become viable and widespread means for providing public education.

## Research and Development Capacity to Shape Education Policy and Practice

The U.S. Department of Education far outspends states in the arena of research and development of new education practices and strategies. This ability allows the federal government to define future directions for educational innovation or, more often, to take an emerging policy direction and greatly accelerate its development. Federal sponsorship for creation of discipline-based content standards in the early 1990s is one example. Federal efforts are likely to focus on identifying and validating research-based effective instructional strategies, which presumably schools would then be expected to adopt.

## The Continuing Roots of Federal Policy in the Equity Agenda

The federal government remains the level of governance most concerned with equity issues. This is appropriate historically and also provides the strongest legitimacy for a broad federal role. Equity is being defined much more broadly to mean that all students are educated in ways that allow them to compete successfully in the economic arena and to be fully contributing members of society. In this sense, equity has come to mean more than eliminating discrimination as it did initially in the 1960s, although much federal policy still focuses on the rights and opportunities of racial and ethnic groups and on the plight of the urban poor.

However, as noted earlier, equity is being interpreted not necessarily as the provision of government programs to the disadvantaged, but as the extension of choice to those (and other) constituents. This radical transformation of equity from the integration of schools to choice among educational settings creates a new tension within federal education policy. Whereas equity-as-integration largely left existing governance structures in place, although disrupting them dramatically, equity-as-choice inevitably will alter governance and organizational structures.

Even the most wholesale federal interventions into the operation of school districts to achieve integration resulted in federal judicial oversight of local boards of education, not the deconstitution of school districts (Vergon, 1988). In fact, the U.S. Supreme Court in *Milliken* v. *Bradley* rejected solutions that would have required changes in organizational structure, such as the creation of "unitary," or fully desegregated, districts freed from court oversight by involuntarily merging urban and suburban school districts (Hudgins, 1975). Choice policies eventually could put the federal government in the role of advocating solutions that could result in dramatic changes in the operation of local schools and in the structure of school districts. This policy tension remains unresolved, but nevertheless illustrates the scope of federal involvement and its likely long-term impacts on governance relationships at the local level.

## WHY HAS THIS INCREASED FEDERAL ROLE BEEN SUSTAINABLE?

The federal role in public education has been transformed over the past 40 years. The net effect has been to establish the mechanisms and mind-set necessary for state and local educational entities to implement federal policy. While numerous studies indicate that the actual implementation process is never exactly (or sometimes at all) what federal policy makers had in mind (Odden, 1991), the influences on local education practices are still significant, in terms of both intended and unintended effects.

The rise of the federal role in education has been supported at different times by two unlikely constituencies—national teachers' unions and the business community. In the late 1970s, the National Education Association (NEA) was one of the primary advocates for the creation of a cabinet-level department of education, thereby severing education's ties with its former home in the Department of Health, Education, and Welfare. This advocacy by the NEA is perhaps understandable, but would not have been possible much before the late 1970s. Previously, the NEA had not been a national political force. With the legitimization of collective bargaining rights for teachers and the shift of the NEA from an organization that represented all educators—teachers and administrators—to one that specifically advocated for teachers, the NEA was able to push for the creation of the Department of Education. The effect this governmental entity would have on local control of schools was not a primary consideration in the political calculus that led national organizations such as the NEA to vigorously support its creation.

In the late 1980s and throughout the 1990s, the business community, or at least the portion that had representatives based in Washington, DC, and had an interest in education policy, promoted policies that were best championed by the federal government. These business groups, which generally favor diminished federal involvement in most sectors of society and commerce, advocated activist federal development of standards, assessments, and programs such as school-to-career. Their support helped jump-start and then sustain the era of standards-based reform from the Bush administration of the late 1980s through the Clinton administration in the 1990s, and into the Bush administration of 2000.

The business community was motivated by concerns about international competition and by their conception of the labor pool as a national, rather than a local, phenomenon. They were far less concerned with preserving local control than they were with producing well-prepared, well-educated individuals capable of serving as productive workers (and contributing citizens, most business groups would hasten to add). As in the case of the NEA, business conceived of education as a national, rather than a local, policy issue, in part because each group was effectively organized to exert influence on education policy at the national level in ways it had not been able to do 20 years previously. In the case of the business community, the change it experienced was the transformation of the U.S. economy from manufacturing to technology. New companies were the spokespeople of the new economy, and they had a different agenda than their predecessors of 20 years earlier.

Federal involvement in and appropriation of education policy in the area of social equity raise fundamental questions about the social utility of local control: Do its benefits outweigh its drawbacks? Can the goal of social equality that is the cornerstone of a democracy be achieved through a system of locally controlled schools, or must a federal government enforce requirements for equal treatment that governing boards at the local level would be reluctant or unwilling to impose? Have the social goals facing the nation risen to a level of complexity and commonality that they demand action at the national, not the local, level? Should the sanctity and needs of local communities override some larger collective good? Or is the collective good the sum total of local interests?

The federal role is far from completely defined. It continues to undergo a rapid expansion and articulation. In the final analysis, this new federal role precludes education from ever again being a totally local issue or policy area, absent some profound retreat by the federal government from this arena, something it has done in precious few other areas once it has established authority.

## THE NEW FEDERAL–STATE RELATIONSHIP

Goertz (2001a) suggests that the federal role in education will be reshaped over the next 10 years due to three factors: (1) After a century or more of debate about the federal role in education, it appears that bipartisan support for and acceptance of a significant, sustained, and even expanding federal role in education policy exists; (2) the appropriate balance between federal objectives, which historically have been equity-related, and state and local control is being reassessed from an era when the federal government used targeted funds, service mandates, and compliance audits to a new strategy based on integration of federal initiatives with state and local education reforms; and (3) federal education policy has shifted its emphasis from procedural accountability to accountability for student learning.

The development by states of content standards and assessments is a test of the new relationship with states. Initially the federal government issued guidance and not regulations on the relationship of state standards to federal programs. State standards and assessments were not reviewed or approved. However, as state assessment plans have been reviewed for Title I compliance, issues such as inclusion and reporting have arisen. The Department of Education has begun to negotiate changes in state policy.

As Goertz (2001a) points out, this is unexplored terrain for the federal government, in which it faces four questions: (1) Who will set the standards for what is an equitable state assessment and accountability system? (2) What are the technical limits of federal policy? (3) What are the political limits of federal policy? (4) What is the cost of compliance?

The Clinton administration during its first term sought to enact policies that directly addressed these questions. While the administration achieved considerable success reauthorizing ESEA and passing Goals 2000 (Pitsch, 1994) and the School to Work Opportunities Act (Halperin, 1994), it also encountered the technical and political limits of federal policy when it attempted to put into place voluntary federal review of state standards and voluntary national assessments. However, barely 7 years later, a Republican administration found itself enacting elements of the Clinton education agenda via the ESEA reauthorization of 2001. Richard Riley, secretary of education in the Clinton administration, said the final version of the new ESEA had a great deal in common with what Clinton wanted. "We submitted a bill that was consistent with this" (Robelen, 2002b).

The passage in 2001 of legislation that would have been politically infeasible in 1995 was due in some large measure to the fact that many states had already adopted standards, assessment, and accountability systems and that the federal legislation simply extended much of what was already being widely attempted at the state level. This illustrates the principle that state policies "migrate" to the federal level. The federal government occupies two distinct roles in policy formulation: generating ideas or issuing challenges that lead to state action, and instituting policy that reflects emerging state practices.

Simultaneously, federal regulations close off much adaptation by schools. While one thrust of federal policy is to promote a focus on student performance and parental choice, other aspects, particularly special education and some Title I regulations, serve to severely limit organizational adaptability in certain arenas. The only solution offered in practice has been a process to waive federal regulations in certain circumstances, a measure that has been largely symbolic to date. Federal policy will face this continuing tension between the needs of particular groups of students who may require extra protection by the federal government, which has been the heart of federal education policy for nearly 40 years, and the notion of education as a general social good and one that the federal government should be promoting through higher, common expectations for all students and through improved processes of schooling.

## WILL FEDERAL INFLUENCE DECREASE AT SOME FUTURE POINT?

Under what scenario could the clock be turned back to an era where states, and particularly local districts, had primary control over education policy? It is difficult to envision such a scenario. The federal government still seems best equipped to guarantee individual rights, and local school districts have had great difficulty absorbing the equity agendas of the past 50 years. Would they maintain these if federal presence decreased? Just as important, can the nation any longer afford truly localized education policy? Can individual districts decide to educate students in ways that equip them only to live in the local community, or should all students receive an education that enables them to leave the local community if they so desire?

Education policy has gained greater prominence at the national level precisely because it is an issue of concern to a significant portion of the populace, including the general population and a range of special interest groups. This makes it appealing to politicians. Furthermore, education policy at the federal level can be pursued for relatively small amounts of money, as a proportion of the total federal budget, but effects can be shown to be widespread and significant. This combination makes education an attractive issue for which political return can be substantial. For this reason alone, education policy is likely to remain a centerpiece issue at the national level.

Rothstein (2001) makes the case that the next logical step in federal policy would be to address interstate inequality of per pupil spending. Just as states have been charged by the courts or taken it upon themselves to address intrastate spending inequalities, so might the federal government move to equalize funding among states. He points out that the highest-spending districts in Kentucky now spend less than the lowest-spending districts in Wisconsin and that interstate spending inequality has changed little during the past 20 years.

Such a policy undertaking would be daunting in many regards, and Rothstein (2001) outlines the myriad issues that an intervention of this nature would have to address. This may be the ultimate federal education policy. As important as such an initiative would be to helping students most in need of equal educational opportunity, it would spell the functional end of local control and would soon limit state control dramatically. However, some would argue that these changes occurred long ago. For example, in 1960, Myron Lieberman (in Campbell, Cunningham, Nystrand, & Usdan, 1990) asserted, "Local control of education has clearly outlived its usefulness on the American scene. Practically, it must give way to a system of educational controls in which local communities play ceremonial rather than policymaking roles: Intellectually, it is already a corpse" (p. 125).

Absent changes in the social and economic structure of American society, it seems unlikely that the current federal role can be abandoned. Its parameters are relatively clear—a demand for higher levels of academic performance and greater equity of achievement among all groups. States, local districts, and schools are receiving their "marching orders" increasingly from the federal level. What, then, is the legitimate role for states and local districts in this new partnership of shared power with the federal government? Forthcoming chapters explore these new relationships.

# Chapter 3

# Power to the States: Why and How States Are More Actively Shaping Education Policy

States have taken to shaping education policy for a variety of reasons. A primary, if indirect, driver has been the movement of responsibility for education funding from the local to the state level. Also important has been an increased public interest in educational quality, business pressure for improvement, and a willingness by states to experiment with new governance methods in search of improved educational results. Notions of systemic reform caused states to examine essentially all of the policy levers available to them to see how to effect large-scale changes in education. Research establishing that schools do have a significant effect on student learning further empowered states to devise policies to improve schools and to expect more from educational leaders. Finally, legislators are beginning to recognize that they can and must link funding and performance expectations if they are to exercise their newfound control over funding in ways that lead to improved student achievement.

## INCREASED STATE RESPONSIBILITY FOR FUNDING AND ITS RELATIONSHIP WITH EDUCATION REFORM

Litigation challenging state education finance systems began in earnest in the early 1970s and can be thought of as occurring in at least three waves. The first wave, including the U.S. Supreme Court 1971 decision on *San Antonio Independent School District* v. *Rodriguez,* was based on the equal protection clause of the U.S. Constitution and was largely unsuccessful. The Court established that education was not a fundamental federal right and that interstate differences in funding were acceptable as long as they were rationally related to a legitimate state purpose.

The action then shifted from federal to state courts for the second wave of legal challenges. California led this wave with the *Serrano* and *Serrano II* cases. In *Serrano*, which preceded *Rodriguez*, the California Supreme Court ruled the state's funding system violated equal protection provisions of the U.S. Constitution. This decision was effectively nullified by the U.S. Supreme Court decision in *Rodriguez*. In *Serrano II*, however, the California Supreme Court required that school funding be determined on some basis other than district property wealth.

The focus in this second wave remained on equity defined as equal funding per pupil. State courts did begin to find state funding systems unconstitutional when disparities in funding per pupil were so great that courts could find no rational relationship in the disparity to a legitimate state purpose.

In the third wave, litigants began to use the education clauses of state constitutions as the basis for challenges. Most state constitutions had a clause that contained what has been described as "substantive component" language, which requires states to provide an educational system that meets certain minimum specified levels or results in certain broadly defined student outcomes. Words like "meaningful," "adequate," and "standard" appear in state constitutions to describe the education that should result from state funding. Here the focus is on what the system achieves rather than simply on per pupil equality in spending. This changed the measure of equity to the level and impact of education programs, not just funding discrepancies.

The general trend has been for challenges to school funding systems to be successful over time as litigants keep trying new strategies and approaches until they find one that state courts find compelling. This has resulted in a gradual shift toward equity being defined in terms of the effects of state funding rather than simple numerical equality of funding. The result of effects-based equity definitions has been to challenge lawmakers to think about how student needs differ from district to district as well as to conceive of the education system as having to be able to achieve certain specified goals.

The transference of funding responsibility from local school districts to the states has occurred in a relatively short period of time. States have not necessarily been able or willing to give careful attention to the unintended consequences of this transformational policy change. No state undertook reform of its funding system with the express goal of increasing state control over local school systems. Lawsuits often were brought by underfunded districts that wanted equality of funding, not state control. The goal in nearly every case was either greater equity of funding among school districts or provision of resources adequate for all students to receive an education consistent with state constitutional requirements (Verstegen, 1998; Whitney & Verstegen, 1997).

Evidence that states have increased their stake substantially in local education funding is illustrated by the increase in the proportion of education spending assumed by states over a 27-year period. The state share of K–12

spending, on average, increased from 38.3% in 1971–72 to 49% in 1998–
99. Local and intermediate sources provided 44% of funding, and the federal government accounted for the remaining 7% (National Center for Education Statistics, 2001). This moved states into the role of primary funders
of local education.

Many states have become more involved in school finance only grudg-
ingly. Their efforts to equalize funding, even under court order, have not
necessarily been successful. Odden (1998) cites research by Evans, Murray,
and Schwab (1997) that shows that although many states have undergone
court-ordered school finance reform in the past 30 years, success in reducing fiscal inequity has been limited. The reforms did reverse the increasing
gap between high- and low-property-wealth districts, but per pupil spending remains related to property wealth. After 30 years of fiscal reform, states
were left with significant inequity of funding along with increased responsibility to provide funding.

Increased state control over education funding and more vigorous reform programs generally have been related. California's SB 813 (Cuban,
1984), the Kentucky Education Reform Act (Steffy, 1993), and the Massachusetts Education Reform Act (Anthony & Rossman, 1994) are examples
of this phenomenon. Throughout the late 1980s and early 1990s, as states
undertook more responsibility for education funding, they tended to launch
ambitious reform programs on a scale not seen when funding was strictly a
local concern.

The challenges to inequitable state funding systems often were mounted
by school districts incapable of generating as much revenue locally as other
districts in their area or elsewhere in the state. The goal of the districts that
mounted these challenges was greater fiscal resources, not loss of local control. However, almost without exception, the effect of moving fiscal decisions
to the state level has been an inevitable increase in the quantity and the impact
of state-generated education policy and a concurrent decrease in responsibility and authority at the district level. Although Fuhrman concluded in 1974
that early finance reform programs did not necessarily establish a direct relationship between increased state funding and loss of local control, subsequent
events suggest that this has been the effect in most cases, if loss of local control
is defined as increased prescriptions of education policy at the state level.

The most recent trends in education finance policy have been for courts
to invalidate state finance systems that do not achieve "adequacy" standards,
which some courts have defined as the level of funding found in "world-class
educational systems" (Verstegen, 1998). During the 1990s, courts in Alabama, Kentucky, Massachusetts, Rhode Island, West Virginia, and Wyoming
all handed down rulings indicating that the state's funding system should be
held to an adequacy standard.

Courts are sending the message that state standards are a good expression of what constitutes an adequate education, and that states must establish a link between finance systems and state education standards and programs (Blair, 1999). The funding system must provide resources adequate to enable students to meet state standards. State legislatures are left to devise finance systems that ensure that the state's schools are providing an adequate education, as defined by the courts, to all children. In states that have adopted challenging educational standards, the effect of state finance litigation and legislation on local district discretion can be seen more clearly. New Jersey presents an example of one extreme, where the courts over a period of 25 years have directed the state to make fundamental changes in education funding, changes designed to ensure an adequate education for all students. Texas is perhaps the other extreme in terms of being a state that has attempted to preserve local control but has had to confront repeatedly the inequities and inadequacies of its finance system. The most recent court actions have indicated that the state's finance system must give consideration to adequacy as well as equity.

The states' increasing control over finances has both preceded and paralleled the movement to adopt academic content standards. The emergence of standards systems has laid the groundwork for making connections between funding and performance. As long as education standards are established locally, it is not possible to compare districts nor is it feasible to determine student performance levels that are accurate or comparable across districts. As state standards have taken hold in states across the nation, they have provided a context within which district performance can be assessed. This information can then be linked back to state spending decisions, with the goal of improving schooling and affecting the ways local school districts instruct students. Odden (1992, 1998) explains that the effect of the national and state emphasis on teaching students to higher standards has been to shift the traditional focus on equitable distribution of resources to an expanded conception of finance policy designed to facilitate the goal of more students reaching high standards.

Odden (2001) contends that many changes will have to occur at the district level in response to a state finance system focused on student achievement of high standards. The state will have to strive to determine what constitutes an adequate amount of funding to enable students to reach high education standards. The state's primary motivation will be to redefine school finance as more than simply providing each district the same money per pupil. The state will need to identify the resources necessary to provide an adequate amount of funding for each student to meet standards, acknowledging that some students are more expensive to educate than others. This will lead to inequity in funding among districts, when considered from the point of view of dollars allocated. The goal will be to bring about equality of results among students.

If this type of redesign of state education finance takes place, it will have significant implications for all school districts in a state. Unless a state is willing to devote new revenue to education, funds will be reallocated from richer to poorer districts. The potential for conflict between districts is heightened, as is the specter of program reductions in high-wealth districts. Texas has struggled with this issue since the passage of school reform legislation in 1993. The finance system earned the nickname of the "Robin Hood" system because it shifts money from richer districts to poor ones. In 2001, 84 property-rich districts surrendered a portion of their property tax revenue to the state, which redistributed the funds to property-poor districts (Keller, 2001). Districts have initiated a series of lawsuits challenging this form of financing, alleging that they would be forced to reduce their programs as a result of the law.

These far-reaching effects of state finance decisions on local district operations are notable in Texas in part because the state has largely resisted the national trend to shift school funding responsibility from the local to the state level. Even with over half the funds still generated at the local level, the state has moved to reduce significantly the spending gaps between districts, consistent with the larger national movement toward greater funding equity. Texas is also a state that has enacted far-reaching education reforms over the past decade.

It is worth noting that education reform in Texas was initiated in 1985, around the same time that finance reform and movement away from the weighted pupil averaging system was undertaken (Verstegen, 1985). Texas also was one of the first states, beginning in the mid-1980s, to develop state standards and assessments. These have been refined several times, each time moving the focus more clearly onto student performance. Even in a state where the majority of funds are raised locally, increased state activity to equalize funding and improve student performance has the effect of strengthening state control.

## EDUCATION REFORM IN THE 1980S

The 1980s turned out to be a pivotal decade in state governance of public education. The effects of school finance reform activities in the 1970s, the call by business to improve the "competitiveness" of American education, and a series of national reports on the inadequacy of the educational system converged to create an environment that stimulated significant education policy generation. These forces served as a catalyst for changes in education that society at large seemed ready to embrace. States commissioned numerous blue-ribbon commissions that often complemented the work of national commissions. The Education Commission of the States estimated that 275 such activities occurred during a 4-year period in the mid-1980s.

Even as the nation endured a sharp economic downturn in the early 1980s, states implemented ambitious reforms (e.g., California, SB 813). As the economy improved in the mid- to late 1980s, many states began to devote significant resources to educational improvements and reform programs. States increased educator salaries, created mentor teacher programs, targeted particular types of districts for remedial aid, and added course requirements that required additional funding.

These state-level activities were an assertion of state primacy in education policy formulation. Most, if not all, states explicitly rejected the notion of federal leadership of education reform. States seized the political initiative. The federal role was primarily to exhort states (and local districts, but primarily states) to improve. Education Secretary William Bennett's famous, or infamous, "wall charts" are perhaps the best example of this phenomenon. Local districts were not the initiators of policy changes and began to assume an increasingly reactive stance to state initiatives.

These state policies and reforms were concerned with equity and quality issues, but not in even measure. While federal policy had been concerned almost exclusively with equity for the previous 20 years, states focused more on quality. Quality was defined as increased graduation requirements, more academic courses for all students, tougher teacher licensing and evaluation requirements, and greater oversight of districts' education programs.

These measures had equity as one goal, but not their sole goal. They were a departure from federal programs targeted to specific groups of students to help equalize their educational opportunities. These reforms affected all schools and students. Some groups may have stood to benefit more than others from an emphasis on quality, but states were concerned more with system improvement than with the needs of one group exclusive of all others.

One indication of this conclusion was the mixed reaction that "opportunity to learn" standards received as content standards were being promoted in the early 1990s (Elmore & Fuhrman, 1995). Opportunity to learn standards stated the conditions and resources necessary for all students to reach state standards. These had significant fiscal as well as social and organizational implications for state educational systems. While some states did increase resources to education, which resulted in additional opportunity for all students to learn, most avoided any specific commitment to providing equal opportunity to learn as a prerequisite to expecting all students to reach high standards. This has created significant tension between districts and states regarding whether it is realistic to expect all students to reach high standards. Here the state maintains its focus on quality as the primary driver of reforms, with equity an important but subordinate goal.

Massell and Fuhrman (1994) assessed the effects of 10 years of state education reforms from 1983 to 1993. They concluded that results were mixed. On one hand, state actions did have the desired effects. Students were taking more academic courses. Remedial courses were being replaced by courses with more traditional academic content, and the content did not seem to be watered down. The proportion of high school graduates going directly on to 2- and 4-year colleges rose from 49% in 1980 to 60% in 1990. Similarly, the proportion of students taking the SAT increased by 8 points to 41%. Overall scores in mathematics and science rose on the National Assessment of Educational Progress between 1982 and 1990. To be sure, many disturbing trends remained, most notably, the gap, which began to increase after closing somewhat in the early 1980s, between minority and White students' achievement.

The reforms were the product of legislators, not of educators. Massell and Fuhrman (1994) note how power shifted and policy making became more removed from practitioners' control. In California, for example, state politicians were the primary initiators of ideas for reforms in 1983, for the first time seizing the leadership that had long been held by educators and traditional interest groups. Teachers found themselves responding to, rather than recommending, proposed policies. More shocking, they found themselves identified as part of the problem.

The policy issue focus shifted from increasing specification of academic requirements toward statements of academic expectations. Although states specified in the 1980s that students take more academic courses, and isolated gains were made, this did not necessarily result in dramatic improvements in learning. This gap between policy and practice was particularly evident when the performance of American students on international comparisons indicated that fewer reached higher levels of proficiency in mathematics and science than in comparable countries (Lawton, 1995b; Stevenson & Stigler, 1992; Valverde & Schmidt, 1997). Students seemed to be mastering basic information, but not progressing beyond basic skills to higher-order, complex thinking and reasoning. Simply mandating more courses did not seem to be the answer.

One interpretation of why American students did poorly on measures of more sophisticated skills is that state reforms narrowed the zone of teacher professional discretion, causing teaching to become focused on basic skills. However, a closer examination of state reforms reveals that few mandated specific teaching methods or curriculum. At most, states provided curriculum frameworks of the type instituted in California that were influential but still voluntary (Cohen & Hill, 2001). The reforms often required that students spend more time studying a subject; teachers and local educators made decisions about how to translate this in practice, which generally meant little or no significant change in the existing instructional program. State policies in the 1980s focused educators on "intensification," or doing more of the same, generally resulting in some improvements for those students who could benefit from more of the same and significantly less improvement for those who needed something different.

Local districts, for their part, often viewed state education policy as chaotic and fragmented, gyrating from program to program, goal to goal, from one legislative session to the next (Conley & Goldman, 1998; Fuhrman, 1993b). In many states, reform requirements had no specific dollars attached to them, which local districts interpreted as an unfunded mandate, while legislators assumed that general fund resources were adequate for reform implementation if educators simply prioritized their expenditures better. In other cases, states did not anticipate the logistical problems associated with a reform such as increasing mathematics requirements, which required that more teachers be prepared to teach mathematics and that enough teachers be available to take on the additional teaching load. Local schools were provided little guidance on what to cut from their programs in order to make room for these new academic requirements. Districts and teachers often took a "wait and see" approach, adapting as little as possible to accommodate the reform requirements while leaving as much of existing practice intact as possible (Goldman & Conley, 1997).

## THE STATE ROLE IN EDUCATION REFORM IN THE 1990S

What has been characterized as the "second wave" of state education reform began in the early 1990s and can be characterized as states setting standards, then "getting out of the way" to allow local districts to develop and adapt creative solutions that enabled achievement of state goals. While the standards and eventually their accompanying assessments were prescribed in ever greater detail, the hoped-for transformation in governance relations failed to materialize. The existing relationships between states and schools were maintained essentially intact.

Often state education departments were to be "transformed" into facilitators of school improvement. While some did offer a much wider array of support services to schools (Lusi, 1997), all retained their traditional oversight responsibilities. As the decade progressed, many even gained new, more powerful mechanisms to control local districts, including the right to take over governance of a district directly, to send in teams to review district practices and critique local boards of education, and to reconstitute individual schools.

The notion that local communities should be responsible for the governance of their schools via locally elected boards received continuing lip service in state legislatures even as the reality of state policy development went in the opposite direction. The new "top-down, bottom-up partnership" for achieving educational results never really materialized. Often the result of this partnership was that the state, under the guise of "empowering" local districts, simply failed to provide details on what schools were expected to do to respond to the reform requirements. Teachers and administrators responded predictably by demanding greater specification of what the state was expecting of local districts or by applying the new nomenclature of reform to traditional practices (Spillane & Zeuli, 1999).

For example, Massell, Kirst, and Hoppe (1997) found that California educators complained that state standards were too broad and general in nature and that district and school staff were assumed to have the capacity, resources, time, and expertise to flesh them out into a local curriculum. Kentucky educators similarly felt that they lacked the time or knowledge to create the kinds of curricular and instructional programs they needed to meet the new state expectations. They demanded that the state provide them with more specific guidance and support, which it did.

The net effect was to strengthen the hierarchical relationship between the state and its local districts. This trend existed throughout the "second wave" of reform, but rapidly intensified during the "third wave," when high-stakes testing and accountability requirements were implemented in earnest. In this third wave, district and school administrators adapted incrementally, and, more important, teachers gradually came to accept that the new standards and assessments were not going to go away, contrary to many initial reactions that "this too shall pass."

Massell, Kirst, and Hoppe's (1997) study of standards-based reform in nine states in 1994–1995 concluded that strong antigovernment sentiment resulted in challenges to state standards, but the standards remained central components of state education policy. While no state undertook major expansions of its standards-based policies, all "stayed the course." All continued to revise their content standards, as did 20 of 25 school districts studied.

One thing states did learn in the early 1990s was how to involve local educators in standards development. The Council of Chief State School Officers (Blank, Langesen, Bush, Pechman, & Goldstein, 1997) reports that in the 1990s, state initiatives to develop state standards and frameworks were designed to ensure widespread involvement of local educators, community leaders, business groups, and political leaders. These more interactive processes had time for dialogue, debate, and review built into them. Classroom teachers were actively involved as well in writing and editing content standards and frameworks. Statewide task forces engaged a range of stakeholders, leading to new alliances among educators and a range of constituent groups, and creating a sense of shared ownership in the standards they developed.

Just as the states had learned, sometimes painfully, how to develop standards that the public would support, so they embarked on the creation of assessment systems that would hold schools accountable for achieving state education goals. While many states had histories of testing programs that allowed local districts to choose the standardized test they would use, others required all schools to use the same standardized achievement test. The results were not generally utilized for significant decisions at the state level. In the new environment, however, tests gradually began to take on additional purposes, moving beyond a "measuring stick" of schools to an unapologetic focus on accountability. This occurred for the most part without input or influence by local school boards, school administrators, or teachers.

States recognized the need to move beyond simply providing a framework within which local districts would achieve state goals by adapting their local programs. One of the first ways states intervened was to change policies that had a direct effect on teachers' ability to enable students to meet state standards and pass state assessments. Policies ranged from teacher competency tests, to alignment of entry-level teacher certification programs with standards, to more extensive and expensive programs designed to support or retrain teachers in the field.

Over time, educators by and large came to accept in principle, if not support in practice, the states' major policy thrusts toward higher standards and greater accountability. Disagreements continue to persist over the specific means by which these goals should be achieved, and these disagreements are substantial enough to put some state programs on hold or to result in significant revisions (Olson, 2001a). However, the basic principle of state direction of the instructional program via standards and assessments has become ever more accepted and institutionalized. The role of the local district and individual school in this new system was not seriously examined or revised. States assumed that school districts had sufficient autonomy to adapt their practices in ways necessary to achieve state goals or, more often, simply ignored the implications for the way local schools were to be governed.

## Waivers and Deregulation

States turned to another policy tool as they attempted to find a new balance between centralized decision making and localized education practice. Schools and districts would be allowed to waive specific regulations, under the assumption that excessive regulation was preventing schools from functioning effectively. Waivers were an attempt to duplicate the successes experienced in the deregulation of trucking, airlines, telecommunications, banking, and other sectors of the economy during the 1980s. Schools were able to request exemption from regulations that hindered their ability to improve student achievement. Examples of areas in which waivers were offered include personnel requirements, curriculum, length of the school day, class staffing, and class structure (Fuhrman & Elmore, 1995).

Between 1986 and 1990, 20 states adopted waiver programs (Olson, 1990), but schools responded with a decided lack of enthusiasm to the opportunity to waive requirements (Fry, 1992; Fuhrman & Elmore, 1992). Policy makers, accustomed to years of complaints by educators about excessive mandates from above, expected schools to jump at the chance to do things differently. But state education department officials reported that they received far fewer requests for waivers than they had anticipated from both the state and district levels. The requests they did receive tended to be for waivers of relatively minor rules and regulations. Many schools found that what they perceived to be regulatory barriers were in fact not even regulations, and that many activities undertaken under waiver programs would have occurred anyway (Fuhrman & Elmore, 1995).

Most state waiver programs did not result in the type of educational innovation and improvement sought. The reasons for this phenomenon are complex, but experiences in Dade County, Florida, are illustrative. Although over 300 waivers were granted in a program begun in 1986, most were related to specific language in the local union contract under which teachers requested more flexibility in how they utilized their time during the school day to plan and work collaboratively. However, many of the requests were to waive regulations that did not exist. A similar trend was noted in other states, including Oregon where the majority of requests to the state board of education for waivers related to nonexistent rules. A study of waivers in Texas indicated that most were requested for staff development to allow a school or district to conduct an additional day or days of staff development in lieu of student instruction, final examinations, course requirements, and exceptions to maximum class-size limitations (Texas Education Agency, 1993).

Local schools in waiver states were reluctant to take action to change, fearing that the state would not really allow them to make changes that deviated significantly from traditional education practice. Schools labor under a set of conceptions about state regulations, real and imagined, that substantively limits adaptation, change, and even improvement. Educators were controlled not only by the state, but also by their own culture and conceptions of schooling. Fuhrman and Elmore (1995) outline the substantial political and practical barriers inherent in deregulation of schools, from waivers to charters to accountability systems linked to broad deregulation. Changing governance structures alone, whether the change was increased decentralization or waivers, did not result in transformation of education practice. States were often in the position of having tried a variety of strategies to restructure the state–local relationship and having invested significant new resources to bring about school improvement, with little substantive improvement in educational achievement or school organization as a result.

## Site-Based Management and School Site Councils

In fact, many states began to implement reforms that devolved power directly to schools. The mid-1980s saw the first attempts by legislatures to change the structural relationship between schools, districts, and the state (Prasch, 1984). This first generation of structural change was based on the transfer of more responsibility to school sites (Guthrie, 1986). By the mid-1990s, site councils were common in states as varied as Kentucky and Oregon.

Known as site-based management or site-based decision making, a variety of reforms were instituted either granting more authority to principals or requiring schools to involve more people in determining the school's program and goals, effectiveness, and even budgeting (David, 1989; Swanson, 1989). These reforms were the outgrowth of advocacy for decentralized decision making that had been around in various forms since the 1960s (Bridges, 1967; Fantini & Gittell, 1973; Murphy & Beck, 1995). Their focus gradually shifted from control by the principal to councils of constituents charged with improving schools in ways consistent with state goals (Peterson del Mar, 1994).

Councils were given various responsibilities, but prominent among them was school improvement so that more students would meet high academic standards. The site council was not simply a management tool; it was a link between the state and the schools. The initial outlines of a newly defined relationship between the state and schools began to emerge. The state was to create the broad policy parameters, provide the resources, and establish accountability measures. The schools were to have authority to make decisions and adapt programs locally in order to achieve state-mandated goals.

Site-based management has run into its share of problems. Legislatures created site councils without necessarily recognizing that school cultures are built on localism and bureaucratic structures unlikely to be naturally innovative or to accept state policy goals readily. Schools for the most part were not particularly eager to take control of their own destinies or to place their decisions into a broad context of state reform programs. Principals had no particular training to lead democratic participative decision-making models. Teachers, parents, and community members were not necessarily ready to devote the kind of time and energy necessary to govern a school and make policy for it (Conley, 1991; Malen & Ogawa, 1988; Taylor & Bogotch, 1994).

Those that did have a modicum of success changing or improving schools often relied on external pressure for improvement emanating from the state. State accountability requirements in Illinois have had the effect of focusing school-based councils on achievement in Chicago, for example (Hess, 1999). Wohlstetter & Mohrman (1994) concluded that where site councils were successful in helping schools to "actively restructure," the schools used state and district curriculum frameworks as one of their strategies to focus reform efforts. Research on site councils indicates that simply creating them does not necessarily lead to improved student achievement (David, 1995/1996; Leithwood, Jantzi, & Steinbach, 1999; Malen, Ogawa, & Kranz, 1990; Wohlstetter & Odden, 1992), although they may have other positive effects on schools (Wohlstetter, Van Kirk, Robertson, & Mohrman, 1997).

Site councils also can be understood as attempts by states to move governance beyond the exclusive control of professional administrators on the implicit assumption that greater involvement by teachers, parents, and community members will lead to greater improvement, defined in terms of the achievement of state goals. Popkewitz (1991) describes this type of power decentralization as a "state steering strategy." Site councils at times are seen as an indirect challenge to the authority of school administrators and local school boards as well, which have responded by enacting provisions to limit the authority of the site councils or relegate ritual duties and ceremonial presentations to them (Ayers, 1991; David, 1994a). As more data on student achievement have been generated by states, site councils have become more important as places where such data can be analyzed and discussed. Since the data derive from student performance on state assessments, the councils' role as implementers of state policy is strengthened (Goertz, 2000).

Site-based management and site councils have not necessarily been a failure and certainly remain quite popular in places where the practices have been institutionalized. The point here is neither to praise nor condemn these practices *per se*. The experience with site-based decision making, however, does illustrate that a focus on governance, absent a sense of how governance changes at the school level interact with the other elements of a complex bureaucratic structure like a school district, will not lead consistently to desired results.

This new relationship, wherein the state sets expectations and goals and schools have greater discretion to create programs to achieve specified goals in return for enhanced accountability requirements, may not be such a good deal for schools. States have not always followed through on their promises to loosen regulations, nor have they necessarily provided resources needed to implement the policies successfully. However, they have retained the accountability requirements. Decentralization of authority to schools has the look of a strategy that paradoxically may yield greater control over schools by the state and more alignment of local education practice with state goals.

Schools will not so much be freed from the control of the district as they will be moved into the orbit of the state. Decentralization of decision making, viewed through this lens, works against, not for, the strengthening of local control at the district level. It also places new burdens and expectations on schools without necessarily providing the conditions schools need to respond successfully to state goals.

## Charter Schools as an Example of a New Governance Mechanism

As schools learned how to adapt to state demands for greater focus on academic content standards and assessments, new governance approaches were being proposed and often implemented in a disconnected, episodic, and controversial fashion. A range of new strategies surfaced, including site councils and private management of public schools, and free-market notions, such as vouchers.

The most distinctive and viable new governance model is the charter school. Charters are an attempt to deregulate schooling while simultaneously maintaining a connection with state goals. The variance in charter school legislation among states is an indication of the ways in which charters are an exploration of alternative strategies for governing public education.

Bulkley's (1999) examination of the ways in which charter school legislation was put into practice in Michigan and Arizona found that in both of those states, agencies outside of the traditional public school governance structure were designated as the authorizers for charter schools. In Michigan, universities emerged as the primary sponsors of charters, while in Arizona, both the State Board of Education and a specially created State Board for Charter Schools could sponsor charters. Bulkley (1999) explains the decision by state policy makers to use sponsors other than local boards as an example of institutional choice. Policy makers believe that sponsors other than local school boards are most likely to approve schools that are consistent with legislative intent.

What often is overlooked in the discussion of charters is their importance in establishing new governance structures and relationships between the state and local schools. Charters bypass the authority of local school boards without creating a state school district. They exist in a sort of governance "twilight zone," where responsibility and control functions are ambiguous. Policy makers who sponsor charter school legislation expect the marketplace to police charters. State education departments have been specifically banned from working with charters in Arizona, for example.

However, Bulkley (1999) suggests that as the number of charters increases, the pressure for more formalized oversight will increase as well. She notes that "DiMaggio and Powell's work (1983) suggests the possibility that in the next few years we may see isomorphic pressures on authorizers that push charter schools further toward more traditional organizational structures and norms." If this is the case, over time charters will become a new and dramatically different form of governance for public education.

## Governing Urban Districts

As external players create continued pressure to be involved in education policy making, the structures for governing urban districts in particular begin to fracture and become more complex. In addition to charters, mayoral takeovers of school districts (Kirst & Bulkley, 2000) represent another example of a move away from the "one best system" (Tyack, 1974) notion of educational organization and governance. State-appointed oversight boards, as in New Haven, Connecticut, or Newark, New Jersey, are yet another variation on the traditional local education board.

The mayoral takeover, however, is a return to the past in many ways, to a time when school systems were more directly connected with city government (Wirt & Kirst, 1989). The current approach has mayors circumventing local boards by changing the governing structure itself. In Philadelphia, the mayor and governor aligned to produce a takeover of the schools and a restructuring of governance that turned over control of the district's 264 schools to a city/state commission. The commission is charged, among other things, with determining whether private contractors should run 45 of the city's lowest-performing schools in partnership with community groups, itself a new governance strategy (Gewertz, 2002).

Plank and Boyd (1994) argue that such challenges to existing governance structures are more likely during times when there is less agreement on institutional goals. In such environments, political advantage becomes more important than institutional legitimacy, as reformers attempt to enforce their goals on the educational system.

The governance of urban districts had been transformed long ago from school boards whose members numbered in the dozens and who represented neighborhoods and political parties to boards with fewer than 10 members, a professional manager, and a large bureaucracy. In theory insulated from politics, urban bureaucracies developed their own inefficiencies and political power, but avoided much of the accountability that had been present in a system more subject to political control. Currently, these bureaucracies and their attendant governance mechanisms, citywide school boards, appear paralyzed and largely incapable of coping with the myriad problems urban districts face. Fractured political power in cities and an intractable educational bureaucracy in control of the schools contributed to a downward spiral in many urban districts.

New York experimented with community school boards from the 1960s on as one way to counteract the centralizing tendencies of large urban districts. These subdistricts have had their share of ups and downs, and frequently find themselves in power struggles with the central administration. Some, District 2, for example, have achieved student learning gains. Others have become swept up in their own internal politics. The solution for urban school governance is yet to be discovered, which means more experimentation with alternative modes of governance is likely in urban districts.

State government has become much less reticent about teaming with mayors in particular to take a more active role in urban educational governance. This is a recognition as much that education problems need to be solved locally as that the formula adopted by progressive reformers a century ago has created its own set of problems. As mayors approach the problems of urban school districts, they find they face a formidable set of opponents who have a stake in the current governance structure. Professional educators and bureaucrats, boards of education, teachers' unions, and even community groups all have a vested interest in maintaining the local control model. The states, meanwhile, are concerning themselves more with results than with the preservation of local control.

## STATEWIDE SYSTEMIC REFORM

Although state power and influence grew during the 1980s, events at the end of the decade and in the early 1990s triggered an additional surge in state authority and policy activity, what has been called the "third wave" of education reform (Murphy, 1990). This third wave is characterized by the movement of the states to center stage and the resulting rise of the notion of systemic reform, initiatives that can be launched and monitored only at the state level and that affect the entire educational system.

The emergence of systemic reform signaled an ownership by the states and, to a lesser degree, the federal government of educational problems and a corresponding willingness to reshape the entire educational system to address these problems. Systemic reform is by definition an acknowledgment that individual school districts are not viable or appropriate governmental entities to solve complex social problems or meet new education goals that states have set for schools and schooling.

Statewide systemic reform programs have at least five components. They clearly identify the goals or standards expected of all students. They develop or identify curricula linked directly to those standards. They make available to schools high-quality instructional materials appropriate to the curricula. They ensure that standards and curricula are accompanied by professional development programs that enable teachers, administrators, and other school staff to understand how to teach the curricula most effectively. They have student assessment systems that are based directly on the curricula (U.S. General Accounting Office, 1993, cited in Verstegen, 1994b).

Statewide systemic reform occurred at the confluence of two important policy streams: (1) the movement toward state education goals spurred by the adoption of national education goals in 1990 by 50 state governors and the U.S. president, and (2) the increasing tendency of courts to link equitable funding with the ability of students to attain comparable educational outcomes from a state-sponsored educational system. Between 1989 and 1994, for example, seven state school finance systems were declared unconstitutional by state supreme courts. Many other states had lower court decisions overturning school financing schemes that were not appealed to state supreme courts, but that served as triggers for legislative action nonetheless (Verstegen, 1994b).

New Jersey courts found in the 1990 *Abbott* v. *Burke* decision that the state must provide course offerings that enable students to achieve a wide range of attributes such as good citizenship, cultural appreciation, and community awareness (Bader, 1991). The decision focused on the imbalances between rich and poor and called not just for equal funding, but for equal programmatic opportunities for all students, noting that what passes as a "regular education" for seriously disadvantaged students is not equal to an equivalent program for advantaged students. The state was responsible to ensure that all students had an equal opportunity to be able to compete in the world beyond schools as a result of a publicly funded education.

Kentucky courts, in finding not just the finance system but the entire educational system unconstitutional, went so far as to identify seven capacities that the educational system should have as its goal for all students to achieve. These ranged from sufficient oral and written communication skills to vocational skills that enabled students to compete with students in neighboring states, gain entry to academic institutions, or obtain jobs (Verstegen, 1994b).

This "new educational equity" called for "school finance systems to be restructured and aligned to curricular improvements, to give to many what has been reserved for the fortunate few: equal opportunity for excellence in education" (Verstegen, 1994b, p. 371). School finance systems had become a tool for educational equity and excellence. This is a long way from school funding determined by a local vote and levied based on local property values.

These new finance systems required a forceful and activist role by states in the determination of a wide range of education policies that would help ensure that the state's schools would deliver upon the promise of greater student achievement. The state's roles as provider of resources and specifier of results were welded together, creating both a mandate and a duty for the state to assume a more forceful role in education policy.

## BEYOND THE COLEMAN REPORT: SCHOOL EFFECTS
## ON STUDENT LEARNING

A supporting reason for a more activist state role in education policy is a shift in belief about the effect schools can have on student learning. Coleman's 1966 study of educational opportunity, commonly known as the Coleman Report, reached the conclusion that schools did not account for much of the variance in student performance, and that home and community factors were much more important. This view of the school as a place with limited ability to enhance student achievement tended to take education policy away from school improvement. Madaus, Airasian, and Kellaghan (1980) noted that the report had the effect of dealing a blow to those who viewed schools as vehicles to close the gap in student achievement that resulted from different socioeconomic differences and it spawned the notion that schools could have little effect on student achievement. While the federal government in particular launched programs to improve neighborhoods and families, the schools themselves were left largely to their own devices to set practices and policies.

The Coleman Report was challenged almost immediately on methodological grounds and by those who believed schools did make a difference (Cain & Watts, 1968; Edmonds et al., 1977; Lemann, 1999; Meier, 1968; Ribich, 1970). While the debate on the report's methods and conclusions raged during the 1970s, its conclusions often were cited by policy makers as a reason not to spend more money on schools (Grant, 1973).

Researchers began to examine more closely the role schools played in student achievement (Edmonds et al., 1977; Levin, 1970; Rutter, Maughan, Mortimore, Ouston, & Smith, 1979; Whitbread, 1974; Wilson, 1980). As they did so, they found many relationships between what teachers and principals did in schools and the learning that occurred (Block, 1983; Cohen, 1982; Edmonds, 1982; ERIC Clearinghouse on Educational Management, 1981; Purkey & Smith, 1983).

This upsurge in research summaries that communicated the power of schools to enhance student learning coincided with an increase in state policy activity that began in the early 1980s. This new sense that schools that followed certain practices could increase student learning regardless of student background served to help stimulate state policy initiatives directed at the conditions and requirements of schooling.

This early work was followed by additional studies confirming the importance of the school as the unit of analysis for determining effects on student achievement and the additional importance of the teacher and the principal in the achievement equation (Teddlie & Stringfield, 1993). This combination of factors helped set the stage for a flurry of major state reform initiatives throughout the 1980s and into the 1990s. This line of research, now well established, has led to what Marzano (2000) calls a "new era of school reform," based on the notion that schools have significant effects that can be measured with some precision at the level of the school, the teacher, and the student. These effects are subject to influence by better education practices, which increase the importance of schools and their organization and education programs.

Establishing that schools could overcome social conditions was a critical prerequisite to state reform programs. If policy makers believed that schools could not effectively educate students from disadvantaged or impoverished backgrounds, it would make little sense to invest significantly in public education. The custodial function of schooling would have been emphasized, and attempts at improvement might have been focused on making school more pleasant or palatable for those who could not really benefit much from an education.

Instead, the effective schools research created a mind-set for policy makers in which schools could make a substantive difference, for students and for society. The fact that much of the research focused on schools in high-poverty neighborhoods served to strengthen the belief that good education policy could be a key vehicle for resolving a host of social problems associated with poverty.

Had this conclusion not been reached, it is likely that resources would have been directed to social service agencies rather than schools. Schools saw increases in funding during the first half of the 1980s in terms of real dollars (Flanigan, 1992). A strengthening economy in the mid-1980s enabled these increases, but the belief that schools could have an effect on student learning supported the political will to allocate dollars and enact programs.

In this new conception of state education policy, schools moved from being irrelevant to being the key vehicle for overcoming poverty and family background (Miller, 1983). This shift in emphasis occurred at a time when large-scale programs designed to eliminate racial segregation and to decrease social and economic inequality were winding down or being questioned on ideological grounds. In this environment, and in light of research indicating that schools could make a difference, the educational system rapidly displaced other social programs as the preferred governmental vehicle to overcome inequality. This new emphasis on schooling as a tool to address a major social problem focused the intensity of the policy process more directly on education and resulted in numerous state efforts to reshape public schooling.

The most recent manifestation of the school as an institution for overcoming the effects of poverty is the "high-performing schools" model. This approach is an extension of the effective schools method and research. It works by identifying schools that outperform their cohort group on specified measures. They are schools that have demonstrated they can educate students from high-poverty backgrounds successfully. Researchers then go to these schools and observe what is occurring to determine why these schools are effective when so many others with similar student populations are not. The thesis is that if these schools can do it, any school can do it.

The Education Trust's publication *Dispelling the Myth: High Poverty Schools Exceeding Expectations* (Barth, Haycock, Jackson, Mora, Ruiz, Robinson, & Wilkins, 1999) contains a listing of schools that meet one of two criteria. They are either (1) "high performing," which is defined as being among the 10 highest-performing, high-poverty schools on state assessments in reading and/or mathematics; or (2) "most improved," defined as being among the 10 biggest-gaining schools on state assessments in reading and/or mathematics. Many of these schools were found to achieve results that rivaled and even exceeded comparator suburban schools (i.e., schools with similar characteristics).

The study found a number of common characteristics among these schools. They used state standards extensively to design curriculum and instruction, assess student work, and evaluate teachers. Student progress on standards was monitored by comprehensive assessment systems, and students received extra support as soon as it was needed. The schools increased instructional time in reading and math in order to help students meet standards. A larger proportion of funds was allocated to support professional development focused on changing instructional practice to help students meet specific academic standards. Parental involvement was focused on helping students meet standards. These schools were all located in states or districts that had accountability systems in place with real consequences for adults in the schools.

Carter's book, *No Excuses: Lessons from 21 High-Performing, High-Poverty Schools* (2000), indicates by its title alone the underlying philosophy of the high-performance school approach: There is no excuse for any school not to enable its students to reach high standards. Carter identified three high-performing charter schools, three private schools, one religious school, and 15 public schools. These schools had principals who were free to make major decisions regarding the school's education program and personnel and who used measurable goals to establish a culture of achievement that at the secondary level focused on college preparation. Master teachers assumed duties such as peer evaluation, lead teacher, assessment expert, and keeper of the vision. Frequent testing provided continual information on student achievement, and teachers then took responsibility for their students' performance. A focus on achievement was key to maintaining good discipline because student self-discipline and self-control were linked to learning. Schools used time effectively and increased time in the school day, week, and year. Parents and principals worked as partners to make the home a center of learning, to support parents' reading to their children, and to provide parents the information they needed to check homework and ask about assignments.

At the other end of the comparison spectrum is the First in the World Consortium, a group of schools from the suburbs of Chicago. This group of schools set the goal to become first in the world in math and science achievement. These schools work collaboratively to benchmark their students against international achievement standards, to identify and implement best education practices to improve math and science achievement, and to create and support learning networks that connect educators within and across districts to share effective techniques (Kimmelman, Kroeze, Schmidt, van der Ploeg, McNeely, & Tan, 1999). This coalition serves to identify high-performing schools, but in this case the comparators are schools in the highest-achieving nations in the world.

Numerous reasons have been given for why American students cannot equal the performance of students in comparator nations, and much has been made of the "achievement gap" (Stevenson & Stigler, 1992). This consortium seeks to prove that American schools can produce results comparable to the best in the world, and it has begun to accumulate evidence that they can achieve this goal, as measured by performance on the Third International Mathematics and Science Study (Hoff, 2001d).

All of these examples of high-performance schools are important from a policy point of view for three reasons: (1) they tend to generate ideas for new policies or requirements that all schools must follow; (2) they set the stage for standards systems that are based on the premise that all students can achieve high and challenging academic standards, and accountability systems that expect all schools to enable students to achieve these standards; and (3) they encourage policymakers to establish a connection between funding and performance, an idea that will be explored next.

## NEW STATE EXPECTATIONS FOR
## EDUCATIONAL LEADERS

About the same time that the capability of schools to increase student learning was being established, educational administrators began to be viewed as school leaders rather than managers. In much the same way that the high-performing schools model increased the emphasis on school performance, the conception of principal-as-leader moved school administrators to center stage as important actors in the educational improvement process. In this conception of educational administration, the principal in particular is expected to possess the knowledge, skills, and abilities to lead schools toward sustained academic improvement. Beginning in the early 1980s, the findings from the process–product and effective schools' fields of research were translated into a series of publications and programs that emphasized the principal's ability to bring about school improvement.

The development of principal-as-leader, the acceptance of schools as environments that had significant effects on student learning, and the identification of exemplary schools that outperformed their comparator schools, set the stage for states to ratchet up their expectations for schools, particularly those that served students from low-income environments. These three factors were absolutely necessary for standards-based reforms and school-based accountability systems. If Coleman's initial conclusions had been accepted at face value, it would not have made sense to expect schools to improve. Similarly, without the effective schools research to pinpoint many of the elements of effective schools, improvement programs would have been impossible; each school would have been assumed to be unique and no statewide policy could have been devised to effect school improvement systematically. Exemplary schools that proved it was possible to have success with a wide range of students helped justify accountability notions in which individual schools were compared with one another and in which all schools were expected to bring about improvement in student achievement.

This combination of increased responsibility, clear goals, and a political consensus to improve schools became harnessed to the effective schools model in a way that energized a broad range of school-based reforms aimed at improving learning for all students. The ability to connect quality with equity was crucial to maintaining continuity with federal policies while simultaneously responding to new demands from the business community and urban activists for more effective schools. However, putting policies of this scope into practice is profoundly challenging for states and for school systems unaccustomed to mandates that reach into the core of schooling.

## LINKING FUNDING AND PERFORMANCE: THE NEXT STEP

The next logical step in the evolution of the two policy streams, fiscal control and academic standards, was their connection through a means to link funding and performance. Whether it is feasible to connect the two has been the source of considerable debate over the past 2 decades.

### Two Views on Funding and Student Performance

Much of the research on the relationship between dollars spent and student achievement has focused on the macro level, connecting average state spending with state achievement scores. Some researchers have reached the conclusion that there is no direct relationship (American Legislative Exchange Council, 1999). They argue that schools have enough money; they just don't utilize their resources effectively and efficiently (Hanushek, 1994).

Other researchers, applying meta-analytic and case study techniques, have reached a different conclusion (Greenwald, Hedges, & Laine, 1996). They find a relationship between spending and performance, particularly when examined at the school level (Murnane & Levy, 1996a). Studies have identified a range of specific factors where there is a relationship between funding and performance and where even modest increases in funding have resulted in improved achievement (Burtless, 1996; Greenwald et al., 1996).

If a relationship exists between funding and performance, it should be feasible to connect state spending and expected student achievement—if adequate data could be collected on how the monies were spent and on how efficiently schools were functioning. A model that captured this relationship would be of potential value to state legislatures accustomed to determining education funding levels based on political horse trading rather than on any rational determination of how much money schools actually need and what results could be expected from various funding levels.

## The Oregon Quality Education Model

The Oregon Quality Education Model (OQEM) is an example of a state funding model designed to establish the relationship between state funding and student performance (Conley, 1999). It is one of a new breed of finance models designed to ensure that states provide all students with an adequate education and to determine how much such an education costs. This form of finance method is known as a "professional judgment" model. The OQEM professional judgment model is a subset of a number of approaches to school finance known as adequacy models. An adequacy model seeks to ascertain the amount of money needed to provide an adequate education to every child in the state (Calvo, Picus, Smith, & Guthrie, 1999).

The OQEM is based on "Prototype Schools"—elementary, middle, and high schools designed to enable students to meet specified state goals. The costs of each of the elements and components required to provide the education program needed to meet state goals are specified for the prototype schools, then divided by the number of students in the schools to attain a per pupil funding amount. The state's projected education budget can then be generated by multiplying this figure by the number of students in the state. In this way, goals can be established for the state educational system, while the judgments of educators and other experts regarding the resources necessary to achieve the goals are used to determine an appropriate level of funding.

The OQEM was made possible by several factors. First, the state had taken over school funding as a result of a property tax limitation measure that capped the rate at which local districts could tax residents. This caused the state to have to equalize funding among districts. The measure also reduced property taxes, moving more fiscal responsibility to the state level. By 1997, the state was providing 70% of education funding out of the general fund, whereas it had provided 30% in 1990. The remaining 30% came from local property taxes that the state effectively redistributed based on its equalization formula. In reality, the state controlled all school funding, which was roughly equalized statewide.

An equalized funding system, in which no district can raise significant revenue independently, was one important prerequisite to the OQEM. The second factor was the existence of a common set of definitions for district and school data, combined with a system to collect such data and make them available in a form that allowed generalizations about the ways in which Oregon schools allocated resources. This helped establish the baseline for the prototype schools.

The third factor necessary for the creation of the OQEM was a set of common measures of student performance. These were available as a result of legislation passed in 1991 that established statewide academic standards and assessments in math, English, science, and social sciences. The assessment system, consisting of multiple-choice tests, performance tasks, and classroom-generated student work samples, offered a range of data that could be utilized to determine student and school performance.

The OQEM is relatively unique in two other respects. First, it identifies a series of factors related to school functioning for which no dollar amounts are assigned, but that are equally or more important in predicting school performance and student learning, and second, it establishes predicted levels of student achievement associated with various funding levels.

These additional nonfiscal factors are labeled "quality indicators." They are a series of measures of organizational functioning, health, and efficiency that help ascertain whether the educational system is indeed utilizing its available resources effectively. If the system is not utilizing existing resources well, additional resources are less likely to make a significant difference. The quality indicators derive from research on effective schools and include elements such as principal leadership skills, parental involvement, effective homework policies, high-quality professional development plan, involvement in decision making, and teachers' perceptions of their efficacy, among others. These indicators help create a picture of the degree to which the educational system is employing effective practices that are necessary or prerequisite to improving student achievement.

The model also establishes predicted achievement levels to accompany various funding levels. Using state assessments as a primary measure, the model forecasts the rate of improvement in the proportion of students who meet standards if the state pursues various funding levels. This element of the model is still under development and will need many years of refinement before this relationship is well established. What is most noteworthy at the moment is that an attempt is being made to connect these two key dimensions of education policy, funding and performance. This suggests the future direction of education policy: a more integrated and systemic approach to managing the state educational system. This also suggests that over time states will collect more and better comparable data from all schools to allow a better understanding and monitoring of educational system performance.

These five factors—state control of education funding, equalized funding, common school data elements, common student performance measures, and the quality indicators—are essential to the model's ability to forecast the costs and effectiveness of the educational system. These factors also demonstrate the increasing reach of the state into the province of local school districts. Oregon had been one of the most staunch local control states in the nation. Before the 1990s, districts were required to have their budgets approved yearly by local voters, who could and did cause districts that could not pass budget increases to cut programs or shorten their school year, sometimes by months, to live within available revenues.

In just a decade, the state's educational system has been transformed into one guided by the state in nearly every significant area. New accountability provisions have been put into place, now that common funding, data, standards, and assessments exist. Schools routinely are compared across districts in "cohort bands." Results appear in local newspapers and on websites. Local school districts are still important governance units, but schools must attend more closely to the expectations of the state.

If legislatures and governors are able to put into place adequacy models of the type the OQEM represents, the practices of local districts and individual schools will be influenced to a much greater degree by the state, but so will the expectations. The state, for its part, will be obligated to fund education proportional to the performance goals it adopts. A model of this nature solves two problems at once: It reduces the ambiguity in the local–state relationship as well as clarifying the state's responsibilities relative to funding school reform and improvement.

Examples like the Oregon Quality Education Model illustrate how state power has been not just extended, but put to entirely new purposes. The education policy environment at the state level is now one that concerns itself with a broad range of interconnected issues and goals. Finance is linked with reform; public education is viewed as a system, not a series of indepen-dent school districts; the effects of schools are debated, but they are assumed to be able to counteract social and economic factors; educational adminis-trators are no longer considered bureaucrats, but key performers in the state's attempt to improve schooling. The new state perspective on education is an activist perspective where even conservative elected officials tend to believe that state government should direct and control the state educational sys-tem. The following chapter explores in more detail the forces operating on public education and the goals and purposes underlying federal and state intervention into local schooling.

# Chapter 4

# THE COMPETING FORCES SHAPING
# GOVERNANCE AND POLICY

Schools are subject to forces seeking to alter who makes decisions about education. The battle over who will decide issues of public policy is known by researchers as institutional choice (Clune, 1987; Plank & Boyd, 1994). This struggle is nothing new; it is an ongoing fact of life for schools. Kirst and Bulkley (2000) describe institutional choice as "complex, uncertain, and subject to continual political change." The balance of control in education is "a series of evolving political bargains and changing perceptions about the capacity of alternative institutions" that "will never be settled by policy makers making a purely local analysis" (Kirst & Bulkley, 2000). This chapter explores the forces operating to generate reforms that affect education policies, practices, and structures.

The competition to control and guide educational governance and policy is intense. Federal, state, and local government jostle for position and influence within the policy arena, as do a range of nongovernmental organizations and interest groups. While the old system of local control is clearly in decline, the dynamics of the new system are not yet established.

The states' role as the primary level of governance for public education is well established. In practice, this has meant very different things in different states at different times. Some states have strong traditions of local control; in others, schools are more accustomed to receiving direction from state education departments. Regardless of their histories, all states are undergoing changes in the relationship between local school districts, the state, and the federal government.

During the past 30 years, the role of states has changed in nearly every important aspect of education policy and governance. States are now initiating policies in areas where they historically had shown constrained involvement or influence, such as finance, academic standards, assessments and achievement measures, teacher licensing requirements, data reporting requirements, labor relations, school-site governance structures, teacher incentives, and school choice options.

The overarching goal of increased state involvement in policy generation that affects local school districts has been to improve student performance. In the 1980s the goal of reforms was to increase the quality of
educational inputs, things like course requirements or teacher certification
standards; in the 1990s it was to get all students to reach high academic
standards.

## FIVE FORCES BEHIND STATE REFORMS

While improved student achievement guided policy development at a
macro level, five underlying forces provided sustained political impetus for
reforms to move through legislatures. These included (1) changes in the goals
of public schooling, (2) increased accountability expectations for schools, (3)
a much more activist role by business groups advocating education reform
at the state level accompanied by the adoption of private-sector notions of
management and governance, (4) concerns about urban school districts combined with public perceptions that education as a system is failing, and (5)
an emerging set of new relationships among the federal, state, and local levels. In brief, these forces helped states to take greater control of education
and to set goals focused on improved student achievement.

It is neither possible nor necessarily desirable to establish direct cause-
and-effect relationships between any one of these complex variables and any
particular action by a state. These stimuli serve to create an environment
within which states have been willing to entertain legislative action on a
widening range of education policy topics. Within any given state, other
factors in addition to these macro factors may be at work. These additional
factors include the state's unique history and method of educational governance, macro- and micropolitical forces within the state, the condition and
stage of development of the state's economy, the forces that control and guide
public opinion, and the nature and goals of the formal and informal leadership structures and interest groups present in the state along with the per-
sonalities of key individuals in positions of power or influence.

To understand state policy making fully requires acknowledgment that
it is not always a completely rational process. The five forces listed previously suggest cause–effect relationships between politically expressed needs
and policy generated to address those needs. Sometimes this is the case. In
other situations, policy results from emotional responses to nonproblems, in
response to the demands of an individual or group with particularly strong
beliefs about the need for a particular action by government, or in response
to special interest groups bent on achieving a particular result beneficial to
their interest group. If these complexities and realities are acknowledged, it

is possible to consider the five forces as important explanatory factors for policy trends that have emerged over the past 20 years, without feeling compelled to accept them as the only forces that operate in the policy arena or as the sole explanation for any particular policy.

## Changes in the Goals and Purposes of Public Education

The state role is changing not just because control of funding is migrating from the local to the state level, as noted in Chapter 3. If the basic goals of a public education system remained unchanged, it might have been feasible to devise a funding system that simply redistributed resources equitably and left districts free to pursue education programs as they saw fit. In practice, this has not occurred because the goals of public education have changed.

Most state constitutions contain provisions for a "uniform and proper" or "standardized" system of education. The primary state responsibility has been interpreted as providing the educational opportunity itself, not considering its effects. Some states specify the general outlines of a curriculum, the time to be spent in school yearly, and the minimum leaving age, and all have compulsory attendance laws. Beyond these general parameters, the tradition of the U.S. educational system has been to allow districts to operate with maximum autonomy in terms of the specifics of their education programs and the effects of those programs.

This has changed primarily due to a new consensus on the goals of public education. While most adults believe an education should still focus on "the basics" (Johnson & Immerwahr, 1995; Weiss, 1999), policy makers increasingly have been able to agree that education is a tool for national, state, and regional economic development. Furthermore, education is viewed increasingly as a means to resolve social problems. Finally, education is judged by the results achieved, not the programs offered. Student learning is more important than school programs. Given the importance of these goals, legislatures are less hesitant to conceive and pass ambitious reforms designed to achieve these goals. School districts cannot ignore these goals or the state activities designed to achieve them.

The linkage between education and workforce readiness was forged in the early 1990s as a national issue (Ambach, 1992; Commission on the Skills of the American Work Force, 1990; Harp, 1991; Resnick & Wirt, 1996; Secretary's Commission on Achieving Necessary Skills, 1991) but perhaps was underestimated as a fundamental force behind states' increasingly activist role in education policy formulation. The rhetoric of workforce preparation has served to drive education reform in a variety of states. For example, Oregon's 1991 Educational Act for the 21st Century was initiated as a means to retool the state's workforce so that the state's economy could evolve beyond natural resource extraction.

States have struggled to decide whether their standards are intended as a minimum all students should and could reach or a set of high, challenging expectations that many will struggle to meet. Within both models is a rationale that links back to slightly differing notions of economic competitiveness. The high and challenging expectations often derive from notions of a "world-class" educational system, which generally is gauged by how well students do in comparison to America's chief economic trading partners. The minimum competency approaches are rooted in a different conception of worker readiness, one that attempts to divine what skills are needed for general participation in the workforce by essentially all potential workers. Debates on state standards and assessments often have been framed as a choice between these two levels of employment readiness, rather than by academic preparation for postsecondary education.

The high school diploma has become the focal point for efforts to enforce standards that ensure that those receiving a diploma are prepared to succeed beyond high school. State testing policies, particularly high school exit exams, have thrown into turmoil long-standing practices of student sorting that resulted in different groups of students learning very different things (Oakes, 1985, 1987; Oakes & Lipton, 1992; Pool & Page, 1995). The expectation that all students need to reach high levels of functioning has caused schools to eliminate or radically redefine traditional grouping strategies even without explicit requirements from the state to do so, because students from certain groups will never pass state tests otherwise. The linkage to economic competitiveness has inadvertently led to a reassessment of the role secondary schools in particular play in sorting students.

The expectation that all students who graduate can meet high standards runs counter to long-standing practices in high schools. James Bryant Conant, president of Harvard from 1933 to 1957 and president emeritus thereafter until his death in 1978, advocated sorting high school students into tracks as a means to meet all students' needs within a larger comprehensive high school. His publication, *The American High School Today* (1959), served as the template for a three-tiered system that sent one group of students to college, another to work, and left a third in a "general" track, which did not necessarily foster college or work preparation.

By the early 1990s it was becoming clear that this experiment in social sorting was not working particularly well in the context of a new economy. States faced the challenge of reshaping the goals and structures of secondary schools that had thoroughly adopted Conant's model and saw little reason to change it. Economic competitiveness arguments proved strong enough to embolden states to adopt high school tests and exit exams for all students.

After 10 or more years of sustained efforts by states to raise performance of high school students, only now is progress being seen in some states, while others still see little change. It is a testament to both the strength of the reforms and the difficulty of changing high schools that this standoff has been in place for so long, while elementary schools have shown consistent, sometimes dramatic gains on state tests.

The dominant American political ideology from the 1980s on, which was popularized in the Reagan administration, has implicitly or explicitly rejected the strategy of providing more social programs or benefits to address a societal problem. Instead, this philosophy favors a focus on results over programs, individual responsibility over government action. Schools are expected to solve a range of intractable social problems, primarily by establishing clearer, higher expectations linked to incentives and sanctions. This political philosophy also favors reducing government in favor of greater reliance on the private sector, which has led to increased pressure on schools to produce improved student achievement or be replaced by contractors or others who can "get the job done."

As Kozol (1991) has so eloquently illustrated, tremendous inequalities continue to exist among schools. While few legislatures have moved decisively to eliminate these inequalities, many do mandate various programs that schools must follow in an attempt to ameliorate or at least recognize the most extreme manifestations of inequality. Often these mandates are not accompanied by new funds proportionate to the challenge, and when they are, it is sometimes a result of court orders (Gewertz, 2001). Educators are left to cope with these mandates in an era of less government when schools are the primary public institution designated to close the gap between social and economic classes. This focus on results leads inexorably to calls for accountability.

## Demands for Accountability

The accountability movement has gained momentum during the past half-dozen years, but its roots can be traced to the 1970s (Young, 1971). It coincides to some degree with the transference of fiscal control to the state level. As states allocated more of their general fund dollars to local education, it was only natural that concerns about how the money was being expended would generate policies designed to hold districts more accountable in a number of ways. Accountability legislation is more complex than simply monitoring how funds are spent; it also derives from equity concerns that schools are not meeting the needs of all students, particularly that schools serving large concentrations of poor and racial-minority-group students are not enabling these students to succeed.

The rush to enact accountability policies was jump-started when state standards and assessments began to be adopted in the early 1990s. The standards served as a common framework of expectations for all districts, and the state assessments provided a common measure. These tools enabled state policy makers to compare and reach judgments about individual districts and school buildings, often for the first time. Since the systems in most instances were tied to state-defined standards, they lent themselves to in-state comparisons and to the creation of student performance categories, such as "meets" or "exceeds standard." Federal law also required all states to provide performance categories for their state assessment systems. To schools accustomed to viewing progress as gradual increases in percentile scores, standards-based accountability systems were full of new and confusing language and expectations.

Fuhrman (1999) identifies this "new accountability" as encompassing the following key elements: focusing on performance and less on compliance with regulations for district and school accreditation; defining schools as the unit of improvement and collecting, analyzing, and reporting data by school; expecting all schools to adopt continuous improvement strategies tied to specific performance targets; focusing state school inspections on teaching, learning, and feedback for school improvement; grouping schools by category, such as "exceptional," "strong," "satisfactory," "needs improvement," and "unacceptable," when determining accountability and establishing clear criteria for student promotion; reporting school performance data publicly on a rapidly widening range of measures; and attaching consequences to poor performance and offering rewards for good performance.

Assessment and accountability systems have become widespread. Forty-eight states employ state assessments as the principal indicator of school performance (Goertz & Duffy, 2001). Most test students at one grade level in elementary, middle, and high school although federal legislation will require all to test at grades 3–8 annually. Twelve test consecutively from second or third grade through eighth grade in the same subjects and using the same assessment instrument. Several test similar levels but utilize different instruments or test different subjects at different levels. The federal influence on state accountability systems can be seen in Title I requirements that states identify at least three levels of performance on state tests, consisting of advanced, proficient, and partially proficient. Most states have gone beyond this requirement to create four or five categories. These categories serve multiple purposes, including public reporting, student retention decisions, and high school graduation standards.

Thirty-three states have state-defined accountability systems (Goertz & Duffy, 2001). Fourteen states expect schools to meet an absolute target relative to the state's accountability system; five require growth relative to previous scores. None focus entirely on closing the achievement gap between ethnic and racial groups, but one requires both meeting a state target and closing the achievement gap, while three expect relative growth and narrowing of the gap. Eight accommodate a combination of meeting a target or demonstrating growth. Two have elements of all three methods (Goertz & Duffy, 2001).

One of the interesting side effects of this diversity has been to make student performance across states virtually noncomparable without some sort of common reference point. The federal No Child Left Behind legislation mandates that increases or decreases on state assessment scores be "confirmed" by comparing them with National Assessment of Educational Progress (NAEP) scores (Olson, 2002c), which allows NAEP scores to be used as a national reference standard (Reckase, 2002). States will then be able to compare the challenge and rigor of their assessments against those of all other states, thereby creating upward pressure on states that set their performance levels lower than NAEP's (Olson, 2002a).

## Public Disappointment in Education and the "Politicization" of Education Policy

The general sense that the educational system is not achieving its goals has been a force in the policy arena since the release in 1983 of the *Nation at Risk* report (Freeman, 1985; Johnson, 1995; National Commission on Excellence in Education, 1983). Amazingly, it continues 20 years later to be a major driver and definer of policy initiatives (Weiss, 1999). While public surveys find a basic commitment to public education, these same polls find relatively high levels of agreement that education as a system must undergo major change, an opinion professional educators do not share to the same degree (Education Commission of the States, 1997; Educational Research Service, 1992; Johnson & Immerwahr, 1995).

This generalized concern has provided support for state policy initiatives such as increased teacher certification requirements, increased graduation requirements, teacher testing, changes in tenure laws, merit pay schemes, alternative teacher and administrator licensing approaches, academic content standards, and other policy innovations designed to affect the system as a whole, rather than individual schools. These state-level systemic initiatives have been launched with some frequency over the past 20 years, with varying effects. They represent a series of forays by legislatures into the education policy arena that challenge the authority of local education agencies to create and manage their own quality control mechanisms. The implied rationale for these policies is that public confidence in educational professionals to solve the "education crisis" is low and the state has a legitimate right to intervene in a comprehensive fashion in areas where vital state interests are at stake.

Public reaction to education is complex. On one hand, nearly every poll taken indicates support for local schools, with decreasing support for education proportional to the distance from the local schools (Elam & Rose, 1995; Elam, Rose, & Gallup, 1994). For example, a recent poll showed 70% of respondents giving U.S. public schools as a whole a grade of C (Rose & Gallup, 2001). On the other hand, longitudinal data indicate that support for public education (as opposed to vouchers) is at an all-time high (Rose & Gallup, 2001). Public opinion is split on the question of whether the nation's schools are as good as they used to be (Weiss, 1999). The public seems to be supportive of some of the major state reforms, including state standards and tests tied to awarding of diplomas, and testing in general (Rose & Gallup, 2001). This complex environment of public opinion has greatly complicated the implementation of education reform. Simultaneously, it has created an environment within which legislators can justify initiating any of a range of reforms and claim there is public support for them. One conclusion is clear: Education remains one of the top policy issues in the eyes of the public and of policy makers. Both presidential candidates in the 2000 election highlighted extensive education reform programs as central elements of their platforms and campaign strategy (Balz & Morin, 2000).

The inevitable by-product of the movement of education policy to center stage in state legislative circles has been the increased politicization of education in the partisan sense. The intense interest in education policy simply has made more apparent the fundamentally political nature of education policy development and implementation. The current era can be characterized as one in which control over education policy is moving out of the hands of education professionals and education interest groups that were much more influential throughout the twentieth century.

Wirt and Kirst (1989) call attention to these changing dynamics as they describe the 1980s, one of the most turbulent in terms of changes in state attitudes toward education policy, as a time when "new definitions of school purposes, new claims on school resources, new efforts to make the schools responsive to certain groups and their values are all giving rise to a larger, more weblike set of political relationships surrounding local schools." In this environment, every element of school governance was fair game for involvement in political controversy.

The widespread public concern for education and its central role on the policy stage are well established. The public appears to be of a mixed mind about the future of public education, rejecting radical solutions like vouchers, but entertaining more moderate proposals like charter schools. Educators now function in much more of a "fishbowl" than did their predecessors of 50 years earlier. Education policy is now fair game for a wide range of interest groups, and educators will need to learn their role in this new constellation of education policy players and mechanisms.

## The Unique Problems of Urban Districts

Urban school systems in the United States have struggled almost without exception over the past 30 or more years. This increase in their problems coincides with the gradual extension of state control over education policy. The net effect has been to put state legislatures on a collision course with urban districts. This can be highly problematic when legislatures dominated by rural and suburban interests make policy for urban schools. Local control is seldom a strong enough reason for legislatures to limit their intervention into urban districts when the fate of the urban area may be closely linked to the state's economic prosperity and social climate.

In those states with large urban centers, the unique and seemingly intractable problems faced by the inner-city school districts have driven greater state involvement in local school district policy. Turnover of superintendents in urban districts is one indication of the volatility of governance in those districts (Reid, 2001a), although Yee and Cuban (1996) point out that considerable variance exists in superintendent tenure, with some lasting 5 to 6 years, well beyond the 2-year average frequently cited. States have intervened to change governance structures or otherwise exercise greater oversight of urban districts, even to the point of taking over management completely (Rettig, 1992). Twenty-three states have laws that allow the state to take over districts in cases of "academic bankruptcy," fiscal mismanagement, and other situations where evidence of gross incompetence exists. However, only 11 states have exercised the option. In most cases the object of the takeover was an urban district (Johnston & Sandham, 1999). Some cities, Chicago being one example, have seen the responsibility for educational governance shift from the local school board to the mayor's office (Kirst & Bulkley, 2000).

Urban schools and their problems remain a major force driving state education policy development. Public perceptions that urban schools remain in a state of perpetual crisis and that more tax dollars do not necessarily result in solutions or improvements for city schools help spur legislatures to action (Weiss, 1999). Cuban (2001) argues that "systemic reform" policies generated at the state level are not the right solution for the problems of urban schools. The problems of urban schools have become generalized to the entire system, the result of "unrelenting criticism" of urban districts, "allegedly ill-managed and controlled by strike-prone, anti-reform teachers' unions." The media have then amplified this critique and applied it to all American schools, and the public subsequently has accepted this characterization.

Tensions exist between large cities and state legislatures over fiscal and policy issues, and even where those tensions abate, funding and performance issues remain difficult to resolve between state capitals and urban centers (Johnston, 2001). These tensions can lead to sweeping legislation or reform programs. The problems of the urban schools can be the impetus for policies that then affect all the schools in the state. The objective may be to improve or control urban schools, but the effect is to create greater state involvement in all schools within a state.

### The Emerging Federal–State–Local Partnership

The federal and state governments are having more influence on local education policy and practice. However, this is not the same as saying that the state and federal governments control the schools. Schools remain vibrant, unpredictable, complex environments that respond to policies in a wide variety of ways, some predictable, some quite unpredictable. Studies have confirmed that state and federal governments must seek a partnership with local schools if policy implementation is to proceed in a way that addresses government needs and accommodates local realities (Fuhrman, Clune, & Elmore, 1991; McLaughlin, 1991). This "mutual adaptation process" (Odden, 1991, p. 4) leads to successful implementation of programs.

Adaptation alone is not sufficient to meet larger reforms aimed at the core values and practices of education. The state must establish the goals, standards, measures, and consequences to create a framework within which site-level administrators have flexibility to bring about the types of changes that refocus education on high performance by all students.

Marsh and LeFever (1997) studied principals operating under two types of standards systems. Option one was characterized by high stakes and common student performance standards. Principals had the authority and resources to bring about school-site changes. In option two, schools were encouraged to create local student performance standards, were provided unobtrusive support for implementing the policy, and worked with less decentralization of authority and resources. Principals who functioned under option one were more successful in leading their schools toward achievement of the policy's goals than those working under option two. The state provided necessary guidance and pressure for change and improvement, but schools had the ability and responsibility to create local programs that addressed state goals.

Beyond providing a framework of expectations, consequences, and rewards, states must be ready to address a range of critical issues as they formulate education reform policies (Boser, 2001). First among these is the capacity of local districts and individual schools to implement the requirements of the reform. States must be ready to determine in particular what is required in terms of time and training to put reforms in place.

Numerous additional important questions must be considered when education reform policy is being developed at the state level. Will the reforms tend to overload teachers or will something come off their plates, lightening their workload so they can assume the duties and perform the tasks associated with reform? Do the reform requirements conflict with any other rules, regulations, or policies? Are they aligned with other elements of the educational governance system? Is there any incentive for teachers to implement the reform or are there only consequences? Are adequate resources targeted directly to the reform's goals and any programs that arise as a direct result of the reform? If not, are there any provisions to reallocate existing resources in a realistic fashion to achieve the reform's goals? Do educators understand what they are required to do and where they have discretion to adapt the reform to local circumstances? Are educational administrators up to the task of leading implementation of the reform or do they require additional training or motivation to do so? Has the state realistically assessed the political capital that must be expended to implement the reform and how much of this will have to come from local schools and districts? These questions suggest the nature of the states' responsibilities in their partnership with local districts to reform and improve education.

Local districts and individual schools have the responsibility to become more adaptive. They need to be able to respond rather quickly to the demands of state reform requirements. They need to be able to provide feedback quickly as well as to let the state know when its reform policies need refining or which specific aspects seem unlikely of working as the state expected. District central offices will have greater responsibility to interpret between the state and schools and to put data collection and management systems in place that allow school personnel to diagnose strengths and weaknesses in order to cope with accountability requirements. Central office staff should be or become adept at identifying low-performing schools and diagnosing the causes of poor performance. Districts should be ready to reallocate resources internally to ensure that low-performing schools improve, rather than allocating resources equally to all schools. District policies, such as teacher placement, should be examined to determine whether the best teachers end up working with the students who most need their skills. Districts should seek out resources for local schools, either internally or via partnerships with other districts and organizations.

School boards need to redefine their relationship to the state, considering how to interpret, implement, and influence state education policy. Rather than focusing primarily on the amount of money the state provides the local district, the board should expand its horizons to be interested in and knowledgeable about state policy development and implementation. Boards also should seek to maximize community and parent involvement via democratic decision-making bodies at the school level. These bodies need to be nurtured and supported in order to thrive. Boards must insist that such entities really do represent their communities and that they are focused on improvement, not maintenance. Boards also will be expected to understand which schools are succeeding, which aren't, and why. They will need to learn how to shape the administrative structure and personnel so that the organization is focused on continuous improvement of schools.

A key federal responsibility in the context of a partnership with states and local school districts is to provide resources adequate to fund federal program mandates, special education and Title I in particular. In fiscal 1997, high-poverty districts received less Title I money per pupil on average than did low-poverty districts, and more than 1,700 school districts that technically no longer qualified for concentration grants received them due to hold-harmless provisions in the law (Robelen, 2001). A federal government committed to improving student performance will make adequate funds available and target them to the places they are needed most.

Additional aspects of the federal role include establishing frameworks within which states must set improvement targets. The No Child Left Behind legislation lets states determine the standards they wish to set and the ways in which each state will determine student proficiency, but improvement is not optional. Quality standards in areas such as teacher preparation programs is another place a federal presence is consistent with national educational goals to improve teaching, but still leaves states significant latitude regarding the content and structure of those programs (Blair, 2001a; Congress of the United States, 1998).

## NONGOVERNMENTAL INFLUENCES ON EDUCATION POLICY, PRACTICE, AND GOVERNANCE

Educational governance in a system as decentralized as the American system is not understood by simply describing local, state, and federal duties and responsibilities. This decentralization and the lack of a strong federal role in education have contributed to a vacuum at the national level that does not exist in countries where central governments direct education policy. To fill the vacuum, numerous nongovernmental and quasi-governmental organizations have arisen that functionally direct, influence, or coordinate education policy in a wide arena. The influence of these entities can be found at all levels of the educational system.

## National Quasi-Governmental Agencies and
## Nongovernmental Organizations

The unique role in the United States of national organizations devoted to education policy formulation and dissemination has been noted by Fowler (2000). Examples of groups representing the interests of elected or appointed state officials include the Education Commission of the States, the National Conference of State Legislatures, the National Governors Association, the Council of Chief State School Officers, and the National School Boards Association, among many others. Another set of organizations seeks to ensure that the viewpoints of professional educators have influence at the national level. These groups include the American Association of School Administrators, the National Association of Secondary School Principals, the National Education Association, and the American Federation of Teachers.

Each of these organizations actively seeks to identify problem areas, formulate possible solutions beneficial to its members, and promote recommendations for specific education policies. These solutions are identified via forums, issue papers, national meetings, and other means by which new or innovative ideas are explored and shared. Most important, these organizations function as networks to connect members across state boundaries. One of the effects of these networks is that policy ideas and programs flow up the communication chain from the state to the national level at the same time information on new policies is being disseminated downward. Since states are "laboratories" for new policies and programs, this type of communication is crucial to maintaining rough continuity in education policy across states in the absence of mandatory federal policies and to generating new policies and practices.

An example of this phenomenon is teacher licensing standards and practices, which vary from state to state but have enough similarity to permit movement of teachers across state boundaries. At the same time, many states are experimenting with a range of variations in licensing. These initiatives can even go in entirely opposite directions within the same state, instituting policies to exempt individuals with particular skills from teacher education requirements while creating incentives for teachers to become "board certified" by the National Board for Professional Teaching Standards. From these experiments other states draw lessons and develop their own programs. Occasionally state policies migrate to the federal level where they influence policy. The Texas model of school reform with its emphasis on basic skills improvements and school accountability is a recent example. The Texas approach was used as a template for much of the ESEA reauthorization of 2001, also known as the "No Child Left Behind" initiative (U. S. Department of Education, 2001). This use of policy generation and dissemination networks is not found in any other country to the degree it is a fixture of the American educational system.

In practice, the importance of nongovernmental organizations is the breadth of policy options that they entertain and the speed with which they identify, formulate, and disseminate policy issues. With the advent of large-scale electronically networked communication, the pace of this process has accelerated. Ideas flow rapidly from state to state via these interlocking networks. Social promotion, site-based management, and K–16 programs are examples of ideas that were rapidly disseminated via these networks and implemented equally rapidly and in a variety of forms by states throughout the nation.

### Controlling the High School–College Transition

The relationship between the secondary and postsecondary educational systems is another sphere where the decentralized nature of governance confronts the need for some systematic means of communicating across organizational boundaries. Higher educational governance in the United States is in some ways even more decentralized than public schools, when the importance of private institutions is taken into account. Even in large public college and university systems, significant differences exist in requirements, programs offered, and administrative organization. Nearly every state has multiple governing agencies for its public colleges and universities, in addition to private institutions that also may behave in some ways like public institutions.

However, these two systems, higher education and secondary education, both decentralized in their governance, have managed to develop systematic means of communicating. The communication historically has been more one-way than two-way, but this may be changing. Colleges and universities have set their entrance requirements and communicated them to high schools, which have constructed instructional programs and instituted systems to transmit academic information to postsecondary institutions.

### SAT, ACT, and ETS

How has this consistency been achieved without a federal presence prescribing practices? Here is an example of how the American system relies on nongovernmental organizations to fulfill key coordination functions. Two large national testing organizations are the College Board, which manages the SAT, and American College Testing (ACT). The two determine the tests American students take to apply to college. A separate organization, Educational Testing Service (ETS), produces the actual tests the College Board offers, including the SAT and the SAT-II subject matter tests. ETS also designs and markets tests for a variety of other purposes and clients. ACT, by contrast, develops its tests internally.

These agencies produce a range of instruments that influence the future of millions and the curriculum of virtually all high schools. They do so while remaining entirely outside of formal governmental control. Starting with the College Board's humble beginnings over 100 years ago, nongovernmental organizations have been a major force in determining how students will be judged for college admission. ACT began in the mid-1950s as an alternative to the SAT and now parallels the College Board's products and functions in many ways, although it tends to address the testing needs of the work world somewhat more than does the College Board. ACT's mission is "to help individuals and organizations make informed decisions about education and work" and to "provide information for life's transitions."

The full name of the College Board is the College Entrance Examination Board (CEEB), which provides much clearer insight into its origins and purposes. The CEEB is composed of representatives from colleges, universities, high schools, and college preparatory academies. It describes itself as "a national, nonprofit membership association dedicated to preparing, inspiring, and connecting students to college and opportunity." It attempts to understand what its members' needs are for programs and tools designed to enhance and determine college readiness.

Both ACT and the College Board have national networks of members organized into regions that have annual meetings, committees, projects, and reports. These regional groups, under the coordination of the parent organizations, function as a network that can influence both national and state policy. ACT and the College Board serve vital functions by linking among states, identifying key policy issues, and creating products for use by their members and, increasingly, by individual states.

ETS is a powerful organization that exerts tremendous influence on the American educational system, yet is not publicly accountable in any direct way. It is a close cousin of the College Board, having been spawned initially to develop the SAT. From these beginnings, it has expanded to produce a range of examinations, including the Preliminary Scholastic Aptitude Test (PSAT), the Advanced Placement (AP) tests, the Graduate Record Exam (GRE), the Graduate Management Admission Test (GMAT), and, most recently, the Praxis tests for prospective and practicing teachers.

ETS defines itself as "the world's largest private educational testing and measurement organization and a leader in educational research" (Educational Testing Service, 2001). Its purpose as a nonprofit company is to serve the needs of "individuals, educational institutions and agencies, and governmental bodies in 181 countries" for which in 2001 ETS developed and administered more than 11 million tests (Educational Testing Service, 2001).

Only in the United States do organizations of this size, power, and influence exist entirely outside of the formal educational governance system (Cohen & Spillane, 1993). This independence has numerous advantages, but potential drawbacks as well. ETS, the College Board, and ACT must sell enough of their products at a price that enables them to cover expenses and simultaneously generate revenue for future product development. This makes them market sensitive, but also creates a strong incentive for them to continue producing testing instruments that have been proven to be successful revenue generators.

This can create potential conflicts of interest within the organizations, for example, when the flagship product of the College Board and ETS, the SAT, is subject to criticism on the basis of perceived negative social effects, not technical deficiencies. These nongovernmental organizations find it difficult to evaluate the relative trade-offs between generating a secure revenue stream and addressing social goals. The federal government, on the other hand, has less of a conflict focusing its education policies on issues like social equity and access to education, regardless of the effects on particular products or tests.

A recent and perhaps more troubling development has been the metamorphosis of the College Board into "CollegeBoard.com." The line between the organization's role as the repository of a certain amount of public trust and its new emphasis on establishing a commercial presence in the area of services to college-bound students has not been firmly drawn, nor is it clear how the organization can maintain a balance between public trust and profit.

While this articulated system is by no means highly aligned, and high schools and colleges retain broad latitude on how they interpret these tests, the system nevertheless is sufficiently connected across the boundaries to allow students to move between high school and college in a relative smooth, although increasingly complicated and complex, manner.

### Business Groups: Continuing Advocates for Educational Change

Continuing pressure by business interests has helped generate and sustain the push for education reform in the face of educator and parent resistance. While states have moderated their timelines, no state has totally abandoned its education reform program. The business community has been an important force in sustaining the push for education reform at both the state and national levels.

It is important to note that in reality there is no one "business community" in the United States. Instead, groupings of businesses and types of businesses exist. Large corporations tend to have a different perspective on education policy issues than do small locally owned businesses, for example. Over the past 15 years, a segment of American business has organized itself to influence the course of education policy, particularly the relationship between schooling and workforce readiness. Driven by larger corporations, this influence has been felt in individual states as well as at the national level. While a range of businesses have relationships with schools at the local level, these tend to center around school–business partnerships rather than being aimed at policy and program redesign.

Large businesses and corporations are structured to influence national and state policy most effectively (Clark & Lacey, 1997; Oregon Business Council, 1996; Weisman, 1991a, 1991c). These organizations have the personnel and resources to mount sustained lobbying campaigns. Furthermore, some CEOs tend to have broader perspectives on the effects of public policy on business. Frank Schrontz of Boeing, Ross Perot of EDS, Louis Gerstner of RJR-Nabisco and IBM, and David Kearns of Xerox were all notable for their interest in education policy and the influence they wielded shaping state and national education reform agendas. Some have issued reports and written articles and books on the topic that have been read widely by policy makers (Gerstner, 1995; Kearns & Doyle, 1988; Toch, Bennefield, & Bernstein, 1996). Their basic thesis has been similar: America cannot be competitive in the world economy without highly skilled, well-educated workers, which American schools are failing to produce.

As the American economy has transformed from manufacturing to information management and service, employers have become increasingly concerned with employee skills (Akers, 1990; Commission on the Skills of the American Work Force, 1990; Secretary's Commission on Achieving Necessary Skills, 1991). Many businesses have redefined their self-interest in terms that include a high-quality public education system (National Alliance of Business, 1989; Stone, 1991). Education quality becomes increasingly important as a variable influencing where companies locate—and where they remain. Business groups reflect these concerns and lobby at the national and state levels, not just for better schools, but for a radically transformed educational system capable of meeting the demands of the new economy (Gordon, 1990; Weisman, 1991b; Zimmerman, Norris, Kirkpatrick, Mann, & Herndon, 1990).

One of the distinguishing characteristics of business' involvement in education reform in the period from the mid-1980s to the present is that business leaders have been offering specific recommendations and strategies for restructuring educational governance that often have then been picked up by education groups (Education Commission of the States, 1988). Business groups have issued reports that go far beyond the relationship between businesses and schools to consider the role of education in society and how best to organize schools and to instruct students (National Alliance of Busi-

ness, 1989). While many educators have been resentful of this appropriation by business of what previously had been their exclusive domain, the
recommendations of business nevertheless have been very influential in shaping the education policy landscape at the state and federal levels and encouraging a range of new policy options and education practices that would not
have been entertained otherwise (Amster, 1990; Ball, 1990).

Several specific examples of the ability of business leaders to define and
jump-start reform efforts at the state level include the Prichard Committee
in Kentucky, which developed the broad outlines of Kentucky's landmark
education reform program, the Kentucky Education Reform Act (Sexton,
1995); the Perot Commission in Texas, which outlined a standards-based,
performance-based educational system that is still being implemented in the
state (Toch et al., 1996); and the Oregon Business Council, which has issued
a series of reports that have influenced the development of the state's decade-
long education reform effort (Conley, 1993; Conley & Stone, 1996; Oregon
Business Council, 1996).

### Parents: An Amorphous But Potent Force

American parents have proven to be influential in shaping the political
discourse on education reform. Some urban reforms, such as in Chicago, have
been spurred on by parents, who subsequently have gained power through
their participation on school-based governing boards. Parents also have arisen
as powerful critics and opponents to reform, as in Pennsylvania in the early
1990s when parent-led protests caused the state standards first to be put on
hold and then revised (Harp, 1993; Rothman, 1992b). Parent protests over
state tests in Texas, Massachusetts, and New York have been vocal and highly
visible (Hoff, 2000; Manzo, 2001).

While national parent groups were not significantly involved in the development of the recent federal legislation, No Child Left Behind, state-level
parent groups frequently are consulted on state reform proposals. This has
helped to mollify parent apprehension somewhat. As the pace and scope of
state reform accelerated during the 1990s, *ad hoc* parent groups sprang up
to raise concerns and lead protests (Manzo, 2001). Because these groups tend
to focus on one state and even one issue, they have not been able to mount
a sustained organizational challenge to education reform as defined by the
business community.

They have, however, given policy makers pause and led to the scaling
back of some of the more grandiose state initiatives, particularly when teachers were angered and students were affected directly. State assessments that
initially generated high failure rates, as in Arizona and Virginia, are examples
of this phenomenon. Conversely, politicians have adopted some reforms, most

notably California's class-size reduction program, that are favored by parents (Johnston, 1996a).

Parent groups also have pushed for more fundamental reform and have supported standards-based reforms and greater state intervention in communities where schools have been failing. These parents contend that local educators have not been responsive to their complaints and concerns, and that external pressure is needed for improvement to occur (Viadero, 1991).

Parents have been influential in the emergence of charters, often as organizers of such schools. They have been able to argue the case for charters effectively, since legislators often do not view parents with the suspicion sometimes reserved for educators. In these varying ways, parents have tended not to lead reform as much as to constrain and guide its evolution. They remain a force to be reckoned with and one politicians seek to avoid angering.

### Private and Public Foundations: Generating Change and Innovation

Private philanthropies are extremely important as forces that underwrite and guide experimentation in public education. A recent example is the Annenberg Challenge, a half-billion-dollar effort over 5 years to bring about significant educational change and improvement, particularly in urban districts. The Annenberg Challenge was designed to be a catalyst that would energize support for education reform efforts across the country through 18 locally designed initiatives. The Gates Foundation has been a more recent arrival at the educational scene, sponsoring projects to create small learning environments and to redesign failing schools, create new effective schools, and replicate proven models of effective schooling. The Pew Charitable Trusts have undertaken a broad array of program initiatives in education during the past decade. While they have concentrated historically on Philadelphia, they more recently developed a national agenda that supported K–16 education linkages as well as early childhood education. The Carnegie Corporation and the Ford Foundation have long histories of jump-starting education reform. For example, the Ford Foundation's support of community school boards in New York City in the 1960s led to their eventual incorporation as a continuing governance structure in the district. The Carnegie Corporation currently focuses on improving urban high schools. Other private foundations with interests in education reform include the Kellogg Foundation and its "New Options for Youth Through Engaged Institutions Outcomes," which emphasizes connections between high school and college, and the Spencer Foundation, which funds research projects. The Millkin Foundation is notable for its awards to individual educators, recognizing their contributions and excellence. At the federal level, the National Science Foundation has long been one of the most influential sources of educational change, most recently with its multiyear, multimillion-dollar Systemic State Initiative project.

These foundations play a key role in a system where individual districts can decide to pursue new directions and initiatives. They solicit ideas and help develop them. They provide room for activities local districts would not fund on their own. They take on problems no one else seems willing to tackle, such as urban high schools. Their impact is great precisely because educational governance is so disjointed. These organizations can elicit responses from dozens of districts and hundreds of schools, which then make changes in their programs. Some go on to become models; many others burn brightly, then flame out. Still others never really get off the ground. The foundations allow this important experimentation to occur, and they truly take advantage of the decentralized nature of educational governance by making changes one school and one district at a time. The challenge they have faced is scaling up and institutionalizing their achievements so that they have effects on the larger system.

## EDUCATION UNDER SIEGE?

The decentralized nature of American educational governance leads to the formation of power and influence centers inside and outside the formal governance system. Educators have the difficult and frustrating task of trying to read the sometimes conflicting signals from these power centers and to integrate and apply them in practice. Historically, the educational system has coped with this fragmentation by making sure change occurred very slowly, which meant fewer demands were made on schools at any given time. The current situation is different because educators are being called upon to change from all sides at once, from the state and federal governments, from the business community, from the public at large, and from a range of agencies and special-purpose organizations. The changes are not necessarily all in the same direction, and sometimes these groups even alter their priorities before schools have been able to respond fully to the first charge they receive.

This is the current environment within which professional educators attempt to operate. One safety valve has been that schools are not entirely subject to these external controls, as the next chapter illustrates. Schools do not change easily, a fact policy makers and interest group leaders are learning, to their occasional frustration and dismay.

# Chapter 5

# WHY IS IT SO DIFFICULT TO IMPLEMENT STATE POLICY AT THE SCHOOL LEVEL?

The simple reason that it is difficult to implement state policy at the school level is that the educational system is not particularly designed to process policy generated centrally, and schools are not designed to change easily. The more complex answer leads to an examination of the nature and process of policy implementation.

Prior to Berman and McLaughlin's (1978) seminal study of the effects of federal policy on school functioning, many assumed that the educational system did or should work in a mechanistic fashion to implement policies promulgated from higher governing levels. This assumption was probably overdue for reconsideration, given that schools were not changing much even though the federal and state governments were promulgating ever more education policy designed to effect specific changes in schools and schooling.

## THE INTERPLAY BETWEEN STATE AND LOCAL LEVELS IN POLICY IMPLEMENTATION

Berman and McLaughlin (1976) reached the conclusion that policy implementation was, at the least, an interplay between the goals of the policy and the priorities, culture, and politics of the local district. Policies were ignored, appropriated, reshaped, adapted, and implemented along a continuum that was related to the context of each district and sometimes each school. Their research suggested that policy implementation was much more multifaceted than had been suspected or acknowledged previously.

Elmore and McLaughlin (1988) extended this analysis further to reach some general conclusions about the role states should play in the formulation of policy that affected local school districts. They recommended that in order to improve the quality of policy implementation, policy makers should charge practitioners with development of solutions aimed at closing the gap between policy and practice and as a way to avoid mandating requirements with little or no connection to the realities of practice. Policies should be designed to accommodate variability and reflect understanding of effective practice better in order to avoid discouraging and penalizing such practices. Policy makers must learn that rules alone cannot prescribe the solutions to practical problems; they can only set standards of fairness. State policy should be designed to see that affected organizations foster and encourage needed reforms in education practices.

These conceptualizations of the state's role in policy assume to some degree local school districts that are striving to improve, or, at the least, are cognizant of the state's general policy goals and somewhat willing to respond to those goals or negotiate the difference between local and state goals. In settings where districts, schools, or educators have little interest in state policy or even go so far as to implicitly reject the state's right to formulate education policy for schools, these nostrums have less utility. This relatively complex and hostile environment is more representative of what states face as they wield authority in ways that are new and sometimes alien to local school districts. Rather than seeking to close the gap between policy and practice, for example, local districts may explicitly reject the policy goals.

However, not all state reforms are greeted automatically with hostility by local districts. The Center for Policy Research in Education (1989) conducted a 5-year study of education reforms in six states that reached the conclusion that school districts did not tend to resist reforms that sought to increase academic requirements. Districts carried out much of the state reform agenda, and some districts used state policies to promote local priorities.

Reactions to state assessment and accountability policies illustrate the limits of the state as the framer of educational goals, and local educators as the creators of effective programs in response to the goals (Schmidt, 1995). It is almost impossible to imagine an assessment and accountability system that is truly negotiated with local districts and even individual schools, and is derived from their best education practices. This is in part because assessment and accountability systems serve multiple goals and multiple constituencies, with educators being only one, and not necessarily the most important, constituent. When state goals conflict with the self-defined interests of local districts and schools, state–local partnerships are very problematic because state goals trump local interests.

In these situations, few effective practices emerge, and a response that educators may view as effective accommodation of state policies, such as intense teaching to a state test, is not always a practice the state wants to promote. When states attempt to avoid detailed rule setting, educators may seize upon the resulting generality as a reason not to implement policies (Massell et al., 1997); then, when states specify expectations in greater detail, educators point out the flaws or problems with the policy at the implementation level (Goldman & Conley, 1997).

Educators have not necessarily created effective systems designed to augment and support state policy goals. Those large state-level organizations that do exist, such as state teachers' unions, find themselves viewing education reform largely in terms of its effects on working conditions and funding. Other groups, such as state administrator organizations, which may be effective at communicating policy intentions, are less accustomed to implementation-related responsibilities. The net effect is that local educators have few places to turn for help even if they do wish to implement state goals.

Educators certainly have not ignored the need to develop mechanisms for collaborative support and improvement. They have created reform-minded groups and networks, such as the Coalition of Essential Schools (Sizer, 1992), the National Network for Educational Renewal (Goodlad, 1994), and Accelerated Schools (Levin, 1989). These loosely affiliated groups of schools have tended to pursue goals set by educators or derived from the vision of a particular reformer. At times these goals may be orthogonal to state objectives or at the least not necessarily congruent. Schools can suffer from reform overload and fragmentation when these educator-generated initiatives conflict with the demands of state policies (Little, Erbstein, & Walker, 1996). Educators at any given moment may be implementing a variety of programs in relative isolation from one another within the same school, with unpredictable results (Little, Erbstein, & Walker, 2001; Prestine & McGreal, 1997).

Attempts to unite professional development and state reform goals have demonstrated that a link between practice and policy can be established, but that this linkage tends to occur more on the teacher's terms than the state's (Jennings, 1996; Little, 1993). Professional development is the nexus point at which state policy is converted into inputs to which educators react. Teachers can become shapers and reshapers of reforms via the professional development process. As Little (1993) explains, professional development designed solely for the purpose of implementing state reform can obscure important questions about the purposes of reform as well as mask internal contradictions within a reform program or tensions between and among several reform initiatives. The effectiveness of professional development should be assessed in terms of its capacity to enable teachers to work individually or in groups to shape, promote, and criticize reforms from a well-informed basis. "The most robust professional development options will locate problems of implementation within this larger set of possibilities" (Little, 1993).

This argument, while entirely logical and appropriate, illustrates one of the reasons policy implementation is so difficult. If a state is to promulgate a policy, design and organize large-scale professional development programs, then wait while all the problems of the policy are identified and the policy is rewritten, then modify the professional development program accordingly and begin the process anew, implementation of necessity will be slow and arduous, if it takes place at all.

This approach also places teachers in a conflict of interest position to some degree. If a reform seeks to make teachers change in ways they perceive as increasing their workload or disrupting well-established routines, they see this as being asked to make life harder for themselves. Few teachers are likely to embrace such a reform with enthusiasm. Teachers may be well-informed critics, but they may be filtering their critique of state reforms through their own notions of desirable workplace conditions.

Teachers most certainly filter reform goals and requirements through their own set of values and beliefs about effectiveness (Conley & Goldman, 1998). This most important of screens is helpful when teachers are well informed about effective education practice and can help the state avoid policy errors. The screen is equally powerful but more problematic when teachers believe, for example, in a practice such as ability grouping, or that certain groups of students can never be expected to master state standards due to their backgrounds.

In such circumstances, the state is challenged to motivate teachers to change. To be motivated, teachers must perceive some gap or dissonance between current practices and policy goals. The gap has to be sufficient and the goals compelling enough to make teachers willing to learn new ideas and put them into practice. This establishes what Jennings (1996) calls a "bewildering loop" in which policies are only what teachers perceive them to be, therefore limiting the ability of a policy to create dissonance. Hess (1995) found that even when dissonance existed within the community at large, the result was not necessarily a more rapid pace of change in schools. In a study of policy diffusion in urban districts, results indicated that education reform was not accelerated by local community dissatisfaction with schools. Teachers themselves must be dissatisfied with schooling for change to take place and reform-oriented policy to be implemented.

Some reforms, like performance pay or charter schools, tend to divide or alienate teachers precisely because they are instituted without attention to teacher perceptions. However, they are not necessarily undertaken to gain teacher approval (Sandham, 1999). Professional development programs, however well conceived, would seem to be of lesser value when teachers do not approve of the underlying goals they seek to support. Granted, teacher objections to reforms may signal fatal flaws within the policies, but objections are just as likely to reflect concerns about changes in the status quo, loss of status or pay, competition from other education service providers, increased accountability, or other public policy goals that do not appear to benefit teachers directly, from their perspective (Viadero, 2001). Should the state therefore not pursue such reforms, or should the state be aware that teacher engagement and involvement may be of a substantively different nature than in areas where general consensus exists regarding needs and methods?

Fullan and Stiegelbauer (1991) highlight the complexity of reform implementation. They identify nine "key factors" affecting implementation that cluster into three subgroups: (1) characteristics of the change: need, clarity, complexity, quality/practicality; (2) local characteristics: district, community, principal, teacher; and (3) external factors: government and other agencies. He argues for "top-down, bottom-up" policy formulation and implementation. However, only one of the nine factors, government and other agencies, is a top-down factor (although an argument can be made that district directives are top-down as well). Policy implementation, in this conceptualization, is the process of turning an idea loose and seeing how it is processed by a range of constituents through a variety of lenses. Reform is particular—an event that occurs at individual schools, even individual classrooms.

Kirp and Driver (1995) warn against viewing the school and the larger system as dichotomous. Policy conversations have a major impact at the school-site level. Practice is defined and redefined locally, but this redefinition takes place in a context framed by policy makers who should understand that what they can do best is situate this dynamic process within broad boundaries and avoid insistence on adherence to minute details and particulars.

## HOW SCHOOLS PROCESS REFORMS

But what is the environment like within which this complex processing, analyzing, adapting, and articulating are occurring? Researchers, including those who emphasize the importance of teacher involvement and top-down, bottom-up partnerships for change, acknowledge that "the vast majority of schools are not conducive to sustained teacher innovation" (Fullan & Stiegelbauer, 1991, p. 55).

Some schools have learned how to achieve the balance between compliance-oriented reaction to state mandates and adaptation to external demands in ways that improve teaching and learning. These schools continue to be relatively few in number, leaving intact the larger challenge for the state (or district) of how to achieve a reasonable balance between top-down policies and bottom-up implementation and adaptation without lengthening timelines so long that the original policy goals are obscured or forgotten.

When the balance can be achieved, student learning gains seem to be the result, as a study of 71 successful high-poverty Title I elementary schools suggests (U.S. Department of Education Planning and Evaluation Service,

2001). Students in these schools made greater gains in reading when teachers rated their professional development highly and said it supported their school's reform program, focused on relevant standards and assessments, and helped them gain confidence in the use of new teaching approaches. Student test score growth between grades 3 and 5 increased about 20% more for classrooms where teachers rated professional development highly than for those where it received low ratings.

Large-scale applications of programs where educators choose a reform model have yielded mixed results to date, although researchers caution it is too soon to draw definitive conclusions (Berends, Kirby, Naftel, & McKelvey, 2001). An evaluation of 163 schools in the New American Schools approach to whole-school models yielded comparisons with state or district test data. Half showed gains in mathematics and just under half gained in reading.

These models are important because they represent a variation on the top-down, bottom-up formula. One of the largest tests of New American Schools models was attempted in the Memphis, Tennessee, school system during a multiyear experiment in which all schools were mandated to select an improvement model from among a number believed to be effective in increasing student learning. In the end, many schools never settled on a model, many that did never implemented it with any vigor or commitment, and some that did had difficulty achieving and sustaining fidelity with their model's key principles (Viadero, 2001).

The program was abandoned as much due to educator resistance as to a transition in leadership at the superintendent level. In its place the district adopted a strategy focused on improving existing practice by developing curriculum frameworks, emphasizing reading, and purchasing more reading textbooks. Teachers were characterized as having complained about the amount of time and "paperwork" associated with the models. The head of the local teachers' union, commenting on the decision to discontinue the models, said, "All teachers want to do is be allowed to teach" (Viadero, 2001, p. 6). Such sentiment does not bode well for large-scale systemic change grounded in partnerships between policy makers and policy implementers.

What generalizations, if any, can be made about the interaction between state (and federal) education policy and teacher behavior in the classroom? Cuban (1993) offers a summary of the cycle of reform to which schools have been subjected periodically over the past century and considers the factors observed to influence teaching during this period. Reforms follow predictable phases, he contends, and generally end up having little lasting effect on education practice. Cuban's phases of reform can be summarized as follows.

Social, political, and economic changes in objective conditions of life or in ideologies create situations that opinion makers in society define as problems. Policy makers, academics, and opinion makers talk about the problems as they see them, and a consensus begins to develop about what the problems are and what solutions are feasible. Groups and individuals outside the schools develop policy proposals and programs to solve the perceived problems. A cadre of reformers emerges and seeks to influence school boards, school administrators, and teachers to adopt and implement reforms. Some policies do get adopted in the form of legislation, school board decisions, and school-level decisions. Efforts are made to move the reforms into routine practice, to "institutionalize" them within schools and classrooms. Growing criticism of educators' seemingly slow or halfhearted efforts to implement reforms gives way to shrinking attention to whether schools are addressing the problems the reforms were designed to solve. Disappointment sets in. Social, economic, or demographic conditions change and the cycle begins anew.

Why is teaching so slow to change and why is change in teaching so difficult to maintain? Cuban's (1993) analysis of the literature on stability and change in schooling reached a number of conclusions. Cultural beliefs about the nature of knowledge and how children should learn are deeply ingrained in the thinking of everyone—policy makers, educators, parents, the general public, even students. Schools are explicitly organized to socialize students into designated niches within the social and economic systems. Policy makers have struggled to construct reforms in ways that successfully change instructional practices, even though it is possible to do so if certain principles are followed. A series of ill-conceived, haphazard policies poorly implemented lead teachers over time to ignore mandates and reform visions of schooling in favor of current practice. The very organization and policies of districts, schools, and classrooms shape and reinforce instructional practices. These organizational choices preclude a wide range of options while favoring and reinforcing specific methods, behaviors, and techniques.

The teaching profession has developed a culture that tilts toward stability in classroom practices (Little, 1982). Teachers tend to be entrepreneurial but operate under strong norms of isolation and noninterference (Little, 1990). Teachers' knowledge of their subject matter, particularly at the secondary level, and their personal beliefs about the role of schooling in society fundamentally shape their classroom practices (Siskin & Little, 1995). If teachers believe students cannot learn one thing before they have mastered a particular prerequisite skill, for example, they will resist changing the order of instruction. If they believe classroom social systems inevitably must reflect the dynamics present in the larger society, they may simply recreate existing social and power relationships, as they perceive them.

These forces operate in an interactive fashion to create a veritable thicket of beliefs, practices, norms, values, habits, prejudices, opinions, and social relationships into which new policies and initiatives are launched. Few emerge on the other side unscathed and unaltered.

## COMPLIANCE-ORIENTED IMPLEMENTATION VS. GOAL-ORIENTED IMPLEMENTATION

Education reforms have fared unevenly. Those that affect students and student learning more directly prove to be more controversial, more difficult to implement, and more subject to interdistrict variation than those whose effects are felt at a greater distance from the classroom (Conley, 1997b; Hess, 1995). Researchers have suggested that differences in the nature of the policies, whether they are developmental or redistributive, also affect implementation (Peterson, Rabe, & Wong, 1991). Developmental policies ask schools to do things they already do or know how to do. Redistributive policies require schools to do things they have not done previously and to allocate or reallocate resources to specific groups of students. Redistributive programs are generally more difficult to implement than developmental programs (Lowi, 1972).

Evidence suggests that the first waves of federal and state reforms were more developmental in nature and that this allowed schools to comply without necessarily changing underlying structures, practices, or relationships (Center for Policy Research, 1989; Odden, 1991). Additional research found that some schools can successfully implement state education reform policy, and that the nature of the reform influences ease of implementation (Fuhrman et al., 1991; Hoff, 2001c).

The wave of policies that were implemented in the early 1990s began to have a distinctly more redistributive bent to it. Conley and Goldman (2000) concluded that teachers were of two minds regarding state reform legislation that had important redistributive elements. While teachers espoused agreement with policy goals, they consistently found fault with the specific methods the state mandated to achieve the goals. Furthermore, two-thirds of teachers adopted a "wait and see" attitude throughout the period the state allotted for teacher engagement and dialogue about the goals and methods of the reform. Teachers tended to process the reforms in terms of the specific behaviors needed to comply with the reform requirements. They did not perceive the reforms as broad goal frameworks within which they were to transform their practice in ways that enabled them to achieve the goals.

Spillane and Zeuli (1999) found that most math teachers who claimed to be familiar with national mathematics education reform ideas had managed to change the "behavioral regularities" of instruction much more often than the "epistemological regularities." Changing behavioral regularities, such as allowing students to work in groups or introducing more problem-solving activities, is difficult enough. Changing the ways teachers conceptualize knowledge and knowing in their classrooms is much more challenging. Spillane and Zeuli (1999) conclude that policy makers and reformers must be concerned with getting teachers to do more than notice and read reform proposals. Teachers must be assisted in constructing new understandings and developing new meanings for existing practice. To do so, teachers must understand reform ideas, and reforms must support teacher learning. Absent this sort of complex conception of policy implementation, teachers will tend toward low-level responses aimed at complying with requirements while not changing practices or beliefs significantly.

This compliance orientation toward state education policy poses a significant challenge where policy goals extend to the restructuring or reculturing of schools. Compliance-based responses work well when the policy specifies the actions that the educational agencies and personnel must take to meet state requirements. Such responses do not serve as well when schools are asked to adopt new goals and assumptions, for example, that all students can reach high levels of achievement and meet state standards. Compliance in this context means adhering to the letter of state policies, not adopting or owning the reform goal and engaging in the transformation of attitudes and practices needed to reshape schooling. Compliance-oriented thinking by educators is one of the key reasons that the "top-down, bottom-up" partnership model for education reform outlined earlier in the chapter has yet to function as envisioned.

## ORGANIZATIONAL CHALLENGES
## TO REFORM IMPLEMENTATION

Schools in general are not designed to be adaptive, and American schools in particular, with their long history of community ownership and local governance, can be expected to be relatively unresponsive to external direction (Sarason, 1971, 1990). They are subject to the constraints of time-honored routines that are difficult to change, what Tye (1987) calls the "deep structure of schooling" and what Elmore (1990) refers to as the "core technologies" of schools. Their structures are relatively static. Roles are well established. All the funds are committed and few discretionary resources are available. Time is perhaps the greatest problem. Few opportunities for interaction and conversation exist within the school day or year. Dealing with reforms is all the more challenging given these constraints. Elmore (1988) notes that educators themselves perceive a range of internal barriers to change, including an unwarranted sense of safety and security in the present structure, a hesitancy to accept responsibility for student achievement of high standards, a focus more on individual work conditions than teaching and learning generally, an aversion to risk taking, and difficulty connecting reform proposals with everyday school life.

State policy initiatives challenge this institutional rigidity by creating pressure for new routines, structures, and strategies. Grouping practices, for example, are linked to schedules, and each in turn is equally difficult to change. In tandem, they can impose a tremendous barrier to regrouping students and to allocating learning time flexibly to allow students to master material at their own pace. State policies can serve as external stimuli to schools to cause them to re-examine a wide range of practices, something that would be unlikely to occur in the absence of the external mandate.

### Education Reform as Redirective Policy

Current state activity does not necessarily follow the "intensification" model of the 1980s where schools were expected to offer more of the same classes (Firestone, Fuhrman, & Kirst, 1991). In this current incarnation of reform, schools are expected to remake themselves by finding new ways to enable more students to reach high levels of performance and being held accountable for student performance.

Education reform for the most part does not seem to be enacted as distributive policy where new resources are added specifically to achieve reform goals (Lowi, 1972). While some states, such as Kentucky and North Carolina, have devoted resources to an extensive statewide reform implementation infrastructure, many others have defined reforms as new tests. While most states provide some degree of professional development to accompany standards-based reforms, few have addressed the perceptions held by most educators that schools should be provided resources for new or specialized personnel to support all aspects of reform implementation, such as testing coordinators, curriculum specialists, or instructional strategy coaches. When school people say that education reform is not adequately funded, they mean at least in part that new positions of this nature, designed specifically to cope with reform demands and requirements, have not been created and funded by the state. Few districts and even fewer individual schools have proven capable of allocating or reallocating resources and authority to such new positions very quickly or effectively.

As a result, most teachers receive scant support within schools to achieve state policy goals unless districts, states, or the federal government specifically authorizes and designates funds for reform-related activities, such as training on how to score student work in relation to state standards, new instructional strategies to help low-achieving students reach standards, or materials that central office staff members can use to support implementation.

Most states have committed at least some new resources to reform programs. In some cases, the total funding for school reform has been truly significant. For example, Massachusetts provided $6 billion through its 1993

Education Reform Act to support a far-reaching set of changes in district practices, new statewide curriculum guides, and a high school graduation test (Daley, 2000). However, many more states have implemented standards and assessment systems in particular without increases in funding other than what is needed to develop and administer the assessments themselves.

Given the uneven and inconsistent relationship between reforms and funding, the notion of developmental and redistributive frameworks introduced earlier does not fit well with this new arena of state policy activity. Such state policies might better be seen as redirective than as distributive or redistributive. They are attempts to get schools to adopt new goals and to achieve new efficiencies in order to improve learning for all children, rather than to reallocate services from one group to another or to implement new programs.

## Education Reform as One More "Unfunded Mandate"

The term "unfunded mandates" has come to symbolize the frustration lower levels of government experience when state or national policies require them to make changes without providing them new resources. This issue is an expression of a larger set of tensions that revolve around the transfer of power from local to state level. Captive agencies such as schools find it difficult and frustrating to absorb redirection from higher levels of government when this means reallocating resources or examining fundamental operating principles.

This sense of frustration is heightened when state or federal policy goals appear to be patently unrealistic and are revised at some later date. Since states have limited expertise in directing reform from the center and since the reform agenda competes with all other governmental priorities for resources, states often have implemented programs without the resources needed to support them and without being able to direct schools to reallocate existing resources. The desire to preserve local control while achieving state goals is once again an underlying source of tension that complicates education policy implementation and school reform.

## Time as a Limited Resource in Schools

The other frustration educators experience, along with lack of resources devoted specifically to reform implementation, is lack of time to process the state mandates and to change their practices accordingly. This is perhaps the largest obstacle to successful response by schools (Conley & Goldman, 1995, 1998). Absent the opportunity to understand collectively the reform in the context of their school and to understand the state's intentions for the policy, individual educators are left to reach their own conclusions and responses (Spillane, 2000b; Spillane & Callahan, 2000). Since few teachers perceive themselves as capable of achieving the sometimes ambitious, even grandiose state goals, many simply give up and resign themselves to "muddling through," making the best of a bad situation.

Collective understandings of what must be done and how each person supports goal achievement have been a nearly universal feature of schools that have been successful in addressing reform goals (Little et al., 1996). Faculties are not asked to achieve the goal alone, nor can they ignore state goals without consequence. This is not always a democratic process within the school, although it can be. The critical component is an institutional willingness to address the structural constraints schools face in responding to external policies and to overcome restraints in ways that engage all staff at the school, and often students and parents as well, in an understanding of the importance of achieving the goals and the strategies to be pursued (Wohlstetter et al., 1997). The reform is seen not primarily as a threat, but as a combination of challenge and opportunity (Reid, 2001b).

### The Increasingly Complex Nature of State Education Policy Focused on the Classroom

This new wave of state policy, what Odden (1991) would describe as the third wave, is more difficult to implement because it is focused on making changes in teaching and learning, not on variables more removed from the classroom. Conley (1997b) and Newmann and Associates (1996) note the difficulties of making changes that are intended to have direct effects on teaching and learning. Odden (1991) observed that earlier reforms, the categorical programs of the 1960s and 1970s, created special programs for particular types of students. As a result, these programs had little impact on the general curriculum. Current reforms, by contrast, attempt to revamp the general curriculum and improve the overall quality of the educational system. Simply implementing programs or policies is not the measure of their success; whether they result in improved student learning is the true test.

In essence, states are redirecting local school districts, attempting to preserve and accelerate whatever equity gains have been achieved over the past 3 decades, while lifting the overall level of student achievement in areas referred to as the "new basic skills" (Murnane & Levy, 1996b; Secretary's Commission on Achieving Necessary Skills, 1991) or in relation to traditional basic skills (Seymour, 2000). These sometimes contradictory and very demanding policy goals can immobilize schools.

The transformation of education policy from a backwater issue controlled by those with a direct interest in education to a mainstream topic as fully contentious as any other major policy area (Kirst, 1984; Wirt & Kirst, 2001) has caused schools great consternation. This trend has only continued and increased in intensity. Spring (1997) asserts that "the 1990s might be considered to be the most politically explosive period for school politics in U.S. history." He identifies 11 major political groups with specific agendas for national education policy. The list does not include the business community, one of the most significant forces of the past 2 decades. The net effect of this increased political "traffic" is to make education policy development infinitely more complex and unpredictable than it had been when almost all policy was developed locally (Stout & Stevens, 2000).

In addition to groups at the national level, each state has seen the rise of interest groups that seek to influence state education policy. These vary widely from state to state, but many promote fundamental changes in education, such as privatization, or in the preservation of traditional values and a basic skills curriculum. This creates natural conflict with educators and even with education reformers on a wide array of issues.

What local districts now face is a policy generation environment at the state and national levels that seems to change dramatically in short periods of time. Even the state policies that are generated may not have strong backing, or may incite heated resistance from one or more interest groups, making their local implementation problematic. This unclear and murky policy environment makes educators even more cautious than they tend to be naturally when considering new reforms or "systemic" change.

### Coping with "Transformational" State Education Policy

Schools have long favored incremental change over discontinuous change (Conley, 1997b). Incremental change is achieved by making small adjustments in the normal routines of the organization in the hope of gradually, but consistently, improving its functioning. This phenomenon is the normative mode of change in schools and has been labeled by Tyack and Cuban (1995) as "tinkering toward Utopia." Policy makers recently seem to be advocating something more akin to discontinuous change, the "reinvention" of schooling, but with little guidance on what this means and little assurance that once changes are made, policy will continue to support the resulting models of schooling.

Massell and colleagues (1997) studied nine states that generated pressure for rapid educational change. During the period of study, the 1994–95 school year, they observed a "disjuncture" between state rhetoric for large-scale systemic change and local response of slow, incremental progress as schools struggled to implement policies requiring standards-based education that states had been crafting over a 5- to 10-year period.

The public for its part is not necessarily aware of the specifics of education reform proposals, even in states that have made education reform the major public policy issue for nearly a decade (Joint Center for the Study of Educational Policy, 1996; Kannapel, 1995). This public ambivalence or even hostility to reform often causes local educators to hesitate or delay in implementing reform requirements because they do not feel pressure locally to make the kinds of dramatic changes being advocated by state-level reforms.

Schools remain "captive organizations" in many significant respects. Their funding is controlled to an ever greater degree by the state, which increasingly sets their goals. They cannot change their business. They are place-bound and subject to regulation and other limitations that restrict their ability to adapt. Consequently, they develop cultures and routines focused on operating within known parameters. When those parameters are changed or, worse yet, when they are unclear, schools often become immobilized while they wait for clarification of the new boundaries and the new regulations that guide and restrict their actions. State reforms at times have created confusion or have not provided the level of clarity that many schools and school districts need in order to process complex changes.

It is important to note that many schools and districts do adapt successfully to state reform mandates (Massell et al., 1997). However, they do so by fitting the state mandates to their own needs, picking and choosing which aspects of the reform to follow most closely and which to use as frameworks for their own practices. They remain limited in their ability to reshape themselves in ways consistent with state goals, in part because the types of sophisticated and systematic training or professional development necessary to enable schools to adapt to change is often lacking.

Massell (2001) found that a few districts did try to align their training and development programs with local or state reform agendas; however, more typical was the smorgasbord model of "inservice." The wide variation in training and development programs was more pronounced where site-based management practices were in place. Here two state policy initiatives, standards-based reform and decentralized decision making, came into conflict over a third component that affected both initiatives, namely, a professional development program, with the net effect of inhibiting the effectiveness of all three policies.

Some long-term, large-scale changes do occur in schools. They are those that can be translated into programs by schools, that have funding attached to them specifically, and that develop a political constituency to support their continued existence. In general, these changes are additive ones, where a new program is added to the school and funded externally, what Lowi (1972) calls distributive policy.

Changes can and do occur in school structures and programs. Universal school lunch programs are an example of a new role schools assumed that was accompanied by external funding and that created an entirely new category in the school organizational structure. Counseling programs were added to American high schools beginning in earnest in the late 1960s, generally with funding targeted to the creation of these positions, which were new to schools. Federal funding of Title I teachers and classrooms is an instruction-related example of a distributive policy that has persisted and has had an effect on teaching and learning.

## RETHINKING GOVERNANCE AS A FIRST STEP TOWARD STATE–LOCAL PARTNERSHIPS

One underlying factor contributing to the difficulty of implementing state policy is the mismatch that exists between early twenty-first-century state policy goals to improve learning for all students to prepare them for life in a complex economy and economy, and an early twentieth-century educational governance system that created schools to socialize immigrant populations, hold children out of the workforce, and train young people for a new industrial economy.

The twentieth-century governance model worked without excessive state intervention into local schools due in large measure to the fact that local board of education members were overwhelmingly drawn from one stratum of society, the "elite" or "successful citizens," that had a high degree of shared goals (Tyack, 1974). Local board actions were consistent with broad state and national values to which local boards subscribed wholeheartedly. They did so with little external prodding or pressure, and when they didn't, newspapers, social clubs, and others brought that pressure to bear. In this environment, the state had little need or motivation to direct local boards in any significant fashion.

The current situation bears little resemblance to the past. States now have clear agendas for public education. Federal goals and programs, which may espouse values quite different than those held by local boards, have become increasingly important drivers of education practices and organizational structures. Local boards, particularly urban boards, are not necessarily composed of like-minded individuals who share the same values. These boards can and do act in ways that are idiosyncratic and unpredictable relative to state and national goals.

### Three Possible Courses of Action for States

This mismatch suggests one of three possible courses of action to redesign local educational governance. One course is to restore local control and reassert the primacy of local values. To do so would require returning fiscal responsibility and discretion to local school districts, since fiscal autonomy has been the historical font of local authority. The problem with this solution is that any return to locally funded schools would result in a resurgence in per pupil funding discrepancies. Since courts have established that systemic disparities are not generally acceptable, it seems unlikely that a return to this pure form of local control can be achieved. A second problem facing this scenario is that federal courts in particular have established a *de facto* set of national values regarding equity that local boards must follow, regardless of board members' personal beliefs. These judicially expressed values have wide-ranging effects on local education practice.

A second alternative is for states to equalize funding, return local control, and then back out of significant policy generation and implementation. Equalization can be used successfully to address court orders to provide more equitable educational opportunity. A number of states have instituted equalization schemes, generally at great political cost and pain. However, equalization and other policies that move funding responsibility to the state level almost inevitably end up with greater state involvement in and oversight of local school districts. Returning or enhancing local control after the trauma of implementing an equalized funding system seems a political long shot. Even if this were to occur, states have already begun to collect information about school performance and to create comparisons among schools and districts. It seems unlikely that such practices could be abandoned completely now that the genie is out of the bottle. Parents and community members are coming to expect such performance information about schools.

The third and most likely scenario is that states will continue to increase their influence over schools. They will seek means to enact policy more effectively as well as to preserve local control as a functional means of governance. To achieve these dual goals will require a rethinking of roles and relationships. What this means in practice is that the authority and responsibilities of all agencies and institutions involved in educational governance will have to be explicitly analyzed, clarified, and restated.

## What's Involved in Redefining the Governance System?

Such a rational process of rethinking the system may prove very much the exception. In all likelihood, governance systems will evolve in practice regardless of whether any conscious process is organized to consider how best to structure them. Examples that this evolution is already taking place are evident and abundant. State boards of education are becoming increasingly prominent and political, whereas only 10 years ago they labored in relative obscurity in most states. State superintendents and state education departments likewise have much greater influence over local school districts, which in the past often sought primarily to avoid interaction with these agencies. Governors clearly have emerged as education policy agenda setters in many states. Education committees and subcommittees in state legislatures address a much wider range of issues and undertake new initiatives on a regular basis. Education interest groups, particularly those representing business, have proven to be very effective at influencing this more centralized process of policy making. Special-purpose commissions have been created to address key education issues in nearly every state. New governance configurations are arising. One state, Florida, has gone so far as to create one governing board for all public education, kindergarten through college.

Schools have found themselves in the limelight, their test scores and statewide ranking published in the local newspaper. Superintendents find themselves reacting to state initiatives and unable to change, alter, or avoid them as successfully as they had previously. Local boards, along with teachers and administrators, struggle to understand their role in this new system and to determine their new sphere of authority and responsibility relative to the state.

Most of this occurs without any explicit awareness that governance relationships are being restructured. Local district personnel and school board members in particular are led to believe that local control is the preferred form of governance. Little is done to help them understand how best to relate to the new state role. Neither does the state carefully consider how to preserve local control or the elements of local control that are most vital and effective.

The fundamental problem that state and federal governments face as they attempt to implement school improvement programs is that the goals of such programs cannot be achieved without the cooperation and effort of teachers and administrators in local schools, who in turn are dependent on the support of their central offices. A fundamental partnership must exist between state and local levels for school improvement to work and for state goals to be achieved. Local educators can follow the letter of state reforms while ignoring the spirit, in which case the reforms seldom succeed. Conversely, local school personnel can embrace state goals as their own, integrate them into their school context, and generally have much greater success achieving them.

Local schools are also the best possible incubation chamber for new programs and strategies. If states eliminate or sharply restrict local initiative, they will end up with fewer options or examples of alternative means to educate students effectively. In the past, much state education policy has derived from successful programs in local schools. Striking a balance between conformity and distinctiveness in local education programs is a difficult goal that few states have yet confronted in a comprehensive fashion.

State–local partnerships also help the state make better policy by providing feedback loops to policy developers from those charged with implementation. No policy can anticipate every situation that might occur as the policy is implemented, and feedback from implementers allows for mid-course corrections. States that have mechanisms to capture and utilize this type of feedback can adapt their policies more quickly and often avoid problems faced when an obvious flaw in a policy is ignored, resulting in inefficient implementation, alienation of local educators, and political resistance to reform.

### Example of a Process to Rethink Governance

Assuming a state wished to pursue the more unlikely path of a rational process to rethink governance on a statewide basis, how would it proceed? It might begin with an inventory of all the institutions, agencies, and organizations with formal governance roles. These would include the legislature, committees within the legislature charged specifically with education policy and funding, the governor, state superintendent, state board of education, state commissions, local boards, superintendents, principals, teachers, regional service districts, teacher preparation programs, and the teacher licensing agency. The current authority and duties of each would be determined.

A task force representing the groups enumerated above would be charged with describing how these entities currently operate in practice in relation to one another. The goal would be to ascertain the places where authority and task responsibility are well matched and where they are not. In places where a poor match exists, the task force would make recommendations that outlined and specified the new relationship and how authority and duties should change accordingly. Additionally, the task force would consider creation of new governance structures and the decommissioning of structures or institutions that no longer were needed.

The product of this task force's deliberations would serve as the basis for a public dialogue and debate about the structure of the state educational governance system. While such debates are often painful and even divisive, public exchange is justified in the current environment where educational governance is being changed in a piecemeal fashion. At the very least, such a discussion will help those whose roles have changed understand how the roles have changed and what the implications are.

One possible positive effect is that the contributions of local boards of education in particular might be recognized and their role and duties more clearly identified, specified, and delineated. A discussion of this nature gives states a chance to assess the drive toward greater control and to ascertain the effects on other elements of the governance system. Ideally, consensus could be reached on how to proceed toward a governance system that reflected a blend of state and local goals and that minimized conflict based on jurisdiction and responsibility.

The relationship between the state and local districts necessary to further state goals while preserving and validating local authority must be carefully developed and nurtured. It requires new structures and mechanisms for communication, decision making, and resource allocation, in particular. Such a process of redesigning governance represents the first step in a conscious aligning of the myriad and diverse forces affecting education policy within states and between states and the federal government. Aligning all of these factors and numerous others is the challenge that is examined in the following chapter.

# Chapter 6

# ALIGNING POLICY LEVERS

Aligned educational systems are ones where standards and assessment are consistent statewide and are linked coherently across grade levels. In an aligned system, curriculum is still controlled locally. The state's primary role is to consider the ways in which all of the policy levers it controls can be arrayed to send consistent messages to local schools regarding state educational goals and the responsibilities of local schools to achieve those goals. Ideally, this alignment also leads to a system in which goal ambiguity is reduced and local flexibility increased. This allows local schools to focus more clearly on both state goals and local priorities.

Fuhrman (1993b) identifies the following key elements in system alignment: (1) states set clear, challenging expectations for students and then develop coordinated instructional policies consistent with stated expectations; (2) states then grant schools greater freedom to organize and conduct instruction to reach state goals; (3) much of the current tangle of state regulations that interfere with schools' ability to adapt is removed or revised; and (4) state instructional policies provide enough detail so that educators understand what is expected of them, but not so much that daily practice is dictated or constrained.

This idealized state–local relationship has not necessarily materialized in most cases. Instead, states seem to be more willing to adopt the first part of the equation, ambitious expectations, than the second, reduction of regulations and avoidance of overly detailed interventions into local practices. States seem comfortable creating a conceptual framework for alignment while ignoring to some degree the difficulty schools will have adapting and aligning their curriculum horizontally and vertically. Furthermore, schools seem ill prepared and poorly organized for the actual task of responding to this new policy framework. The lack of detailed state direction in the arena of curricular alignment to meet high standards has been an obstacle for many schools and teachers, accustomed as they are to operating in isolation from their neighbors and to making decisions with relative autonomy.

## PLUSES, MINUSES, AND LIMITATIONS OF ALIGNMENT

The notion of curriculum alignment is not new, but has gained renewed popularity during the past 2 decades (Glatthorn, 1981, 1999; Scott,
1983). What is new is the change of focus from coordinating within a school
or among local schools to aligning local curriculum and instruction with
state standards and assessments.

Discussions of state education policy first began to include the concept
of policy alignment in the early 1990s. Since that time, scholars have debated
the degree to which the current policy system sends coherent messages to
educators (Fuhrman, 1993a). Clune (1993a) states that education policy as
currently structured in the United States is incapable of producing major
increases in student achievement because policy is "extremely fragmented
and ineffective." The policy system produces numerous "uncoordinated
mandates, programs, and projects that provide no coherent direction." The
net effect is to increase the complexity of educational governance while con-
suming human and fiscal resources. The American system, Clune (citing
Cohen, 1990) contends, "produces the largest quantity of educational policy
in the world, and the least effective." Even the notion that states should be
considering the cumulative impact of all of their policies on local education
practices and on the achievement of state educational goals is a relatively
new phenomenon. It is one with significant implications for the relationship
between local school districts and the state.

### What Is Gained from an Aligned System?

An aligned system can have many benefits. Common standards allow
educators within a state to share curriculum, teaching techniques, and effective organizational practices across schools and districts. Smaller districts
benefit from the work of larger districts. Parents develop a better understanding of what is expected of their children, and students can be placed more
accurately when they change schools, both of which are valuable in areas of
high mobility.

In a 1999 study of states' use of standards and assessment, the American Federation of Teachers (1999b) found that states' overall commitment
to standards-based reform remains strong and that the overall quality of the
state standards continues to improve. Every state except Iowa, Montana, and
North Dakota is measuring student achievement toward state standards.
Many states describe the level of mastery students must demonstrate to meet
or exceed the state standards. In order to make standards count, 14 states
have consistent statewide policies designed to end the practice of passing
students from grade to grade regardless of whether they have mastered the

standards. Twenty-three states have in place or are moving to develop incentives such as advanced diplomas or reduced college tuition in order to motivate students to achieve higher standards.

Alignment of teacher licensure or certification requirements with state standards helps ensure that prospective teachers possess the knowledge and skills necessary to instruct students successfully toward achieving the state's standards. Similarly, alignment is promoted by textbook selection processes that are geared to identify materials consistent with state standards. Educators benefit by being able to communicate with a common language to describe key learnings students must master.

Advocates contend that an aligned system is more equitable than the current system, where some schools have high expectations for students and others have low expectations (U. S. Department of Education, 2001). Grades mask the differences between what students in a school with high expectations really know and can do compared with those in schools with low expectations (Steinberg, 1996). With the same expectations for all students, it becomes less justifiable to track groups of students into different curricula based on questionable criteria, the effect of which is often to relegate the poor and those from ethnic and racial minority groups to substandard educational experiences that lead only to a dead end (Oakes, 1985).

In fact, decentralization of decision making often exacerbates differential expectations; one reform stream contradicts another (Wells & Oakes, 1996). Alignment represents the imposition by the state of a set of expectations that supersede the authority of each school to decide how capable its students are.

States can successfully raise expectations, for example, in high school mathematics courses (White, Gamoran, Smithson, & Porter, 1996), but high schools, in particular, have strong forces arrayed against common expectations, including differentiated, hierarchical curriculum structures and cultures committed simultaneously to offering a common education and to accommodating differences (Goodlad, 1984, 1987). This tension plays out in a highly political environment where adult needs are overlaid upon these conflicting goal systems (Blase, 1991).

## What Is Lost to an Aligned System?

Critics do not generally attack the notion of alignment directly. Instead, they object to the most visible and political manifestations of alignment, namely, state standards and assessments. In general, critics are concerned about the loss of teacher discretion in the classroom and a redirection of teaching toward test preparation (Thompson, 2001). Governance issues, such as local control, are generally a secondary consideration. The primary concern is that teaching will become guided by state tests. The critics argue that no system of standards will ever be able to take into account the range of students present in schools, and that the purpose of education should be development of the individual student in the ways that individual teachers deem most appropriate, rather than the measurement of all students against common, externally derived standards (Ohanian, 2001).

Darling-Hammond (1994) asserts that content standards aligned with tests are the wrong starting point for systemic school change aimed at improving teaching and learning for all students. She offers three reasons (Xu, 1996). First, when states specify content that will be tested, teachers' options to organize instructional programs appropriate to their students are severely limited. Second, local communities will not engage in their own conversations and considerations of the tough choices required to set standards if the state does it for them. Third, the tremendous inequity in the opportunity to learn that exists among schools is a bigger problem than a lack of state tests.

Darling-Hammond (1994) further contends that rather than building a system around content standards and assessments, policies should seek to develop, as the beginning point, a system focused on improving teacher knowledge and equalizing the capacity of schools to educate all students. Rather than a focus on standardized state tests, more authentic forms of assessment are needed, with open standards developed locally and a focus on student self-evaluation and public presentation of work.

Another danger of alignment is that it can lead to institutionalization of values and beliefs. Once policies are centralized at a state level, it becomes easier for interest groups to have influence out of proportion to their presence in the larger society. State standards can be turned to the uses and views of particular groups, as occurred when the Kansas Board of Education revised the state's learning standards to reflect the board's view that evolution should not be taught, an act that subsequently was reversed (Blair & Hoff, 2001; Hoff, 1999). Without mechanisms to allow standards to be developed in an orderly fashion that ensures that they reflect broad societal values, alignment can lead to an increasing politicization of the curriculum.

Equally problematic in an aligned system is the inverse problem: the potential exclusion of various interest groups. If a group's point of view is totally excluded, its members can feel alienated from the schools and may pursue other educational options. This phenomenon may be one of the forces driving the charter school movement and leading to the phenomenally rapid increase in the number of home-schooled children. Ethnic and racial minority groups and others who do not have access to power or to the standard-setting process can see their perspective missing or inaccurately presented in state standards. English and history standards have been particularly difficult to formulate because of problems reaching consensus on what literature all students should be expected to read and what history events and interpretations all students should be expected to learn (American Federation of Teachers, 1999c).

Others caution that state assessments in particular drive schools toward a narrowed conception of curriculum, choosing to focus on test preparation and items that will appear on tests (Boser, 2000; Smith, 2000; Williams, 2000). What is sacrificed in the bargain, they say, are programs not directly related to the tests, like music and art, along with teacher creativity to devise lessons based on student interests (Borsuk, 2000).

These voices also assert that it is fundamentally wrong to expect all students to be good at the same things or to master the curriculum in a way that will be demonstrated on tests. In states where students must pass multiple tests, they contend that it is unrealistic to expect all or even most students to be adept at such a wide range of subjects and knowledge bases. The goal that all students will reach these standards is unrealistic, and special needs students and second language learners in particular are not well served by tests that they cannot hope to complete successfully. The net effect will be to destroy the self-image, confidence, and desire to learn for many students, while simultaneously affirming the mastery of students who were already successful in the system (Thompson, 2001).

Koretz (1991) raises an additional warning based on a study of the generalization of performance across high-stakes state tests. Third-grade students in a large high-poverty urban school district showed little evidence that high scores on a state achievement test generalized to other tests for which the students were not explicitly prepared. The findings suggest that when teachers focus on content specific to the test used for accountability, rather than on trying to develop student cognitive abilities more broadly, improvements do not generalize to other areas or other tests.

## Limitations of the Concept of Alignment

The concept of system alignment is appealing in principle to state policy makers regardless of ideological bent because it provides a way to promote a consistent, comprehensive view of the state education system as if it were one integrated mechanism. It is appealing as a policy strategy because it seems on the surface to be something that can be attained without increases in resources. However, in practice alignment is difficult to achieve for several reasons.

Alignment does not occur all at once. It occurs over time as various dimensions of educational governance and practice are reconfigured. This occurs because a time lag accompanies the implementation of any state policy. As a result, schools receive policies over time and implement them based on conditions that exist at the moment they are received, not the time they were conceived. The net effect is that the actions of the policy implementers will always be out of step to some degree with the current priorities of the policy generators. As one portion of the system is aligned with another, a third area may be evolving independently or the circumstances that initially motivated the alignment may change.

For example, many states undertook education reform to enhance work-force readiness in order to transform state economic bases. During the past 10 to 15 years, many state economies have undergone significant transformation while their schools struggle to implement the rudiments of standards-based reforms passed 10 years ago. The economic system did not wait for the alignment policies to take effect; the larger social system continued to evolve at a much more rapid rate than schools.

This gap between policy intention and implementation can be labeled policy drift. This occurs when policy goals change or evolve even as programs first generated to address the initial policy goals are still being implemented. In education this is illustrated by the way in which the focus of state standards and accountability systems has shifted gradually from ensuring that all students possess necessary academic and work-readiness skills to holding schools accountable to the state. The basic aims of better student performance remain, but successive policies have shifted the focus subtly to a new goal—accountability. This has the effect of reshaping the policy's function and effects within the educational system. Educators, some of whom are still debating the merits of the original policy, find that the policy goals have changed. Their schools often are still struggling to understand, implement, and achieve the initial goals.

Policy drift is abetted by term limit laws that shorten legislative institutional memory and by the movement of education policy into mainstream partisan politics. Legislatures and governors seek to leave their own unique mark on the schools. In highly partisan states this leads to policy fragmentation, the rapid gyration from one policy approach to another.

California's experience with testing and accountability systems is an example of policy gyration and also suggests the difficulty of achieving policy alignment. The California Learning Assessment System (CLAS) was developed in the early 1990s only to be canceled in 1994 shortly after its implementation. The state had no statewide assessment again until the legislature adopted a new program in 1997 and implemented it in 1998 (Lawton, 1995a, 1996). The state accountability program, Standardized Testing and Reporting (STAR), was based on tests for which schools had less than a year to prepare (Betts & Danenberg, 2002). In 2001, California found itself with more than 10 different examinations in use for K–12 testing to determine achievement, proficiency, and college eligibility placement (California State Postsecondary Education

Commission, 2001). The norm-referenced measure administered since 1998 as the basis for the STAR program was replaced in 2002 by a different norm-referenced instrument, which in turn was replaced by a standards-based test. During this period, accountability was increasing, as were the stakes of school-level performance on these ever-shifting assessments.

In many other states, legislatures tinker with or modify a previously adopted reform strategy, sending it in a slightly different direction just as schools are managing to put the first elements into place. Kentucky's landmark education reform effort has seen policy drift as the original plan to have schools make sustained gains over a 10-year period was replaced with an accountability system that judged schools on a year-to-year basis and that extended the deadline for all schools to meet a specified standard to 2014 (Abercrombie, 1999).

While mid-course corrections are clearly necessary when large policy initiatives like statewide testing are undertaken, this sort of change in the underlying measurement means and standards promotes a "this too shall pass" mentality in schools. The press to implement the original reform requirements often recedes in favor of more pragmatic approaches by educators to the new requirements and procedures. This pragmatism is manifested in the form of a continuing waiting game and calls for clearer, more consistent, stable, and unambiguous signals, which are not going to happen given the realities of policy drift. If a state truly wished to align education policy and practice, new mechanisms would be needed to shorten the time between policy formulation and implementation.

McDermott (2000) describes a related phenomenon: partial implementation of the many competing programs and reform initiatives vying for educator attention, particularly in urban districts. "Path dependence," the way in which a sequence of small events affects institutional structure and functioning, can be nearly impossible to modify significantly. Initiating new programs is a way to circumvent existing structures and simultaneously mollify particular constituencies. Following the programs through to full implementation may not serve the interests of local educators whose goals were more to defuse a particular political issue than to change the system.

These sorts of temporal and organizational limitations make alignment of the type that exists in countries with more centralized educational governance essentially impossible. Other nations have systems that are capable of putting new policies into place relatively rapidly in a comprehensive fashion and sustaining them until they are institutionalized. Americans have not shown much interest in adapting educational governance to achieve these goals. The likely outcome, absent a rethinking of governance structures and relationships, is that state education systems will continue to operate in loosely coordinated fashion, attempting to manage a range of sometimes conflicting but more often mildly contradictory education policies. Schools will be challenged to process education policy more quickly and to reconcile the differences among a series of slightly differing manifestations of a larger state policy initiative.

## Putting Alignment into Practice

Given the limitations of the concept, what does it take to make alignment work as well as possible? Traditionally policy has been disseminated via bureaucratic channels. Little thought was given to how the policy was received by "street-level bureaucrats" (Lipsky, 1980), like principals and teachers. Recently states have begun to pay attention to the ways in which educators interpret policies, how this affects educator willingness to implement policy, and how this process relates to the policy's ultimate effects on education and schooling.

Educators require opportunities to make sense of externally imposed policies in terms of their local realities, personal teaching practices, and values (Conley & Goldman, 2000; Jennings, 1996; Spillane, 2000b; Spillane & Zeuli, 1999). For this process to occur successfully, several things are required from the state.

First, policies must be clear enough for educators to perceive the links between and among them. Second, policy levers need to be aligned simultaneously or within a short period of time. Standards, assessments, and accountability in particular need to be carefully coordinated. Third, educators need to perceive that they can implement the policies successfully. When teachers in particular feel that state goals are unrealistic or unattainable, they react by rejecting the goals or adopting compliance-oriented behavior. Fourth, adequate time must be allocated for teachers to comprehend the policies and their implications for practice. Fifth, teacher perceptions must be captured and factored back into the policy adaptation process.

States can help this process by creating new communication structures. In addition to traditional one-way "dissemination" systems, more active and engaging forms of communication are necessary. A cadre of policy "interpreters" and "translators" has to be organized and mobilized. Its function would be to explain policies and to assist educators in making sense of them. Additionally, the individuals constituting this cadre would collect input from practitioners to help identify potential flaws and pitfalls in the policy as it moved into practice. Other more interactive forms of communication, such as state-sponsored websites where questions are answered quickly and accurately, also aid the meaning-making process. Such approaches let educators create the connections between broad state goals and effective programs at the district and school levels.

## WHAT ARE THE LEVERS FOR SYSTEM ALIGNMENT?

States have at their disposal a range of policy levers that they can arrange so that the schools receive a more consistent message about state priorities and goals. The most prominent levers and issues surrounding their use are described below.

### State Standards and Assessments: Key Policy Tools to Drive Alignment

The primary tool states are using to align schools accustomed to operating in a highly independent fashion is a system of content standards and assessments that span the curriculum from kindergarten through high school. States have adopted standards and assessment systems precisely for the purpose of aligning instructional efforts within the school system. These systems serve to focus curriculum and instruction and to provide common measures of school system performance that are comparable over time.

Forty-nine states have adopted some form of content standards, while 35 have state-level assessments designed to determine student knowledge on state standards (Education Week, 2001). Alignment is achieved as schools focus on state standards and assessments. In theory, schools retain significant flexibility to use local control to adapt their program to learner needs. In practice, using assessments to align the system has proven highly controversial (Massachusetts Coalition for Authentic Reform in Education, 2002). Its effectiveness as a policy strategy is yet to be fully proven, although states such as Connecticut and Texas are showing signs of consistent improvement on state measures.

### The Challenge of System Alignment for Teachers

In some states teachers have not necessarily been given adequate training or support relative to the new standards and assessments. How to educate students who fail to meet the standards after receiving conventional instruction is also a particularly vexing problem. Selecting content from among a welter of state standards can be perplexing for teachers accustomed to moving sequentially through a textbook. Diverting time to what teachers consider test preparation is viewed as a diminution of instruction. The state assessment is not viewed as an integral part of the learning process, but something that stands apart, separate from what teachers do for most of the time in their classrooms.

An additional and often overlooked reason teachers may object to state assessments is that they have never before in their careers been subjected to such direction by the state. Most state policies are blunted before they reach the classroom. State assessments in fact are penetrating the classroom and affecting education practices (Firestone et al., 1998; Olson, 2002b; Viadero, 2000).

This is indicative of the psychological dimensions of system alignment. Veteran teachers in particular have a mind-set relative to their own classroom and the state's proper role in directing their activities. While most teachers do not object to the notion of state standards, the assessments in particular often are seen as unnecessarily invasive. Some also view heightened state accountability demands, which they often associate with the tests, as insulting or not relevant to their situation. This reaction may be entirely justified based on individual teacher circumstances, but is also to be expected when the rules of the game are changed on a profession for whom autonomy has been an integral component.

Herein lies an additional irony. An aligned system requires not just compliance, but greater cooperation and interaction among teachers. This potentially more beneficial aspect of state standards and assessments is often not experienced by teachers in schools that do not redesign in ways that focus planning and program decisions on state standards and assessments. Left to their own devices and provided minimal support and direction, teachers tend to work in isolation and teach to the test. It is perhaps only natural that many object to a system that seems to make demands on their time and expect them to acquire new professional skills while surrendering their autonomy in the bargain.

Schools that have adapted successfully to this newly aligned system are relatively few in number currently, but appear to be growing rapidly. Principal leadership frequently is cited as a key dimension to successful adaptation (Goertz, 2000; Olson, 1999; Reeves, 1998). Principals set the tone and provide the opportunities for teachers to work collaboratively to redesign or adapt programs and to communicate about their successes and challenges in teaching to state standards.

### Role of Networks in System Alignment

It is perhaps ironic and even a bit counterintuitive that a key dimension to aligning a system may be the creation of formal and informal networks of educators who share strategies and techniques for adapting successfully to the new system (White, 1999). Networks are not necessarily hierarchical, but are driven by common interests. They may or may not be controlled by the state, but are organized and facilitated by interested members (Jennings, 1996). They may set their own agendas and function in their own ways. Smith and Wohlstetter (2001) describe these as affiliation networks. Such networks are created to enable participants from different organizations who have membership in some common voluntary group to work together to solve a problem that is too large for any of them to address individually. The focus of these networks is on interorganizational collaboration rather than individual professional advancement, which is the focus of several other types of educator networks.

Networks may be organized *ad hoc* or sponsored by consortia of school districts, regional education labs, colleges and universities, and philanthropic foundations (Wohlstetter & Smith, 2000). A few state education departments sponsor such networks, which serve the purpose of bridging the gap between individual teachers operating in isolated classrooms and statewide goals and programs (Firestone & Pennell, 1997). The networks also provide teachers with an additional source of information beyond what their building principal might provide. Studies of teacher networks indicate that they are powerful tools for shaping teacher attitudes and practices (Lieberman & Grolnick, 1996; Smith & Fenstermacher, 1999) and that networks can be vehicles to promote teacher understanding of state policies (Adams, 2000; Pennell & Firestone, 1996).

Networks can be a key component in an overall strategy of system alignment because they allow participants to learn from one another and to operate under norms of collaboration and cooperation, which are more familiar to educators than state-generated mandates. Networks create more "social capital" among schools (Smith & Wohlstetter, 2001), enabling them to solve problems or access resources they otherwise might be unable to obtain (Wohlstetter & Smith, 2000). These networks even have the potential to help mitigate ineffective principal leadership by opening up the flow of knowledge to teachers, parents, and others in the school community.

States also can organize or sponsor networks, particularly among content-area teachers (Cohen & Hill, 2001). This type of network generally is focused on a specific element of state education policy, such as a new curriculum framework or a state writing assessment. Adams (2000) describes a teacher network focused on implementing a new statewide mathematics curriculum. Teachers utilized the network to gain common understandings as well as to bridge between state policy and classroom practice. Clune (1998) explains how networks in the National Science Foundation State Systemic Initiative contributed to teacher understanding and to greater policy coherence. Firestone and Pennell (1997) analyzed state-sponsored networks in California and Vermont and reaches the conclusion that such networks can help teachers address state reform goals while simultaneously improving their knowledge and motivation and empowering them to make better classroom decisions.

## State Accountability Systems as Alignment Tools

Accountability systems are not necessarily undertaken with system alignment as their primary goal. However, in practice, accountability systems are powerful drivers of educators' behavior (Lashway, 2001). These systems exact a tremendous cost in terms of educator resentment and hostility and may create quite perverse results in some instances (Harrington-Lueker, 2000). Nevertheless, accountability systems serve to generate system alignment (Kelley, Odden, Milanowski, & Heneman, 2000).

Evidence seems to suggest that state accountability systems have a particularly strong effect when the goal is to increase equity of student achievement. Skrla (2001) reports a study of Dallas, Texas, teachers that found particular configurations of state accountability requirements and testing can have a positive impact on teacher expectations of students and the instructional methods they use to improve the achievement of minority and poor children in particular. These may produce long-term cumulative effects that extend beyond a single-year assessment.

The amplification of effects over a multiple-year assessment is another powerful reason for system alignment. Sanders and Horn (1998) present evidence of the cumulative effects that teachers and schools have on student achievement in the context of a statewide assessment and accountability system. Tennessee students who had effective teachers for 2 to 3 consecutive years significantly outperformed students who had ineffective teachers, even after adjustments were made for race, socioeconomic level, class size, and classroom heterogeneity.

## Incentive and Reward Programs for Schools and Teachers

The flip side of sanctions is incentive programs. These tend to fall into two broad categories: programs providing incentives and rewards to individual schools or teams of teachers, which exist in 14 states (King & Mathers, 1997), and those targeted to individual teachers or administrators (Odden, 2000). In theory, incentives should prove highly effective as a means to elicit desired behavior from educators. In practice, they can conflict with any number of existing factors in schools, including teacher isolation and noncooperation norms, and fall short of their desired goals. Teacher organizations and groups of teachers in states that have launched incentive programs have been vocal in their opposition to such programs on the grounds that teaching is a collective and collaborative activity and that each teacher and school contributes to the success of others. However, research on the use of these programs has concluded that they can be effective. Fuhrman (1999) and others observed that monetary bonuses can be motivating and that sanctions also can have a motivating effect: "Both get teachers' attention."

The use of incentives is not new and was an integral component of many education reforms in the 1980s (Cornett & Gaines, 1994). For example, by

1986, 29 states were either implementing or developing career ladder or teacher incentive programs targeted to student performance (Cornett & Gaines, 1994; Cornett & Gaines, 1992). The current generation of incentives focuses more tightly on how well students perform on state tests as the metric by which rewards are determined and distributed. Combined with programs of sanctions, they appear to be bringing about greater system alignment, although many educators and others argue strongly that the system may be aligning around the wrong things (Cuban, 2001; Meier, 2000; Ohanian, 2001).

### Aligning Teacher Preparation with State Standards

Teacher preparation programs may prove ultimately to be the pivotal link in system alignment. Educational change is slow, almost generational in nature. Given the difficulty inherent in changing the beliefs and methods of many veteran teachers, it seems only natural that the state would move to ensure that the next generation of teachers is proficient in the skills needed to teach successfully in an aligned system. Achieving this goal is much more difficult in practice than in principle.

Teacher education is spread throughout the postsecondary system in most states, occurring in public and private institutions both large and small. Control over the content and quality of teacher education programs also is dispersed between at least two entities, accrediting agencies and the state teacher licensing authority. Accrediting agencies visit colleges of education periodically to ensure that their programs meet specified professional standards. Accreditation is important to most teacher preparation programs, which devote considerable time and effort to preparing for accreditation visits as well as responding to resulting recommendations. Before the era of strong state involvement in education policy, accreditation visits were the primary influence on the design and content of teacher preparation programs and on efforts to improve them.

Recently, accrediting agencies have adopted policies and standards more in line with many state reform efforts (Wise & Leibbrand, 2000). However, accreditation still stands somewhat outside state processes for approving institutions that recommend candidates for teaching credentials. State agencies that approve teacher education programs also can exert significant influence on the content and evolution of teacher preparation programs and, by extension, of the skills and attitudes their graduates take into the public schools. Credentialing agencies review the content and design of preparation programs before they are approved as meeting state requirements for a teaching license.

Changing teacher education in concert with K–12 education reforms is difficult under the current governance structure. In addition to credentialing agencies that may or may not be working in concert with the state education department, the postsecondary system is almost always governed by a different board than the K–12 system. Colleges are accustomed to asserting a certain degree of independence in the design of their preparation programs and in their adaptation to state goals. The profession's own major reform efforts, including the Holmes Group's report, "Tomorrow's Teachers" (1986), and the Carnegie Forum for the Advancement of Teaching's "A Nation Prepared" (Mertens & Yarger, 1988), have led some but by no means all colleges to redesign their teacher education programs consistent with report recommendations. Nor have they inspired new teacher preparation or licensure policies in states. Some colleges point out that the demands of national accreditation agencies limit their ability to serve state needs exclusively. Others prepare students to teach in a number of states and contend it is difficult if not impossible for them to design their programs to align with one state's goals and needs. Postsecondary institutions in general resist whenever they feel state agencies are attempting to intervene politically into areas subject to academic freedom. Even when programs attempt to adapt, they may find they come up short against state expectations (Blair, 2001b). Still others simply express philosophical objections to the entire program of state reform and indicate that academic freedom permits them to decide what they will teach and how they will teach it.

The federal government has exerted its influence on teacher education through Title II of the Higher Education Act of 1998, which requires colleges and universities with teacher preparation programs to file "report cards" with the federal government. These requirements yield more information on who participates and who graduates from these programs. The goal is to enable better public determinations of the quality of prospective teachers prepared in these programs (Blair, 2001a). This new federal interest in teacher quality is driven by findings that confirm the difference well-qualified teachers make in terms of student learning (Wenglinsky, 2000).

A conundrum faced by preparation programs that do wish to align with state policies is that even if the preparation program is redesigned to be consistent with state goals, few faculty may possess the skills needed to teach in such a program. Given the rapid implementation pace in many states, even fewer practicing teachers who develop expertise in achieving state goals will be available to serve as mentors, models, and supervisors for student teachers. Professional development schools are one possible strategy to help preparation programs remain more in touch with problems of practice (Darling-Hammond, Bullmaster, & Cobb, 1995; Petrie, 1995). Such relationships between postsecondary and secondary institutions are notoriously difficult to structure and maintain (Myers, 1997).

States turned in the 1980s to testing teachers as a means to ensure basic skills mastery. By 1990, essentially every state had such a system in place. The tests used were frequently norm-referenced instruments of general knowledge in English and math and proved problematic for several reasons (Harrington, 1999). The tests were not aligned intentionally with the state's content standards. As a result, prospective teachers were not tested on specific knowledge and skills needed to teach the state content standards. The tests also proved to be a barrier to potential teachers from a variety of backgrounds where additional teachers are needed. Passing rates on state tests differ significantly among racial/ethnic groups (Darling-Hammond, 1985; Goertz & Pitcher, 1985).

More recently, states have sought to align the tests with their standards and assessments as well as to use more sophisticated measures of prospective teacher performance. In Oregon, for example, applicants for an initial teaching license must produce a portfolio of work samples that demonstrates their ability to elicit student learning and to enable students to meet state standards (Schalock & Cowart, 1993). This is in addition to a requirement to pass a basic skills achievement test and a teacher knowledge test.

Despite all the shortcomings of teacher testing programs and angry reactions from teachers (Harrington, 1999), the pressure for testing to improve the quality of those admitted to preparation programs and the teaching profession is so pervasive that one of the major teachers' unions now publicly advocates for such tests (Zernike, 2000).

## K–16 ALIGNMENT: WHAT IS IT AND WHAT DOES IT LOOK LIKE?

One other way of thinking about alignment is the notion of a K–16 system of education. In such a conception of education, the goals and key performance expectations are articulated from kindergarten through college. Assessments, curriculum, teacher preparation and certification, and education policy generally are aligned not only in primary and secondary education, but across the boundaries of the K–12 and postsecondary systems. This type of alignment is relatively common outside the United States. The American system, with its emphasis on local control, has been able to function with secondary and postsecondary systems joined tenuously through a series of *ad hoc* mechanisms that may be showing signs of wear and tear.

Some argue the lack of alignment between precollegiate and postsecondary systems is intentional, that one of the primary purposes historically of the high school–college transition has been social sorting (Lemann, 1995). Secondary schools have been assigned the task of identifying those who can go on to higher education, but not through the more formal, exam-based means seen previously in many European and other national educational systems. The American system has been portrayed as holding out hope to all and as a social equalizer by which those from lower economic classes can improve their social standing. The assumption has been that if students do what is asked of them in high school, they can go on college.

This loose conception of alignment has operated via a set of quality control measures that have become increasingly suspect as means to link the two systems. Course titles, Carnegie units, teacher grades, class standing, recommendations, and extracurricular activities combine with tests from nongovernmental organizations like the College Board, ETS, and ACT to provide the information used to articulate the two systems. This information is analyzed, categorized, ranked, and weighted in differing ways by different postsecondary institutions. Secondary students and teachers have a general idea of what colleges expect, but each teacher is free to designate and teach the specific knowledge and skills she or he deems necessary for students to succeed in college.

The net effect is to favor those who understand this complex and sometimes contradictory measurement system over those who assume they should just do what high school teachers and counselors tell them to do, or those who receive no guidance at all (Ziebarth & Rainwater, 2000). Furthermore, the system encourages a checklist approach to learning, one that often discourages development of the very attributes favored by many colleges and universities (Conley & Bodone, 2002). Students may seek easier courses or easier teachers in order to get better grades. They may pay for test preparation courses for SAT or ACT, tests that were designed initially to identify college aptitude independent of high school performance. These tests tend to correlate with student socioeconomic status more than any other single factor. Admission occurs so early in the senior year that some students may choose to avoid academic coursework during the final semester of high school (Kirst, 2000).

Postsecondary education is really more of a series of systems unto themselves, segmented into 2-year and 4-year, public and private institutions, often with different governing boards and funding sources for each system or even institution. This mix of service providers, combined with the optional nature of postsecondary education and the extensive choice available to consumers, makes postsecondary education very different from the elementary/secondary system, which is compulsory and largely monopolistic in nature. This basic incompatibility in system structure and governance has helped make articulation and alignment problematic.

## Closer High School–College Connections

One strategy has been simply to loosen the barriers between systems, particularly between high school and college, rather than to attempt to articulate across systems. Most notable have been postsecondary options programs. These programs allow high school students to begin to accumulate college credits through a variety of arrangements. Options include dual enrollment, where students enroll in high school and college simultaneously, taking classes at each; on-site college courses taught to high school students by specially certified high school teachers or by college instructors; middle-college high schools, which are secondary programs physically located on a college campus that engage students more directly with the college transition; and, increasingly, Internet-based classes that may include both high school and college students. Some states are allowing early matriculation by students who complete their high school requirements ahead of schedule.

Postsecondary options programs have proven popular with students and parents and less popular with educators who are concerned about losing some of their best students and the state funding that accompanies them. Colleges are often concerned about accommodating adolescents or overcrowding in classes where full-time, regular students have difficulty enrolling. Prominent examples include Minnesota's ground-breaking 1985 initiative (Archibald, 1990), Colorado's program begun in 1987 and subsequently amended (Christenson & Conley, 1993), and Washington's Running Start, initiated in 1992 (Washington State Board for Community and Technical Colleges, 1997). All of these programs are similar in that they allow students to take college classes while still in high school. They differ in the specifics of which students can participate, whether students can get dual credits for the courses, and the degree to which high school teachers can teach courses at the high school for which college credit is granted. The percentage of students enrolled in each state is in the range of 5% of the state's seniors, but the programs are extremely popular with the public. High schools continue to raise concerns that the programs siphon off the best students or make it more difficult to offer honors or advanced placement courses, while postsecondary institutions in these states have developed a range of strategies to accommodate these students with limited impact on college programs. Student interest has spread beyond high achievers to include a much wider range of students who participate in broad spectrum of college programs. Postsecondary options programs have received support from those interested in more choice in education and have been opposed by those in education who fear losing students or funding (Archibald, 1990; Nasstrom, 1986).

One can predict bitter battles over postsecondary options programs because they are difficult to construct as win–win propositions. Since high schools are affected much more than colleges and in a more negative fashion, groups representing high school interests can be expected to unite to oppose such programs or to modify them in ways that have the least negative impact on high schools as currently conceived. Without a redesign of high schools or policies that create continuous transitions from high school to college, it will be difficult to take full advantage of postsecondary options programs and their potential for greater system alignment (Conley, 2001, 2002b).

### Smoothing the Transition for all Students

Angus and Mirel (1999) assert that high schools lost their focus on college and vocational preparation long ago and came to be concerned primarily with custodial care of adolescents. High school reform has tended to push high schools toward a core curriculum model on one hand (National Center for Education Statistics, 1997) and specialty schools-within-schools or academies on the other hand (Raywid, 1996).

If high schools are to accommodate a wider range of student interests and learning styles, they will likely increase what is referred to as contextual learning (National Alliance of Business, 2001; Steinberg, Cushman, & Riordan, 1999). Internships, mentorships, field-based experiences, project-based learning, and applied academics are all examples of contextual learning (Souders & Prescott, 1999). Programs of this nature will be of potential interest to all students and will serve the purpose of helping young adults develop greater maturity and the ability to function in an adult world. Such skills will be important to students who want to take advantage of postsecondary options programs as well as those who choose to enter the work world.

To enhance system alignment, high schools will have to learn to construct experiences that include both college-bound and non-college-bound students. Activities that develop student maturity and provide real-world experiences will open more opportunities for students to transition smoothly from high school. This new notion of articulation defines readiness more broadly than simple academic preparedness, and articulation more broadly than coordinated course requirements.

### The Interaction Between College Admissions and High School Reform

Attempts to create stronger and more rational articulation between precollegiate and postsecondary education are beginning to cause ripples in both environments. As states pursue standards-based reforms, they begin to make changes in secondary schools independent of college admission standards. Rather than adapting to the needs of postsecondary education, state reforms are creating new expectations for learners and new means of gauging student performance. These new measures do not translate well into the traditional admissions process. If states pursue greater alignment in their educational systems, the historically asymmetrical relationship between colleges and high schools regarding admissions criteria will undergo a rebalancing.

State education reforms in the 1980s were geared toward increasing the academic focus of a high school education. In general, states increased the number of years of mathematics and science required for a high school diploma. These changes caused few problems for universities, which already stated their admissions requirements in terms of courses taken. These actions did prompt some state universities to raise their own requirements in these areas, but the changes were what Grossman, Kirst, and Schmidt-Posner (1986) refer to as "intensification"—basically more of the same.

Education reforms in the 1990s began to pull high schools in the direction of state standards and assessments (Olson, 2002b). Interestingly, the standards in essentially every state were not constructed with the explicit purpose or goal of preparing more students to enter college. A survey of the standard-setting process nationwide (Conley, 2002a) reveals that higher education was not involved systematically in standard-setting activities, although individual faculty members or token representatives from admissions offices on occasion were included on standard-setting panels. The net effect of the lack of focus on college admission is that state standards and assessments currently do not necessarily line up well with university admissions requirements in terms of their substance, and not at all in terms of how they are measured. States specify knowledge and skills students are to learn and the standards they must reach, while college admissions requirements identify courses students must take and grades they must receive in order to be considered for admission.

This lack of systematic connection between high school standards and assessments and college admission holds the potential to aggravate articulation issues and to stress the entire standards-based reform effort. If high schools begin to focus instruction on state standards and assessments, and if these are not consistent with university admissions requirements, high schools might end up neglecting college preparation for test preparation, or preparing some students for state assessments and others for college admission. Neither approach helps high schools or colleges achieve their goals.

The tension between state expectations and university requirements has not yet been fully resolved in any state. Accommodating these two different systems for measuring student knowledge and skills is a critical unresolved issue that must be addressed if system articulation is to proceed to include both precollegiate and postsecondary systems.

## P–16 Projects in the States

At least 24 states are engaged in P–16 activities to unify their educational systems from preschool or kindergarten through college (Ziebarth & Rainwater, 2000). The key strategy is to eliminate the traditional boundaries between different educational levels and institutions by adopting a common system of standards and assessments that generates data useful for admission or placement into the next level in the system. Ideally, students will be able to move from grade to grade and school to school as they meet standards. Chronological age need not be the key determinant of movement within the system. More important, the adults in the system can have clearer expectations for students and the tasks in which students should engage to ensure success at the next level.

The first step toward a K–16 system in a number of states has been to bring together educators from all levels to engage in common discussions and dialogue regarding their expectations for students and the means by which student progress might better be determined. The most notable example to date has been Oregon's Proficiency-based Admission Standards System (PASS) (Conley, 1997a).

Oregon adopted a sweeping program for high school reforms in 1991. The goal of the reforms was to create better articulation not necessarily between high school and college, but between high school and the work world. As the reforms have evolved, the goals have expanded to include postsecondary articulation. PASS, which was established in 1994, seeks to address this lack of articulation between K–12 reforms and university admission. PASS organized collaborative planning teams consisting of high school teachers and university faculty to develop proficiency-based standards for university admission, designed to take the place of traditional course requirements. These proficiencies align with the state's tenth-grade Certificate of Initial Mastery standards and assessments as well as those for the Certificate of Advanced Mastery, which is focused on grades 11 and 12 and emphasizes contextual or applied learning.

This linkage between PASS and the two certificates blurs the distinction between "applied" learning and traditional academic courses, allowing high schools to implement new curriculum that offers students preparation for the work world and college simultaneously. These reforms create a framework within which Oregon students can move from high school to postsecondary experiences more seamlessly as they demonstrate their readiness to do college-level work. Those who choose not to go directly to college have more options open to them, and in almost all cases have already met some proficiency requirements, thereby making it more feasible for them to complete college entrance requirements at some later date.

Georgia has established a number of P–16 Councils to enhance articulation between high schools and 2- and 4-year institutions (Henry & Kettlewell, 1999). One of the key initiatives of the Councils is the Postsecondary Readiness Enrichment Program (PREP). Statewide goals for the Councils and for PREP include increasing the number of high school students successfully completing the gateway courses of algebra and geometry by the end of tenth grade; increasing graduation rates in high schools, technical institutes/ colleges, and colleges and universities; and closing the gaps between the expectations set for students who graduate from high school and enter college and those who enter technical institutes and work.

Kentucky adopted legislation in 2001 that directs the state's Council on Postsecondary Education to help enable the establishment of local P–16 Councils charged with the responsibility to promote teacher preparation and professional development, the alignment of competency standards, and the elimination of barriers that impede student transition from preschool through baccalaureate programs.

The Missouri K–16 Coalition will focus on grades 11 and 12 and the first 2 years of higher education (Rainwater, 2000). The coalition is charged with promoting quality performance standards; encouraging faculty agreements on content and expectations in the major disciplines, beginning with mathematics; supporting full articulation within and across educational sectors; and identifying strategies for enhanced performance based on preparation and ability (Stein, 1999).

Another notable example of a state-level effort to enhance articulation between high school and college is Illinois, which administered its Prairie State Achievement Examination to all juniors for the first time in April 2001 (Allen & Banchero, 2000). The exam consists of three distinct parts given over 2 days: (1) tests developed by the State Board of Education and linked to Illinois content standards in writing, science, and social sciences; (2) two Work Keys tests, Reading for Information and Applied Mathematics, that measure skills employers feel are critical to job success; and (3) ACT, which tests English, mathematics, science, and social science knowledge for college entrance purposes. This set of assessments will provide information useful to employers and colleges, and, most important, will provide students better information on how well they are preparing to achieve their post-high school goals.

The Maryland K–16 initiative has a number of dimensions, including a project to develop end-of-course examinations that eventually will link with university admission and placement (Shapiro & Haeger, 1999). University faculty members have been very involved in developing the standards for these examinations. The goal is to be able to use the results for placement purposes and to help ensure continuity between high school and university curricula.

New York high school students now have to pass Regents examinations in English language arts and mathematics in order to receive a diploma from their local school district. These exams were developed specifically to be useful in the college admissions and placement process. Some universities in New York are beginning to use the results from the exams instead of their own placement tests.

Washington State has adopted a Certificate of Mastery (CoM) at grade 10 that will be linked with university admission sometime after 2008. University faculty have developed "exit competencies" that students must master in addition to the CoM, if they wish to go to college, thereby creating greater alignment between high school and university expectations.

### Examples of National Projects

In addition to these state-level responses, a national project called Standards for Success (Olson, 2001c) seeks to clarify university entrance expectations and examine new possibilities for system alignment. The Association of American Universities, in partnership with the Pew Charitable Trusts, launched this 3-year effort to identify in detail the "key knowledge and skills for university success."

Standards for Success convened a series of meetings at research universities throughout the country to gain input from faculty who teach first-year courses. The faculty were asked to identify the knowledge and skills necessary for success in those courses, to submit examples of student work that meets that standard, to annotate the work to illustrate how the work meets the standard, and to contribute course outlines and assignments that identify more clearly what students are expected to do in those classes. This information was analyzed and synthesized. From it, a brochure and CD-ROM were assembled and distributed to every high school in the nation. The goal of the project is to create standards statements that for the first time express the expectations of university faculty in language that parallels that of state high school standards. Standards for Success also analyzed state high school assessments to ascertain the degree to which they yield results that might be of use in the college admissions process. In addition, the project produced resources that can help high school teachers and district curriculum committees make the senior year truly challenging and engaging for all students by helping teachers focus on curriculum that prepares students for success in college.

## ALIGNMENT: MORE ENERGY, BETTER RESULTS?

Alignment brings with it a series of challenges educators and policy makers alike must face. As fragmented as an unaligned system is, it possesses the relative advantage of allowing each level to pursue its own goals and programs in relative isolation from the needs and requirements of others. This "simplifies" the system's operation in the sense that less energy is needed for coordination and articulation or for attention to the needs and demands of groups external to a particular level. This also helps insulate the system from imposition of one set of values or beliefs system-wide.

The emphasis on articulation will result in new demands, structures, relationships, and procedures, which may in turn trigger changes in roles as well as in education programs. Alignment is not likely to succeed absent large-scale changes in the authority and responsibility of all the existing layers in the governance system. Simultaneously, the somewhat informal control over important aspects of national education policy held by privileged nongovernmental organizations is certain to fall under much greater scrutiny. No force seems capable of derailing the alignment train. However, getting education to function as one system after centuries of separation is a formidable undertaking. Effecting improvement in student learning immediately while alignment is still under way is even more of a challenge. Greater alignment will have profound effects on all governance levels. These effects are the topic of the next three chapters.

# Chapter 7

# CHANGES IN ROLES AT THE STATE LEVEL

The roles, duties, and structures of state policy bodies like legislatures, governors' offices, state education boards, and education departments are already in flux and will continue to evolve in response to the new power and responsibility that have accrued at the state and federal levels. Understanding how these offices of government function relative to one another and to local educational systems is now much more important for educators, whose professional lives are affected more directly by the actions taken at the state level. Each of these entities is discussed in turn.

## THE CHANGING ROLE AND STRUCTURE
## OF STATE POLICY MECHANISMS

Governors and legislatures have emerged as the key players in education reform. Their involvement brings a stronger connection between politics and education. However, they also reflect the needs and concerns of constituencies that are affected by education policy but have not necessarily had access to the educational system. Governors and legislatures ground education policy in a broad-based perspective on the goals and purposes of school systems. They also enter an area of great complexity and difficulty where creating cause-and-effect relationships through state policy can be elusive. The challenge has not deterred activity among governors and legislators, who seem to be learning incrementally how to utilize the political and policy processes to manage state school systems.

### The Emergence of Governors as Education Reform Leaders

The shift in funding to the state level and the extended critique of public education as a failing institution have caused voters to question who is in charge of and responsible for the schools. The answer, in the public's eyes, is often the governor. This has led governors to assert their authority over education policy (Johnston, 1999). Governors have tended to put forth specific education reform policy proposals as well as to provide political support for continuing implementation of sometimes controversial education reform programs (Stricherz, 2001a).

Some governors are no longer enamored of local control. California governor Gray Davis, a supporter of public schools who campaigned for state bonds to fund new school construction and whose budgets recommended increased education spending, has not been hesitant to criticize local control, which he describes as an "abject failure" (Johnston & Sandham, 1999). California is an example of a state where power has shifted to the governor's office, which has not been hesitant to exercise this newfound authority. A stream of education reforms now emanates from the California governor's office, whether it is occupied by a Republican or Democrat (Stricherz, 2001a). The state board of education and state superintendent of public instruction, each of which used to operate relatively independently of the governor's office to formulate education policy across a range of issues, find their power at once amplified and challenged as policy making moves to the state level and is initiated increasingly by the governor's office. This has led to tension and conflict among the governor, board, and superintendent. The solution from the governor's perspective in California was to create a cabinet-level education position and invest it with authority to develop education policy. Here is another example of a new structure being created and overlaid on a system without resolution of the overall governance structure and power relationships.

Oregon's governor from 1994–2002, John Kitzhaber, has preserved the state's ambitious and sweeping education reform program by fending off all legislative attempts to eliminate or alter it significantly, while simultaneously working to bring about modifications that have made the reforms palatable to a broad range of politicians and citizens (Sommerfeld, 1995). The State Board of Education, all of whose current members were appointed by Kitzhaber, also has rejected all attempts to weaken or turn back reforms. The two different state superintendents elected during the governor's term in office, both nominally Republicans in this nonpartisan position, have worked cooperatively with the governor and would have been much less effective without the governor's leadership and support.

Florida Governor Jeb Bush initiated a redesign of educational governance in the state, resulting in one governing board with authority for all public education—elementary, secondary, and postsecondary—and a state education secretary, both appointed by the governor (Richard, 2002). Georgia Governor Roy Barnes authored a comprehensive program of school reform that proposed abolishing tenure for new teachers, creating an independent office of education accountability, allowing parents to transfer their children out of failing schools, cutting class sizes to 11 students per teacher in the early grades for low-performing schools, requiring teachers to pass basic technology tests before they are hired or recertified, and instituting signing bonuses to attract teachers to hard-to-fill areas such as math and science, and to rural schools (Jacobson, 2000).

## Legislatures as "Incubators" of Reform Programs

While governors provide the leadership, state legislatures have been the incubator and nursery for many programs of education reform. The impetus for charter schools, for example, has come primarily from legislatures, and charter school legislation varies widely across states (Hanks, 1997; Nelson, Berman, Ericson, Kamprath, Perry, Silverman, & Solomon, 2000). A wide variety of ideas and approaches have been generated and implemented in different states. These differences are consistent with the values and political traditions of the respective states.

From these legislative-based initiatives, spring a wide variety of programs and policies. These variations among states, districts, and schools yield useful examples of what works and what doesn't, and those examples often are adopted or adapted by other states and the federal government. This is consistent with the American model of public policy development, where states experiment with new ideas before they are generalized to other states or the national level.

Legislatures have taken their cue from commissions or consultants who recommended particular packages of programs. The effects of reports from a state-level commission such as Kentucky's Prichard Committee or a national group such as the Commission on the Skills of the American Work Force, which issued *America's Choice: High Skills or Low Wages* (1990), have been profound within and across states. Legislatures have functioned as forums where the business community in particular is able to exert influence successfully and build political coalitions for the passage of education reform programs. In Oregon, business leaders endorsed passage of the Oregon Educational Act for the 21st Century in 1991 and were among its primary supporters and defenders in the legislature throughout the decade when it came under fire in nearly every legislative session. The reforms, while still controversial, have been largely institutionalized, and the governor and legislative leadership utilize them as the framework for state education policy.

## Relationships Among Policy-Making Bodies at the State Level

Education policy and governance structures vary in many important respects from state to state. At least four distinct configurations have been identified (Ziebarth, 2000). Twelve states employ a model in which the governor appoints the state board, which then appoints the chief state school officer. Eight states have elected boards that appoint the chief. In 11 states, the governor appoints the state board, while the public elects the chief state school officer. Eight other states have governors who appoint both the state board and the chief. In addition, 10 states have variations on these four models that include no state board and a chief appointed by the governor (Minnesota); a state board composed of five members appointed by the governor and two apiece by the lieutenant governor and speaker of the house, which then appoints the chief state school officer (Mississippi); and a state board with 16 members appointed by the legislature, one by the governor, and an elected chief state school officer (South Carolina).

The historical intent in most states was to have educational governance stand separate and aside from a partisan legislature and at arm's length from a partisan governor's office. One of the effects of education's migration into the mainstream of state policy has been the *de facto* politicization of state boards and education chief executives. Politicization occurs when the actions of boards and education CEOs become more aligned with specific political parties and philosophies.

Furthermore, education policy decisions now have more significant and immediate effects on other areas of state government, particularly budget-related implications. Education policy is now linked more directly with economic development policy, for example. Urban renewal and educational improvement are often flip sides of the same coin. K–12 education reform competes head-on with postsecondary education for state fiscal resources. As school improvement becomes a higher priority, dollars are redirected from other state agencies and initiatives to education, while improvement policies increasingly emanate from the state level.

With the firm establishment of education as a state issue and the initiation of attempts to harness schools in the service of state goals, more conflict is generated among state-level players. Governors on one hand and elected superintendents or commissions on the other hand compete to see who will provide leadership for education policy. Georgia provides an example of this phenomenon (Jacobson, 1999). At one point, the state superintendent, governor, and state board of education held conflicting positions on a range of education issues and on the authority each legitimately possessed (Hoff, 1999).

While competing governance units are a safeguard against excessive power accumulating in one place, these three entities vying for control over education policy—governor, state superintendent, and state board—are all part of the executive branch of government. The degree to which conflict exists among them suggests a policy system that is not synchronized or designed in a way that produces coherent policy consistently. The resolution in some states is to change the way boards and state superintendents are selected. The measure of success will be the degree to which the executive branch is capable of speaking to the legislative branch in something approaching a single voice and of sending clearer, more consistent policy intentions to schools.

Whether this leads to "better" education policy is largely in the eye of the beholder. These changes do signal the fuller integration of the educational system into the larger body of state government. This integration provides additional evidence that education policy is becoming fully institutionalized at the state level and that any sort of return to local control as it historically has been practiced is highly improbable. Indeed, one of the criticisms of more streamlined governance systems is precisely that they do not allow local districts as much of a voice in state policy as the districts once had and that education policy making should not be terribly efficient or rapid (Clune, 1993a).

States are just now learning how to formulate and manage education policy centrally. As states become more adept at generating policy in a coordinated fashion, schools can expect to see a range of new initiatives that will be increasingly more carefully crafted and effective in employing all of the tools states have to enforce their wills. Ironically, these new initiatives may be justified as ways to promote more local control or consumer choice, but in the end the result will be to consolidate the state's hold on education policy. In some states, the legislature is already being referred to as a sort of "super school board" (Stout & Stevens, 2000) due to its increasing influence on local education practices and the range of education issues on which it now sits in judgment, from the macro to the micro level.

However, as noted earlier, schools continue to lack the capacity to adapt rapidly to new policy initiatives. They have been designed to be conservative and to change slowly. Increasingly state policy makers will have to come to grips with the mismatch between their desires for educational change and the organization and culture of schools as they exist today.

## THE NEW ROLE OF STATE BOARDS OF EDUCATION

State boards of education are one of those educational governance mechanisms that are uniquely American. State education boards were relatively obscure in many states before the past decade, to educators and noneducators alike. Most boards have had a limited range of authority focused on developing the rules and regulations that accompany state legislation and the minimum standards surrounding such things as high school diplomas and length of school year. State boards also provide direction to and general oversight of state education departments.

Before the 1980s, few outside the education policy community paid a great deal of attention to how these boards were constituted, what their duties were, and what potential influence they could wield over state education policy. Notable exceptions existed in Texas, California, and New York, where the state boards had long histories of choosing textbooks and making other significant education policy decisions that placed them in the public spotlight with some regularity. Even in these states the scope and visibility of the state board of education has increased dramatically during the past decade.

State boards of education seem to be one of the "winners" in the restructuring of educational governance, if winning is defined in terms of power gained or lost. During the past decade, most state boards of education have seen their duties and responsibilities increase in a number of areas. These include approving state content standards; approving and monitoring state assessment systems; designating failing schools, in partnership with state education departments; approving individual charter schools, hearing appeals when local districts deny charters, and even sponsoring charter schools; setting state educational goals and performance targets; and approving state accountability reporting systems, including school report cards and other rating systems. These functions are nontrivial in the eyes of local school boards, administrators, teachers, and the general public. This enhanced visibility allows them to shape the larger public policy debate about public education aims, purposes, and goals.

Additionally, they may be linked much more closely with governors' offices than are education departments. In 31 states, governors appoint the entire state education board, and in four other states they are responsible for the appointment of at least some members. Of the 31 boards selected by governors, 14 choose the chief state school officer. Of all school boards, appointed or elected, 26 appoint the state superintendent of education. From 1930, when 33 of 48 states elected their state school chief, the number is likely to decrease to 14 of 50 in 2003 (Stricherz, 2001a). Ten governors appoint state education chiefs, twice the number since 1983 (Johnston, 1999). State board influence increases when the superintendent is appointed by the board or by a governor who appoints the board, rather than being elected independently of the board.

The relationship among state board, state superintendent, governor, and legislature also has not been seriously re-examined and restructured for close to a century. In states that have appointed boards, these boards now represent the education agenda of their respective governor's office more directly and prominently. The increased power of state boards occasionally has put them in the middle between governors and superintendents who have been in conflict. Governors have moved to restructure a board when it stands in the way of the governor's policies, as in the case of Michigan's Governor

Engler, who initiated legislation to transfer the powers of the elected board to an appointed superintendent. In other cases governors have sought the resignation of board members and then moved to change from an elected board to an appointed one (Johnston, 1999; Johnston & Sandham, 1999).

These high-profile incidents obscure the fact that little has really changed regarding how boards are organized and staffed. Boards are overwhelmingly voluntary part-time positions with meager professional support staff to assist them in their preparations and deliberations. Boards are asked to pass on a wider range of ever more complex and high-stakes issues, while operating with the same time, expertise, and resources they had when they were much less central to state education policy.

Business groups have shown greater interest in having their representatives on state boards in order to further the educational improvement agendas of the business community. Similarly, membership from racial minority groups has increased as issues of unequal educational achievement and failure of urban schools have become more prominent. Political party affiliation also has become more of a factor in state board composition, although most boards are still officially considered to be nonpartisan.

State boards can play an important role by providing a forum for public input into education policy, by offering a sounding board for professional educators frustrated by state policies, by translating state policy into practices that make the most sense for educators, by managing specific innovations such as charter schools, and by attempting to retain some distance between public education and partisan politics. If they fail to fulfill these roles and come to be viewed as impediments to coherent education policy development and implementation or as political threats, it seems clear that governors in particular will move aggressively to limit or reallocate their powers.

However, it appears more likely that they will continue to come more under the wing of governors and will become an outlet for the expression of gubernatorial policy goals. This is consistent with a structuralist view of organizations that would contend that organizations tend to create new structures and change the duties of existing structures based on new power relationships.

## THE CONTRADICTORY GOALS OF STATE EDUCATION AGENCIES

Few, if any, state education departments were designed with the goal of improving local educational systems. Most departments of education have been relatively weak and small in size. Even in states with histories of more state direction of education, education departments have remained relatively modest in size and authority relative to the number of students and schools in these states (Lusi, 1997).

State education agencies have been viewed with suspicion by local school districts and by state legislatures whose members reflect concerns of local constituents. Here again, the traditions of local control and locally generated tax revenues for schools served to shape the state agency's role and structure. This has meant that state education departments have been concerned with a relatively constrained set of responsibilities focused on local district compliance with state policy.

When state education agencies did become more interventionist in local districts from the late 1960s onward, it was as a result of the expanded federal role in education policy. This expansion began with the Elementary and Secondary Education Act in 1965. At the time this act was passed, the federal government had no effective means to implement education policy nationally. The implementation strategy adopted was one of working through state education agencies instead of setting up a large federal mechanism designed to coordinate and oversee national education policy.

To this day, the U.S. Department of Education has only modest regional presences throughout the nation and relies almost entirely on state education departments as the agents to implement federal education policy. In many states nearly half the positions in the state education department are funded by the federal government for specific purposes such as overseeing a range of federal policies including Title I, special education, bilingual and migrant education, vocational education, and, most recently, school improvement programs.

State education agencies have evolved from simply interpreting federal regulations and monitoring local compliance to spurring improvement in schools and organizing and enforcing accountability systems. These contradictory roles create tensions within education departments between the personnel assigned these conflicting tasks as well as in the way the agency presents itself to the field.

The oversight function is reinforced in traditional state education agencies in many important ways. State legislatures tend to allocate funds to education departments to monitor or implement specific programs. Local education agencies are familiar with compliance activities and requirements, and are comfortable with or have resigned themselves to interacting with the state education agency along these dimensions. Only in the past 20 years have education agencies been called upon to provide leadership for school improvement, curriculum development, standards creation, assessment design and implementation, and accountability systems.

Needless to say, this type of cultural upheaval in rule-bound bureaucratic agencies has played havoc with the internal dynamics of these agencies. Tensions can exist between the traditional compliance-oriented departments and those units charged with the newer improvement-focused responsibilities. Education departments are called upon to adopt a service-oriented culture, both toward school districts and the general public. Understaffed and burdened by a structure that does not support innovation or rapid adaptation, most education departments struggle to accommodate to the radically new role that legislatures have implied or mandated for them as a result of heightened state activity in education policy.

One of the places where the contradictory role of education departments comes into sharpest focus is in the area of school accountability. Most state accountability systems are still evolving. However, a common thread throughout is the notion that an accountability system serves both to provide information schools can use to improve and to identify poor-performing schools in need of state assistance or intervention. The state education agency is put into the impossible position of implementing the same system to improve schools and to punish them.

This dynamic creates an ambiguous relationship between education departments and school districts; some would characterize it as schizophrenic. Should a district reveal weaknesses to an education department in the hopes of gaining assistance, or will doing so make matters worse? Educators seem more inclined to take a chance by acknowledging weaknesses and accepting assistance, particularly in states with high-stakes accountability systems (Grant, 2000). In essence, schools have nowhere else to turn when facing the need to adapt to specific state mandates. Local districts have little precedent for working collaboratively to solve mutual problems, since most operate in relative isolation. Their primary common contact for information or training related to state reforms is now the education department, which must be approached for assistance even as it holds the power to impose sanctions or publicly embarrass the schools.

## TRANSFORMING DEPARTMENTS OF EDUCATION

What will it take to transform state education departments? Although blueprints have been offered (David, 1994b; Lusi, 1997), few state education departments have been able to reshape themselves significantly. Many have added new duties or personnel, but their basic functioning and relationship with schools remain remarkably consistent over time.

### Whom Should Education Departments Serve?

Can a transformation be accomplished or is some entirely new structure needed for state-level control over local education? To answer this question requires a reconsideration of the constituency of state education departments. Whom do they serve? Are they the agents of the legislature, of the governor, of the state education board? Are they to implement state policy and exercise control over schools? Are they to facilitate school improvement design and administer a system of common standards and assessments that generate data on school and district performance? Are they to provide assistance to those who cannot improve their schools, facilitating the sharing of ideas and the networking of teachers and resources? Are they the advocates for local districts in the legislature, attempting to maximize the funds schools receive from the state budget? Are they "partners" with local school districts, and, if so, what does it mean to have such a "partnership"?

These complex and even contradictory functions still overlook one possible role: advocates for student learning rather than for public schools. An education department whose mission was to advocate for student learning would look dramatically different from one that monitored or even improved schools. In order to advocate for student learning, education departments would have to be organized to ensure that all students had equal access to high-quality learning environments. Whether this took place within a traditional public school or another setting would not be the primary consideration. The preservation of local districts or individual schools would not be the ultimate goal of the education department; nor would the abolition of local control and neighborhood schools be a goal. Instead, education departments would acknowledge that educational structures needed to be matched with communities' needs and capabilities, and the state's role was to ensure that all students had access to quality learning opportunities.

Charter schools are perhaps the first test of whether state education departments can focus on students' needs rather than solely on those of schools. The instinct of most education departments is to organize to monitor or regulate charters, even though the purpose of charters is to escape traditional regulation. Evidence suggests that some states are, in fact, moving toward giving their education departments greater authority to monitor charter schools, setting the stage for tension between "negotiated compliance" and "enforced compliance" (Vergari, 2000).

Will charters be encouraged to innovate and adapt to constituent needs, or will charters become increasingly standardized to meet the regulatory urges and mandates of state education agencies? Can education departments hold charters accountable for results without intruding into their operations? Does the state education department have a responsibility to help ensure that charter opportunities are available to students in all communities, not just those that are the most able to establish charters? How should charters be nurtured? Some education departments have taken tentative steps in this direction, setting up offices with responsibilities for some of these issues. How these offices and their responsibilities evolve will be suggestive of the ways in which education departments more generally will evolve and redefine their roles.

## What Would a New Department of Education Look Like?

How specifically would a department of education look different if it were to transform into a structure that might faithfully implement state policy while simultaneously advocating for school improvement and student learning? One of the primary functions newly redesigned education departments must master is the mediation of state policy goals for local educators and the general public. State-level education policy has tended to be drawn in broad outlines, leaving considerable necessity for interpretation. Education departments have struggled to provide the level of specificity necessary for schools to make sense of state policy, while not straitjacketing local discretion and initiative. As noted earlier, teachers have tended to resist implementing state reform until it has been translated into a level of detail suitable to define exactly what teachers must do at the classroom level. Often this level of detail stifles or subverts the original reform goals. Schools need much more clarification in a timely fashion to allow them to process policies and provide feedback on their effects at the local level.

Most education departments are highly centralized operations located in state capitals. However, electronic communications and the Internet in particular are fostering direct communication with schools, parents, and educational advocacy groups. Rather than being limited to infrequent mailings to school districts, education departments can now disseminate information widely and rapidly, and update it regularly. Few state departments of education have taken full advantage of this capacity, although all have websites of varying quality and utility. Few have well-developed strategies for comprehensive communications, interactions, and data dissemination that meet consumers' needs. Changing the organizational culture of the agency along with the behavior of school personnel and the public to interact via electronic means requires significant refocusing and reorganizing of traditional communication structures and dissemination modes. Educational administrators in particular are accustomed to personal presentations by education department personnel at regularly established intervals.

This new conception of point-to-point communication needs to be coupled with a radically decentralized agency oriented primarily toward local constituencies. This more community-based agency would be responsible for understanding the needs and challenges faced locally. Such knowledge would help the agency discern the effects of state policies and identify the ways in which policy might be better shaped to achieve its goals and to harmonize those goals with local desires and conditions. Staff that remained in the state capital would be charged explicitly with managing political relations between the agency and state government.

To succeed in this new role, education departments need vastly improved policy analysis and generation capacities. They need new data systems that generate comprehensive information on student learning and profiles of school performance. They then need to become much better at analyzing the data that such systems generate. This analysis capacity need not necessarily be housed within the departments themselves but could be conducted by a broad network of service providers, including universities, regional education labs, independent institutes, intermediate service agencies, and even some school districts themselves. Many of these entities already conduct policy analyses independent of the education agency. Coordinating this activity would lead to richer and more valuable policy information.

This enhanced policy analysis and development capacity would be complemented by an improved program evaluation ability driven by the dramatically increasing range of data on student learning that is or will be available. These data will allow education departments to identify the strengths and weaknesses of the educational system along with short- and long-range trends in student achievement, to recommend policies for school improvement, and to suggest new programs or approaches that address specific problems. They can help legislatures make better decisions about which practices to centralize, which to decentralize, and how to measure success more generally.

Furthermore, education departments may find themselves in the role of overseeing a much wider range of education service providers, ranging from traditional school districts to charter schools, home schoolers, and educational contractors. In addition, state education agencies would encourage new quasi-governmental structures, such as networks that focus on a common purpose, like home schoolers or charter schools, or even public schools with like interests. Education departments are uniquely situated to initiate new structures that facilitate a wider array of education service providers.

One other dimension of education department restructuring has yet to be considered seriously by any state. No department has yet been held accountable for specific increases in student achievement. This responsibility has been placed on schools and school districts, where it has been traditionally. If education departments were expected to be directly responsible and accountable for improved student achievement in specific increments, much as schools are, their perspective on the functioning of schools and the urgency of school improvement might change.

## THE ROLE OF COMMISSIONS AND
## EXTRA-GOVERNMENTAL AGENCIES

Education functions like a closed system in many respects. Major changes rarely emanate spontaneously from within schools without some external stimulus. One mechanism that states, the federal government, and citizen advocacy groups have used to challenge this insularity is the special-purpose commission. The most notable and influential example is the federal commission responsible for the publication of *A Nation at Risk* in 1983. Subsequently, numerous commissions and reports have been instrumental in identifying educational problems and, increasingly, setting policy in specific areas.

The far-reaching effects of the National Commission on Excellence in Education, which produced the *Nation at Risk* report, cannot be underestimated. A closer examination of the work of the Commission reveals that it compiled its data primarily from hearings it held around the nation, commissioned papers and presentations, and discussions among its members. The Commission was composed of educators, higher education professors and administrators, business leaders, and heads of associations or organizations, a mixture typical of commissions that have been constituted over the past 2 decades. Its co-chairs were a university president and a school board member. The Commission met 17 times, mostly at institutions of higher education, where its members discussed commissioned papers or took testimony from a wide range of individuals, most with ties to public schools or universities. Their conclusions were not necessarily derived as much from empirically derived data as from the testimony they heard and papers they commissioned.

In many ways, this description is typical of similar *ad hoc* groups that have been convened in the past current era of education reform. Some have had fewer educators as members; some have had a clearer charge. They exist in most cases to critique the current system and offer alternative solutions to educational problems. Commissions can be the source of policy ideas or simply can create an atmosphere within which discussion and debate about educational goals and purposes take place. The commission structure has been utilized effectively in several states to formulate reforms as well as to offer an alternative governance mechanism for implementing reforms, a mechanism that stands outside the state's education department and sometimes outside of government altogether.

The use of commissions is another concrete example of how educational governance is in a period of flux. Commissions are much more common in times of transition than during periods of normal functioning of governmental agencies. They are often a harbinger of transfer of authority from one level of government to another. They may be a signal that a vacuum exists at some level of governance and that something new is needed to fill the vacuum.

## Examples of Commissions and Their Effects

Kentucky's Prichard Committee for Academic Excellence was perhaps the first and most influential of all the state commissions. The Committee is relatively unique in that it is a nonpartisan, nonprofit, independent citizens advocacy group. It was founded in 1983 to improve education in Kentucky at all levels, preschool through postgraduate. The group is privately funded and continues to the present.

The Prichard Committee worked outside the existing governance system. It held town meetings simultaneously in each of the state's 177 school districts in 1984 in order to create political momentum in support of a special session of the legislature to deal with education. The Committee's 1985 report, *The Path to a Larger Life*, helped define the parameters of the debate, including dramatically increased investment in public education, expanded early childhood education, vastly improved teacher quality, and restructured schools, and set the stage for the elimination of patronage from school management. The Committee went on to build public support and train local citizen groups in support of its goals (Prichard Committee for Academic Excellence, 1990). The Committee also took legal action against the state in 1989 that led to a decision by the state supreme court mandating education reform. The result was the 1990 Kentucky Education Reform Act, which the Committee helped shape and support. Subsequent to passage of the Act, the Committee has monitored results and helped encourage public support (Sexton, 1995).

The State of Washington presents an example of a state-initiated, single-purpose commission. Its 1993 school reform law established common learning goals for all students. To develop and administer the reform program, the law created the Commission on Student Learning, a state agency governed by an 11-member commission appointed by the governor and the state education board (Holayter, 1998). The Commission was separate from the Office of the Superintendent of Public Instruction, the state education agency. It was charged with developing clear, challenging academic standards, assessments and other ways to measure student achievement, and a system to hold districts and schools accountable for achieving results with the new standards and assessments. By statute, the Commission expired on June 30, 1999, at which time the Office of the Superintendent of Public Instruction took up its duties.

The Commission had a clear agenda, authority, and a timeline by which it had to complete its tasks. This stands in contrast to traditional education departments that are highly bureaucratized, are slow to respond, and have great difficulty producing on tight timelines. In addition, the Commission's work was complemented by other state boards and a range of additional special work groups and task forces, including the Family Policy Council, which developed community health and safety networks to integrate services targeted to families and children; the Workforce Training and Education Co-ordinating Board, which created a plan to integrate vocational training opportunities with academics; the School-to-Work Task Force, whose goal was to encourage career preparation throughout the educational system; the State Board of Education, which developed new certification standards for teachers and administrators; and the Higher Education Coordinating Board, which adopted new admissions standards aligned with the state's new standards and assessments. Other agencies, including the State Board of Community and Technical Colleges and the Superintendent of Public Instruction, lent assistance and provided resources to support the Commission's work.

In this model of governance change, the Commission served as a catalyst and traffic cop of sorts, energizing disparate segments of state government to unite around a common theme that transcended organizational boundaries. The Commission existed both to address issues of turf and to circumvent them at the same time.

In 2001, Oregon established the Quality Education Commission (QEC). Its purpose is to determine the amount of money schools need to achieve specified levels of student achievement. The Commission utilizes the Oregon Quality Education Model (OQEM), which was introduced in Chapter 3, as the basis for making such determinations (Conley, 1999). The OQEM creates and employs prototype schools as the basis for determining funding and performance levels.

The driving force behind the OQEM and QEC was a governor who wanted a more rational method for establishing state budgets in which education funding constituted over half of the budget. The OQEM as a concept was appealing in part because each successive legislature was under greater pressure from local school constituencies to provide adequate funding, but no one knew what constituted adequacy. Legislators, in turn, were increasingly concerned about accountability for school funding and resulting performance, but also sought to preserve some vestiges of local control.

The QEC fills a need that did not exist 10 years previously when education funding was primarily a local responsibility. It provides a relatively objective analysis of school needs and school performance, which helps satisfy both those who require explanations of how the money is being spent and those who advocate that the state determine the real costs of the programs it has mandated for local schools and then provide funds at the level required to achieve state goals.

The QEC is appointed by the governor and is separate from and independent of the state board of education. However, both the QEC and the state board send messages to schools and to policy makers regarding state educational goals and priorities. The QEC responds to new demands that legislators as well as local schools be accountable for their fiscal decisions.

One of the challenges for local schools will be to determine how to process the messages sent by two different state-level bodies, the State Board of Education and the QEC, which now have somewhat overlapping responsibilities. While the QEC meets a state need, its creation also runs the risk of fragmenting the policy system so that schools will find it more difficult to discern state goals and intentions. The State Board of Education and the QEC will need to send consistent messages regarding state goals and priorities.

## What Commissions Can (and Cannot) Accomplish

The three commissions just discussed pursued different paths toward similar goals. The Prichard Committee worked outside the traditional governance structure and sought to uproot that structure. It depended on broad-based democratic participation and public opinion to create pressure for fundamental change. It eventually developed enough institutional history to become a player in its own right within the state education policy formulation system. Throughout the past decade, the Committee has been free to pick its issues and to conduct studies and direct attention to the areas it feels need to be addressed. This lack of institutional affiliation allows the Committee the latitude necessary to continue to prod the system to remain committed to large-scale, systemic change.

The Washington commission worked within state government but without the need to defend any particular agency or constituency. It served as a focal point to coordinate the efforts of a range of governmental entities. It also translated a policy concept—state standards and assessments—into governmental action. The Commission had ownership of a particular issue and pursued that issue in a single-minded fashion. The Commission operated under a deadline at which point it was "sunsetted." The result was that it produced policy that crosscut a number of agencies without allowing the effects on any individual agency to become the primary criterion upon which any particular idea or recommendation was considered.

The Quality Education Commission was designed to take on a new duty in cooperation with the existing state education board. Its purpose is to meet the new need legislators have for better information upon which to make budget decisions. The QEC serves as a bridge among three elements of government—the governor, legislature, and schools—which previously had not communicated very directly on education policy issues. It serves to articulate the values of each and to negotiate among these branches of government. It fulfills a need that came into existence as a result of a rapid increase in state control over education finance and policy.

Not all commissions end up changing education practice. Some can and do get overtaken by political forces. California's Academic Standards Commission, established by the legislature in 1995, was charged with the "central responsibility to develop academically rigorous content and performance standards to be used in public schools maintaining kindergarten and grades 1 through 12" (Bell, 1998). To meet this charge, the Commission held numerous hearings and considered varying, competing philosophies of education standards. When it did present its recommendations to the State Board of Education, controversy quickly engulfed the mathematics standards in particular. The State Board of Education commissioned an alternative set of mathematics standards that emphasized basic skills and traditional mathematics principles and practices, which it subsequently adopted (Lawson, 1998). In the end, educators resented the imposed standards, although they were voluntary in nature. The Commission had not been able to overcome the highly charged political environment that existed in California at the time.

## Governance Implications of Commissions

The widespread creation of commissions suggests that the current governance system is undergoing self-renewal and a transfer of power for policy making from the local to the state level. The function of nearly every commission has been to identify state-level problems and concomitant policy solutions. While the role of local school districts is not ignored and recommendations may seek to strengthen the local role, the decisions are being made on a state level and the problems are being identified as state problems. Commissions represent one more example of how key aspects of policy formulation are migrating from the local to the state level.

The commissions also illustrate the need for new mechanisms at the state level to govern and improve education. Commissions offer the advantage of drawing from a wide range of constituents, having a single charge, and often being outside of cumbersome bureaucracies. The challenge for commissions is how to function without losing mission focus and becoming ensnared in the larger bureaucracies and partisan political system that surround them. Those that achieve their goals will do so by dealing with a rather well-defined set of issues, establishing a clear relationship with the rest of the governance system, and maintaining the level of independence needed to pursue their defined mission. In this fashion they can come to fulfill new governance functions effectively.

The danger of a system with more than a few such semi-independent mechanisms is increased fragmentation. Commissions that pursue their goals too independently will end up sending a set of messages that is largely unaligned with the rest of state education policy. This is controllable to some degree when the members of commissions represent a range of constituents and work in the open, solicit broad input, seek to understand the complexity of problems before offering solutions, and consciously coordinate their activities with all other branches of the policy system.

Commissions potentially offer forums where local and state viewpoints can be exchanged and arbitrated more thoroughly than through existing structures like state education boards. They also create opportunities for noneducators to engage in education policy formulation in a constructive fashion. The business community, in particular, will likely continue to find commissions to be a valuable route for influencing education policy at the state level. Governors will likely see commissions as a structure that taps the expertise and ideas of a wide range of constituents to address policy problems not well managed within the current educational governance structure and to suggest ways governance should evolve to meet new duties and responsibilities. Politicians will likely find commissions an appealing way to take the heat off elected officials to make difficult and often unpopular recommendations for educational change and improvement.

## WHAT'S NEXT FOR THE STATE LEVEL
## OF GOVERNANCE?

The state level of educational governance has been subject to more turbulence in the past decade than the local level. State institutions are struggling to comprehend and master their new responsibilities and relationships within a turbulent educational governance system. This has resulted in more overt conflict about education policy issues among different state entities than has been the historical norm. Over time the conflict will subside as new power relationships are established and new responsibilities clarified. The current period is one of great opportunity to define what the state level should be doing and whether the existing governmental structures can accomplish the desired goals. This is the time to redefine the role of entities such as state boards of education and state education departments as well as to consider creating new forums such as commissions that address one area only. This is also the time for governors and state legislatures to accept the fact that they are regularly making important decisions that affect local schools and school districts profoundly, and that to make such decisions well requires careful study, adequate staff, and clarity regarding the limits of state power and local responsibility.

The next two chapters suggest the changes that need to occur at the local level in response to the new realities of the state role. These changes will be possible only if states clarify and institutionalize governance at the state level and create a new structure that is in line with state expectations and goals for the public education system.

# Chapter 8

# CHANGES IN ROLES
# AT THE DISTRICT LEVEL

If the state is the winner in terms of power redistribution, then the local school district is the loser. It is important to distinguish between the district, which comprises the board of education, the superintendent, and central administration, and the individual school building. Schools are not "losers" in this power equation in the same way boards and superintendents are. Schools are "where the action is," from the state's perspective. Local school districts, on the other hand, are to some degree a structure in search of a purpose, the rhetoric in support of local control notwithstanding. What must boards and central administrations do to remain important elements of school governance and vehicles for achieving state goals and improving schools?

## LOCAL BOARDS OF EDUCATION

The most fundamental and as yet unanswered question raised by the movement of power and control of education policy from the local to the state level is: What role will local boards of education play in an educational system directed increasingly from the state and federal levels? What is the role of a local board in an educational governance system influenced by market-based conceptions? What roles can local boards fulfill better than any other level of governance? How can local boards harmonize their roles with state authority, rather than compete with or contradict it?

One national report recommends that school boards focus on goal setting, hiring the superintendent, advocating for the interests of children, and ensuring that high and appropriate standards are in place and being achieved. Boards should then avoid micromanagement of districts, instead building a collaborative team relationship with the superintendent, whom the board then evaluates periodically (Goodman & Zimmerman, 2000; Reid, 2000).

If the role of boards can be honed and refocused, they can play a critical role as the linchpin between schools and the state. Following are examples of the types of responsibilities upon which boards might want to focus.

## Taking Responsibility for Local Accountability and School Improvement

Nowhere is the change in the role of local boards likely to be more profound than in the area of school accountability. Boards have had a very spotty record in holding local schools accountable for meeting standards of student achievement, often choosing to ignore for years tremendous performance differences among schools within a district. While some urban boards recently have moved more aggressively to cope with failing schools, few boards have embraced broad notions of accountability for all aspects of the local district without external prodding. Historically, boards conceived of accountability in terms of competent fiscal management and orderly schools. Formal accountability for student learning has been markedly ambiguous or unclear. Schools that attracted too much negative attention, for whatever reason, garnered some form of *ad hoc* intervention, often the removal of the principal. Root causes of poor student performance or organizational dysfunction rarely were confronted.

Under an expanded accountability role, the board puts into place plans and procedures to review the effectiveness of each school yearly. The board reviews school progress, calls for diagnostic data to determine the causes of poorly performing schools, approves improvement plans where necessary, reorganizes ineffective schools, and ensures that each school is operating at peak effectiveness.

This conception of the board's more activist role in school accountability derives from the fact that numerous states are implementing school accountability systems in which intervention by state education departments is the dominant means for addressing failing schools. This approach circumvents the local board and assumes it has failed to improve local schools and is not capable of doing so.

While such an assumption may be warranted in some cases, this bypass approach to accountability robs boards of one of their key responsibilities—ensuring that their community has quality schools. If the local control model of educational governance is to be retained and have any real meaning, boards will have to shoulder ultimate responsibility for school accountability. Rather than bypassing local boards, state education departments could instead provide more and better data to boards about how their schools are functioning and, where appropriate, the causes of local school failure. Boards can utilize such information as a basis for diagnosing the causes of school failure and for pursuing remedies tailored to the local context.

In the past, boards relied on locally administered standardized tests as their only measure of school functioning. Many state assessments offer data on student performance, information that local districts can supplement or build upon. A wider range of tools and technologies exists to gather information on student performance and school functioning. Local boards can develop data systems that yield supplemental information on school functioning. The data can reflect the values and priorities that the local district wishes to emphasize, in addition to any state requirements.

State education departments can be organized to provide progressively greater amounts of technical assistance and guidance to the local boards as they work to improve local schools. Assistance would need to include means to review schools and set up internal systems of accountability. The administration would receive assistance in how to establish effective management information systems. Such systems would yield much more detailed and timely data on student learning as well as on the status of the organization as a whole. The board would share information with the community, which would be the final judge of the board.

Boards could reasonably be expected to devote larger blocks of time to reviewing school performance and to spend proportionately less time on management and maintenance issues. This will be a challenge to boards inclined toward micromanagement and administrivia. Learning how to discuss, gauge, and ultimately judge school performance will not be easy. Boards have an opportunity to help ensure that school accountability remains at a level that is accessible to the average citizen. Boards can serve to reflect citizen values and understandings of what constitutes a good school. Information on school performance can be reported locally in ways that are comprehensible to constituents.

States still must take a leadership role in school accountability when a local board proves unwilling or unable to improve schools and local voters fail to make changes in the board. With the movement of funding to the state level, local boards increasingly are spending state money. The state has a legitimate right to intervene to ensure that state taxpayers' monies are being spent wisely and that students in the district are being educated properly. At the point where local boards are no longer doing their jobs effectively, state power legitimately supersedes local authority.

States have begun to intervene in local districts over the past 15 years, although they have had markedly mixed results in doing so. Their reasons for intervening are complex. A recent example in Prince George's County, Maryland, illustrates the complexity and challenge. When the local board attempted to fire the superintendent, the governor and key state legislators blocked the firing and moved to reconfigure the local elected board to include members appointed by the governor. A "crisis-management board," appointed by the governor, state superintendent, and county administrator, assumed major responsibility for managing the district in the interim (Keller, 2002). The precise motivations are subject to interpretation. However, what is not in dispute is that state authority is superior to local, and that the state in this case was not afraid to intervene forcefully when it perceived its interests were not being well served by a local board, to the point of reconstituting the board's membership.

No mechanisms exist currently that would help a state to know when a local board is not capable of holding its schools accountable for improvement. School test scores, not local school board performance, trigger current state interventions. A new governance system that valued and sought to preserve local boards of education would need to develop the means to assess the functioning and functionality of local boards and to resort to state intervention as a final option only after conclusive evidence that the local board was unlikely to exercise its authority effectively to improve its schools.

### Changing from Standardizing Conditions to Overseeing Improvement and Adaptations

Local school boards tend to standardize conditions among schools rather than to nurture and encourage schools to adapt to the needs of their students. Even in districts that practice site-based management, many more policies and procedures are common than are site-specific. This tendency to standardize exists for good reason. Parents or educators often demand to have the same programs that other schools have. Transportation, food services, even textbook purchases all function better in standardized environments. Labor contracts specify common practices for many education policies. These forces in combination tend to create schools that are more similar than different and that tend to remain so (Tyack & Tobin, 1994).

Given the argument that local districts are seedbeds of innovation and of local solutions to local problems, this standardization is perhaps somewhat troubling. Local boards will need to examine their role as standardizers within their own districts, particularly the degree to which standardizing limits schools' ability to adapt to the demands of state standards and assessments. Increasingly, schools will be compared with other schools within the state, not within the district. As a result, each school may need its own unique strategy to improve. If district practices prevent necessary adaptations, only some schools will improve, namely, those whose culture, student population, and practices benefit most from the particular conditions imposed by the local board. All other schools will suffer.

The board's role in helping schools adapt is more complex. Local boards need to be able to distribute funds differentially among schools based on what is necessary for each school to meet state standards. Allocation schemes that are not based on "equalization" are extremely difficult to accomplish politically, but critical nevertheless. For example, when schools are budgeted based on FTEs (full-time equivalencies) rather than actual costs of personnel, experienced faculty tend to accumulate in schools serving more advantaged students, while less experienced teachers end up concentrated in schools serving the poor. If schools had to pay the actual salary costs of their teachers and had a fixed sum allocated for that purpose, veterans would be less likely to congregate in a few schools, at least not without increasing pupil–teacher ratios in those schools. The Seattle public schools utilize a model of this nature based on three principles: (1) resources follow the student; (2) resources are in dollars and not based on full-time-equivalent staff; and (3) resource allocation varies by the characteristics of students (Seattle Public Schools, 1997).

Boards also can support school improvement by examining a variety of operational dimensions of schools, beginning with the effectiveness of school leadership. Every school must have qualified, quality leadership among its administrators and teachers as the absolute prerequisite for improvement. Boards can hold schools accountable for high-quality improvement plans that contain school goals appropriate to the student population and at a high level of challenge. Through the budget adoption process, the local board can provide funds for innovation and adaptation to those schools proposing new and potentially effective programs. Boards must take care not to adopt contract provisions that excessively limit the ability of schools to adapt to changing student populations, to improve student performance, and to respond to state policy expectations.

## Approving Curriculum That Reflects Both State and Local Goals

Local boards have had relatively wide latitude on curriculum choices in most states. With the imposition of standards, assessments, and accountability systems, a local curriculum must at least acknowledge state standards and assessments. In states with strong accountability systems, the curriculum will be more directly influenced over time by the demands of the standards and assessments.

Does the local school board still have an important role relative to curriculum in such a system? Standards and assessments do offer the advantage of making explicit what is to be studied and when it is to be studied. This articulation of "scope and sequence" of the curriculum has been difficult to attain in many places. This could present an opportunity to boards to move beyond textbooks as the sole or primary source of the curriculum. Districts that have relied on an array of loosely connected textbooks as the foundation of their curriculum now have a framework that provides a progression of learning that is more consistent and apparent from grade to grade. Local teachers can create curriculum frameworks and learning material specifically adapted to local needs and values. Curriculum development can become a part of the district culture and structure. The central office can be organized to support local adaptation while maintaining high expectations for all students.

Districts with well-conceived curricula would be able to provide teachers with tools that would simultaneously help students meet standards and prepare them for assessments. Addressing this need to balance between the standardizing force of the state and the local capacity for adaptation and creativity is a role local boards could become adept at filling.

## The Unique Challenges of Governing Urban Districts

Urban school district governance has begun an evolution that can be expected to continue for some time. The most recent trend has been to bring urban boards more under the control of mayors and legislatures (Hill, 2001; Kirst & Bulkley, 2000; Ziebarth, 1999). This tends to occur where cities provide direct fiscal support to the schools, and states provide additional funds to cities. Such a shift in power and control also can be viewed as an acknowledgment that cities need healthy school systems if they are to revitalize themselves and improve their livability, and that states need healthy inner cities for their metropolitan regions to prosper.

Perhaps the most striking recent example of this trend for governors and mayors to revamp urban school governance is the Philadelphia school system. The "school reform commission" that was appointed in 2002 to govern the district is charged specifically with seeing that student learning improves. Three of the commission's members are appointed by the governor, two by the mayor. The commission is committed to experimenting with the use of contractors to consult with the district and to operate troubled schools (Gewertz, 2002).

The politics of urban districts remain dense and complex. Urban school boards often are reduced to being just one more element in the political calculus of the city. Their credibility is frequently diluted by in-fighting, factionalism, or personality conflicts that play out in the press. The challenge for these boards is to exert the types of leadership for improvement expected of all local school boards under this new state–local partnership. Taming the bureaucracy will be job number one for any urban board intent on reshaping education in a large urban district. Similarly, negotiating among competing interest groups will be a significant challenge in urban educational governance settings. Boards that have the backing of mayors and city councils may be more capable of coping with the profound challenges they and their schools face.

In those cases where schools cannot adapt and improve, boards have begun to turn to outside contractors, a trend that is evolving in fits and starts. Hartford, Connecticut, and Baltimore, Maryland, both abandoned contractors after a series of protracted problems, although scores had improved in three Baltimore schools being run under contract. The Inkster, Michigan, school district refused to pay the Edison Corporation in a dispute over enrollment figures and financial records (Sack, 2002). Boards are still learning how to organize competitive bidding to run schools, to oversee contractors, to mediate between contractors and current employee groups, and to hold contractors accountable for achieving specified goals. As challenging as it is turning out to be, overseeing a contracting process may turn out to be more manageable for urban boards than functioning as micromanagers of an unresponsive bureaucracy.

Urban districts are the only part of the educational system where the creation of new, smaller districts seems to be a distinct possibility. Consolidation was the touchstone of American educational governance throughout the twentieth century. As school districts enter the twenty-first century, consolidation of small rural districts continues.

Simultaneously, various forms of decentralization have been attempted in urban districts. The Los Angeles Unified School District, for example, has implemented a subdistrict model by transferring some elements of governance to regional superintendents without necessarily creating separate education boards for each subdistrict, a scheme that was pioneered by the New York City schools in the late 1960s and continues in place. This strategy has proven problematic when its effect is to upset the fragile racial balance among schools within the subdistricts, which subsequently end up being composed predominantly of one or two racial groups.

The challenge will be to find ways to govern urban schools that acknowledge the diverse values and goals present in American cities, while ensuring that urban schools produce results comparable to those in surrounding suburbs, a major challenge for urban boards of the future and one at which they cannot hope to succeed without a partnership with other parts of city government as well as the state.

## The Viability of Local Boards as Democratic Institutions

Local boards are one of the most grass-roots levels of democratic participation in the American political system. Without revitalizing the role of the local board and affirming its importance, it may begin to fade into obscurity, limited to advisory and ceremonial functions. If the local board is to remain a viable and vibrant component of the educational governance system, its role as a bridging agent between the state and local schools will have to be reinvigorated and strengthened.

The key distinguishing feature of local boards as democratic institutions is citizen involvement. For local boards to play a key role in a reconceptualized governance system, they will to need be forums where state mandates can be adapted in ways that support local goals and that weave community values into state policies. Boards can then develop long-term visions for districts that combine state and local priorities. This type of citizen involvement promotes ownership of schools locally, which has been one of the defining characteristics of American education. This sense of ownership is important for a variety of reasons, including some rather utilitarian considerations, such as willingness to support local funding of new school construction and capital improvements paid for with bonds that must be approved by the general public within the district.

The ultimate question that any serious discussion of American educational governance must confront is the continued viability of local boards of education. They have seen their initial purpose of organizing, funding, and administering a local education program surpassed and in many places overridden by the state.

Local boards existed in part because school districts represented distinct geographical areas, communities, or regions. Boards now exist to some extent because they have always existed. It requires significant energy to organize, elect, and maintain them within each district. They direct administrator efforts toward preparing for board meetings and responding to board requests. They are easily sidetracked into the micromanagement of district affairs and onto noneducational issues with which many board members are more familiar and comfortable. They are subject to appropriation by special interest groups adept at pressure politics or the electoral process, or even to the whims of a particularly truculent individual with a single issue to pursue.

At the least, local boards continue to address a range of administrative responsibilities that states are loath to assume. Among these are due process hearings for employee dismissals and student suspensions, school closure decisions, local school construction, student transportation systems, and school calendars. Whether these types of tasks will become the primary focus of boards and whether anyone will want to serve on a board focused solely on these sorts of responsibilities remains to be seen. Will local boards simply become agents of the state, charged with implementing and overseeing state policies that govern most important aspects of schooling, or will they retain a vital role in school accountability and improvement and in local adaptation of education policy?

For all of their faults and limitations, they represent the best and most cherished traditions in American democracy. They are the unit of government closest to the community. They have the potential to reshape schooling or stubbornly defend the status quo. Their position in a newly redefined and evolving educational governance system is yet to be fully defined. One thing seems relatively certain. The role of boards of education will change more rapidly in the next 20 years than it has in the past 100.

## Local Boards as "Boards of Directors"

One possible way to reinvigorate boards and bring them more into line with their new role in a reconceptualized governance system is to move away from management and micromanagement activities and into policy, strategic planning, and accountability-related tasks. Accordingly, boards would no longer meet with such frequency. They would be restricted to perhaps four meetings per year. Each meeting would have a different focus: one to set annual district goals in light of state goals, another to adopt a budget, a third to review the long-range strategic plan for the district in relation to state and national educational objectives, and a fourth to determine whether annual goals have been met and to decide what to do if they have not been. Meetings would take place on a Friday evening and all day Saturday to provide adequate time for discussion and to allow broad-based citizen attendance and participation.

This type of board would focus on reviewing the performance of educational administrators charged with managing the enterprise of schooling. Board members would have access to much more detailed data on school operations and student learning than they have currently. Subcommittees consisting of board representatives and additional community members would be constituted to handle tasks such as reviewing the annual budget in anticipation of its adoption. Boards would no longer sit in quasi-judicial capacity to hear appeals or personnel dismissal proceedings, since such roles are clearly conflicts of interest that combine executive and judicial functions simultaneously. Board members would maintain a cautious distance between themselves and the district administration in order to judge more impartially the effectiveness of the administration and to disentangle board members from internal district politics.

Serving as a member of a board of education constituted with these responsibilities might be more appealing to a wider range of candidates. The reduced time commitments and clearer focus on fewer things also might be attractive to individuals who want to contribute to their communities by focusing on big ideas, such as long-term goals for the district. Making running for a board position more appealing could help limit the number of special-interest, one-issue, and "stealth" candidates by encouraging those with broader visions to take on the task. Boards that meet less frequently and interact less intensively with the superintendent and central administrative staff have a better chance to maintain their allegiance to the community and are less likely to become co-opted into reflecting the perspective of the district's professional administration. Detachment is useful if boards are to be mechanisms to connect between states, local communities, and local schools. Understanding and accepting the board's roles as a connector between states and schools would enable members to spend less time being distressed about the loss of local control and more time dedicated to school improvement and to communicating to the state the real needs and concerns of local school boards.

## SUPERINTENDENTS AND CENTRAL OFFICES

From the creation of the superintendency to the present, superintendents have had a relatively clear sense of their duties and obligations. They were hired by and beholden to local boards of education and felt little or no allegiance to state education departments. Their longevity was directly related to their relationship with their boards. To this day, one of the perennially popular topics at superintendents' professional meetings is what is euphemistically referred to as "care and feeding" of board members.

### Balancing the Demands of Multiple Masters

Superintendents are now beginning to be asked to serve more than one master. As state and federal governments continue their incursion into domains previously the exclusive province of local school districts, superintendents must decide whose agenda will guide their actions and whose priorities they will follow. Some urban superintendents find their lives further complicated by mayors who have become active in superintendent appointment and removal. As more of their options are limited or dictated by regulations and laws promulgated beyond the local level, they find themselves at times frustrated and unclear about how to reconcile the sometimes conflicting demands of their local board with policies and priorities of state and federal governments.

One of the effects this conflicting tug-and-pull has is to fragment policy at the district level. Each policy—local, state, and federal—can end up being processed independently, even when it proves to be contradictory. For example, federal Title I policy that requires "pull-out" programs of a particular nature are often in conflict with the structure, philosophy, and practice

of reading instruction within a district or school. Superintendents find themselves facing conflicts that are functionally irresolvable. What results is a form
of policy free-for-all, where schools are left to their own devices to sort out
the impact of a range of policies on practice. Often this is done under the
guise of site-based management.

Corcoran, Fuhrman, and Belcher (2001) encountered a form of schizo-
phrenia and role confusion in central offices as those in central administration struggled to understand their role in implementing state reforms. Should
central office staff encourage schools to adopt best practices or allow them
to make their own decisions? Should schools be pointed in the right direction, at least, or left entirely alone? Should schools be given information about
specific programs and research or allowed to make discoveries on their own?
Using evidence and data as a basis for decision making proved to be a problematic transition in all districts studied.

When district staff did take a more activist or prescriptive role, the results were often disappointing. The culture of central offices and of school
districts more generally tends to favor politically expedient solutions, often
based on personal preference, over those generated from empirical evidence.
Although district staff members were more willing than site-based educators to seek and utilize research and data, they faced serious limitations in
their ability to do so. In this atmosphere, advocacy disguised as research could
be used to justify endorsement of a wide range of approaches and programs
consistent with the beliefs of staff. Externally developed programs that
brought with them funding and national reputations were favored over locally developed solutions, which in any case were evaluated more stringently
than the external programs. In other cases, no recommendations at all were
made to schools for fear of being too "prescriptive."

Schools tended to rely on teacher craft knowledge while paying lip service to research on a particular topic or program. While the central office
mandated specific practices in some instances, such as the creation of smaller
learning communities, the schools then implemented them in a fashion that
led to an unintended outcome consistent with craft knowledge. In the case
of small learning communities, this resulted in a new form of tracking that
limited access of certain groups of students to high-quality teachers and challenging curriculum. School staff had even more difficulty than central office
staff accessing research in a usable form, interpreting it in a way that applied to the school's situation, and sorting out conflicting claims and sources.

In the final analysis, decentralized decision making, in combination with
a central office that restrained its role in order to support school-site knowledge generation, ended up undermining rather than promoting the use and
application of knowledge. School staffs were influenced more by colleague
testimonials than by data. While teachers were clearly interested in program

effectiveness, they defined effectiveness in terms of the degree to which a program was consistent with their own educational philosophy and definitions of good practice and their current teaching methods and techniques (Corcoran et al., 2001).

Some superintendents and central offices avoid policy ambiguity by adopting the opposite extreme from site-based decision making; they constrain access to policy knowledge and then promulgate detailed implementation plans with which school-level educators are obligated to comply. The emphasis in these organizations is on compliance behaviors, specifications of what each member of the organization must do in the various situations in which the policy applies. This approach works reasonably well when policies are simple and unidimensional, and have clear outcomes. It is less effective when the goal of a policy is systems change or reinvention of education practices, as many state reforms seek to achieve.

How will superintendents apportion their loyalty in a system where the state sets accountability standards but local boards make employment decisions? The seemingly obvious answer is that superintendents will remain loyal to local boards but increasingly will be looking over their shoulders to monitor external policies that have the potential to cause embarrassment (or worse) if they are ignored. Compounding this trade-off is the fact that local boards change their composition, sometimes rapidly. Superintendents may find it more advantageous to rely on state policy to justify at least some actions and as a way to insulate against changes in board makeup. Superintendents who follow board direction only to be singled out for failing to meet state or federal standards will still suffer negative publicity and loss of credibility in the eyes of a public that seeks to assign responsibility to someone for failing schools. As state power grows, superintendents and central office staff can be expected to be much more cognizant of and responsive to the demands of these external policy generators. While they will not necessarily become direct agents of the state, neither will they continue to be exclusively responsible to local boards of education.

### New Skills for Superintendents, New Structures for Central Offices

A 2-year study of 22 school districts in eight states identified four key strategies employed by central offices that were successful in building the capacity of schools to respond successfully to state reforms and to improve continuously (Massell, 2000). Central offices focused schools on interpreting and using data to identify areas in need of improvement. Superintendents and area superintendents required schools to include state accountability data in school improvement plans and to be aware of the research that informed improvement in areas identified by the data as priorities. Nearly every district had some sort of professional development program aimed at building teacher knowledge and skills. Central offices utilized nontraditional forms of professional development, such as teacher and school networks, peer-mentoring programs, and professional development centers, to create norms of continuous learning within schools. Improvement and alignment of curriculum and instruction was viewed as a key responsibility for the central office. Alignment was achieved by a "patchwork of loose and tight central control," which often varied by subject matter. The central office was the hub from which alignment was organized and facilitated. These districts also targeted particular school buildings to receive extra resources and intervention by the central office. Low-performing schools received extra staff or were assisted by special teams created by the central office. In addition to targeted assistance, all districts had special programs for students who required help reaching state standards.

This sort of support role requires central office personnel to possess a range of skills that add value to the school improvement process. Central office positions increasingly require knowledge of effective educational models, curriculum development, organizational structures, facilitation, mediation, and state and federal policies, including policy goals and intentions. Some school-level administrators have some or all of this knowledge; many do not. Central office administrators will require much more specialized training and education to acquire the complement of skills needed to serve schools and school improvement. They also will be called upon to act as a bridge between schools and resource providers outside the district, including successful schools and programs or organizations and consultants who possess needed technical skill to revise a curriculum or increase student achievement.

The historical reliance on hierarchical relationships will need to be supplemented with an emphasis on collegial interactions to solve problems. This does not imply the abandonment of line authority, but acknowledges that forces external to the district are increasingly important to both the central office and schools. As state accountability systems become more sophisticated, and more information is available to the public at large via state report cards and a variety of websites, the pressure to demonstrate continuous improvement will increase for all. Even the very highest-achieving districts will find themselves subject to local pressure to equal or exceed their peers. In every situation, educational quality and achievement are more likely to increase when line authority is organized to support school-based improvement processes and activities.

It is naive to suggest that superintendents and central office staff are going to transform themselves into agents for state policy implementation eagerly and willingly. However, they will be called upon to do much more interpretation of state policy, helping district personnel to make meaning out of and adapt to the policy in the context of the district's culture and goals. Central offices that are organized to achieve this task and explicitly charged to do so will be more effective in mediating between governance levels on behalf of educators at the school level than those that view state policies with scorn or as unwanted intrusions into local control. State intervention is a reality. Reorganizing and re-skilling to cope with it may be the most functional strategy a central office can adopt in response. Murphy's (1994) study of school superintendent reactions to the Kentucky Education Reform Act suggests how difficult such a process will be, for both the state and superintendents.

## Actively Reshaping the System

Superintendents and central administrators can play an additional key function in a redesigned governance system. They can accumulate evidence of the effects state and federal policies have at the local level and be prepared to suggest improvements and alternatives. They can offer a vision for new directions in state and federal policy. They can utilize their expertise and direct experiences with schools to provide an "on the ground" assessment of policy effects as well as to generate alternatives that will work in the real world. Local central office personnel can be key fixtures in the two-way flow of information and ideas between state and schools. This type of upstream communication has few formal structures in most states since little reason has existed to communicate from the local level to the state.

State education policy over the past 2 decades has been generated from anecdote, idealism, and general data on system functioning. Few reforms have been based on the experiences of districts that have successfully improved student achievement. Large problems and grand ideas can be useful starting points for policy development, but local school districts can contribute to more systematic policy formulation if they learn how to provide feedback to state policy bodies.

To do this, local districts must systematically evaluate the effectiveness of their efforts and understand what is working, what isn't, and why. States and the federal government will need to develop more formalized channels for information to flow upward and be incorporated systematically into the policy development process, in part by making better use of program evaluation data and findings. Superintendents' councils or similar advisory groups do exist in some states, but an expanded and more formalized version of such assemblies can serve a new and more important function mediating between state and local levels. In other states, professional organizations seek to fulfill this role. These bodies often focus on traditional issues such as funding more than on providing systematic feedback designed to shape and evolve, not to blunt or block, state policy development.

If this type of partnership relationship with the state can be established and institutionalized, school boards, superintendents, and central office staff will have a clearer sense of their roles, and states will tend to develop policies that are more likely to be implemented successfully.

# Chapter 9

# CHANGES IN ROLES AT THE SCHOOL LEVEL

The primary purpose of state education reform policy is to bring about improvement in student learning. This cannot occur without affecting those who work in schools. Principals and teachers, from whom state policies have been distant forces, will be affected more directly in ways they cannot control or necessarily predict. The effects may well be contradictory. On one hand, state standards, assessments, and accountability systems are likely to reduce the discretion school-site personnel have had to operate autonomously. On the other hand, schools focused on state goals may be places where principals and teachers can develop higher levels of professionalism by using data and knowledge of best practices to make programmatic decisions, particularly if states follow through on promises to reduce rules and regulations.

Autonomy has been the hallmark of the teaching profession. American education has not been subject to school inspectors common in European and British-influenced educational systems. The ratio of teachers to principals makes close supervision of classrooms difficult. Similarly, the ratio of principals to central office administrators means that little direct oversight of school buildings takes place. Even in highly centralized school districts, individual schools and classrooms operate in relative isolation and privacy unless problems arise. The new governance and policy environment in which schools are treated as elements of a statewide system ensure that the scrutiny schools receive will increase. Accountability for performance is manifested through data-reporting systems that publicly disseminate information on student learning. Principals and teachers will find it necessary to change how they conceive of their jobs, how they work with their colleagues in the school, and how they think about their relationship with their school district and with their state education department.

## PRINCIPALS

The role of the principal has been evolving continuously over the past several decades. The principalship has been identified as one of the most important and influential positions in schools seeking to improve their education practices (Hallinger & Heck, 1998). Considerable research has been conducted on the behaviors and leadership strategies effective principals employ (Office of Educational Research and Improvement, 1999). Many of the same methods necessary to improve schools also will lead to success in an accountability-based system. What is new is that these skills are no longer optional or simply desirable for principals; they form the prerequisite or baseline for defining a competent school administrator. States that expect schools to improve in response to standards and assessments need to engage principals as agents of implementation and change. As such, principals must understand how to lead in a new educational governance environment that has not yet reconciled the new relationship between schools and the state.

Principals are accustomed to mediating a complex mix of sometimes conflicting forces that attempt to exert influence on them. The formal line of authority emanates from the school board and flows through the superintendent and central office supervisory staff to the school level. Principals must balance the mandates of line authority against pressures and demands that emanate from school staff and the local community. Federal and state policies generally have been filtered through the line authority structure. Now states and the federal government are exerting a stronger and more direct influence on schooling at the building level. Although the central office is not circumvented, schools nevertheless must be more responsive to externally generated policy.

In essence, principals, like boards and superintendents, are accountable to more than one master within the governance system. These masters may be sending conflicting messages and setting incompatible priorities. Teachers and even parents and students may not understand or agree with the messages and priorities. Learning how to mediate among these varying demands and policy mandates is an important skill for principals. To do so while bringing about sustained educational improvement will require a masterful application of many current skills, acquisition of new skills, and a shift in role perception.

## Principal as Policy Processor and Interpreter

Principals will be called upon to process and interpret policy to a much greater degree than they do currently. Taking a page from the private sector, principals as middle-level managers will be expected to understand organizational goals and to judge all decisions in terms of how each contributes to achieving those goals. It is reasonable to expect that over time school districts will learn to align their goals with state goals or at least develop processes that harmonize local goals with state goals. As this occurs, principals will face less goal ambiguity than they do currently. Their task will be less to decide among conflicting initiatives than to understand how state and local policies and goals can complement one another. To do so, principals will need to understand state and local policy environments better in order to judge the purposes of policies and their relative importance. Learning how to attend more closely to externally generated signals and demands will be a key skill as principal evaluation becomes tied more closely to school performance, as districts and now states have begun to do (Sack, 2000).

## Principal as Networker

One of the advantages principals potentially have over teachers is greater flexibility in their schedule. With this flexibility principals can leave the building and interact more with others outside the building. This ability has been observed among effective principals (Conley & Goldman, 1994b) and is increasingly important as schools are held accountable to achieve state goals and need to learn from one another. The interactions that occur as a result of networking yield access to resources, ideas for new programs, contacts with like-minded educators, and greater knowledge of how to respond to new policies and requirements (Wohlstetter & Smith, 2000).

States are indirectly promoting networking by comparing schools with one another. Accountability systems report results using groups of schools with similar characteristics, called "comparator bands." Schools that do well relative to those in their comparator band can appear successful, even if their absolute performance may not be outstanding. Interacting with other schools within a comparator band makes sense because the solutions used in one school may transfer well to another. When schools are judged against others spread throughout the state, it makes sense for principals to connect with administrators in these schools to an even greater degree than with neighboring schools in their own districts.

Another key reason for principals to develop extensive networks is to gain access to resources. Effective principals have been shown to be good at securing grants, technical assistance, community support, and other tangible contributions that provide more flexibility for the school to innovate, adapt, and improve (Conley & Goldman, 1994a). State and federal reforms expect improvement from schools even when increases in resources are not provided. In such an environment where resources are fixed and limited, schools capable of obtaining marginally more money or help than their peers have a greater potential to improve their performance.

### Principal as Site Innovator and Policy Adapter

The new mantra of state education policy wherein the state sets general goals and schools achieve those goals by exercising their local control to adapt has not automatically made schools more adaptable, and in many communities local control tends to be just that—another layer of control. The sort of flexibility the state envisions for schools to achieve state goals has proven to be illusory. This does not lessen the pressure on principals to show that they have adapted their programs to reflect both state goals and local circumstances. The good news is that when schools can become adaptable and flexible, they can have a greater positive impact on student learning.

Managing the process of flexibly adapting state goals and policies to local realities and objectives is politically much more challenging than managing in a bureaucratically structured environment where most decisions are rule-driven. When decisions are routine and predictable, life is easier for administrators. However, when more aspects of the organization's agenda are negotiable, the potential for conflict increases. For example, schools that have true control over their budgets can choose how many credentialed teachers to hire in combination with noncredentialed experts, classroom assistants, tutors, and other personnel. Rule-bound settings preclude such options in favor of formula-driven staffing models. Managing a model that allows flexibility in how personnel are arrayed to support student learning offers the potential to match the personnel structure with the needs of students, but also risks conflict with the current system. Managing this tension is a skill principals will need in environments where they are granted greater flexibility to organize and manage instructional programs in ways that lead to achievement of state learning goals.

### Principal as Information Manager

As states institute accountability systems, principals and teachers will have access to more sophisticated data on student performance. The state, for its part, will be responsible for ensuring easy access by school staff to usable data. From these data schools will be able to develop profiles of the strengths and weaknesses of their student population. This information will provide a framework for modifying the education program to match learner needs. Many schools have some experience in this process already.

Principals will need to make sure an effective information management system exists within the school. They will be responsible to oversee the flow of information, and to ensure follow-through by teachers so that data lead to changes that enhance student learning. Knowledge of state data systems and of analysis tools to make the best use of data will be critical to fulfilling these roles. Principals will not necessarily need sophisticated knowledge of statistics or of the technical aspects of data systems, but will need to be able to interpret the most relevant data beyond a surface level.

### Principal as Team Member and the Paradox of Shared Responsibility

As principals are held more accountable for student performance, they are more dependent on teachers, who, after all, actually teach the children. Teacher buy-in becomes even more important as principals are increasingly judged on their teachers' successes and failures. In most cases, principals have no new tools to motivate teachers but nevertheless are expected to get better results. Some states have instituted teacher or school incentive and reward programs, but principals rarely control the distribution of these. Simply mandating teacher behaviors rarely results in improvements that last any length of time.

The challenge for principals is to create high-performance learning communities in which teachers are leaders as well as followers, where collegial interactions and norms work to reinforce the commitment to enhanced student learning, and where teachers truly believe they can make a difference in student learning. Researchers have identified places where this occurs and have documented many of the conditions under which it occurs (DuFour & Eaker, 1998; Little et al., 2001; Oxley, 1997; Rollow & Yanguas, 1996; Shields, 1996). In spite of the existence of effective and successful models, school improvement and implementation of statewide reform policies remains a phenomenon that occurs one school at a time. The principal is a key player in this drama.

## TEACHERS

Almost no one went into teaching with the primary goal of implementing state policies. Nevertheless, teachers now find themselves called upon to be the primary agents of state reform implementation, with the reforms having direct effects upon classroom-level decisions and prerogatives. Teacher reactions to these demands have been complex, as have been the changes in the role of teacher that the reforms trigger.

In general, two types of policies affect teaching the most: reforms that enhance the quality of teaching and those that focus teaching and learning on state assessments. States that invested in teacher quality in the 1980s and 1990s, such as North Carolina and Connecticut, saw some of the strongest increases in NAEP scores. Test scores showed little improvement in states that relied more on testing and accountability systems and less on improved teacher quality, such as Georgia and South Carolina. Although Georgia and North Carolina both increased teacher salaries during the 1980s and early 1990s, Georgia's teacher preparation and licensing standards did not increase as much as North Carolina's, nor did its investment in teacher development (Darling-Hammond, 2000).

That the role of teacher is changing is clear (Olson, 2002b). How extensively it will change remains to be seen. Standards-based reforms in particular run counter to the "loose coupling" (Weick, 1976) relationship that has existed among educational governance levels and has served to buffer the "technical core" of teaching from external intervention (Elmore, 1999). The current generation of teachers has shown little enthusiasm for greater state control (Blair & Archer, 2001; Conley & Goldman, 1998). Their reactions to specific reforms have been complex, ranging from acceptance to ambivalence to rejection. They function as "engaged mediators" (Cohen & Hill, 2001) between policy and practice.

States, for their part, have initiated assessment and accountability programs that often have been poorly conceived and implemented, resulting in protests by educators and concern by parents and others over the increasing prominence of the state in directing local education practice with what appears from the local perspective to be a clumsy and heavy hand (Ohanian, 2001; Thompson, 2001). Teachers voice support for standards in principle, but object to high-stakes tests in practice (Public Agenda, 2001a, 2001b).

Teachers have great difficulty perceiving how they can ever achieve the goals states profess for standards-based systems of education, assessment, and accountability. They express concern that a generation of students will be lost to the new standards (Siskin, 2001). Schools are just beginning to respond to offers of greater flexibility or reductions in regulations adequate to spark redesign (Stricherz, 2001b). States, for their part, often have failed to make reforms clear enough or to provide adequate technical assistance or time for teachers to master new requirements successfully.

The fundamental issue is that policy makers, district administrators, and teachers can and often do have differing understandings of and perspectives on state education reforms (Spillane, 1998, 2000a; Spillane & Callahan, 2000). They process information and make meaning in ways that lead to very differing conclusions about the problems facing schools, the necessary solutions, and the apportionment of responsibility for what needs to be done for state reforms to be implemented successfully (Conley & Goldman, 2000).

At a basic level, policy makers and educators may even lack agreement on what the purposes of an educational system are. Is education to achieve the goals of business and society, or is it to meet the needs of individual students? Should education produce citizens capable of participating successfully in the economic and social systems, or should it seek to enable each individual to develop to the fullest in a personal fashion, perhaps in ways that are not readily apparent or measurable? States and the federal government have focused their definitions on specific goals, while teachers may still be addressing a much wider array of purposes.

In the final analysis, teacher objections to a tightly focused educational system may well limit the degree to which states and the federal government can reshape schooling, in part because teachers are organized politically to influence policy and because they continue to be credible sources of information for parents and others whose views on these issues may still be forming. Their objections also may help states and the federal government to avoid or eliminate potentially fatal flaws in reform programs.

However, even if current policies are modified substantially, it seems highly unlikely that teaching will ever again be as independent from state guidance as it has been throughout its history. Although teachers already feel constrained to some degree by district policies, textbooks, adopted curriculum requirements, and sometimes the culture of their school, they must now add a new force—the state—into the mix. The entry of a new player competing to direct teacher behaviors raises a series of questions. Will state expectations mesh with other demands on teachers? Will state policies pull teachers in entirely new directions or can they be shaped to complement teacher autonomy and support teacher creativity in the classroom? What changes can teachers expect as a result of sustained state and federal focus on a performance-based educational system? To cope with the issues suggested by these questions will require new teacher skills and behaviors, the most important of which are discussed here.

### Dealing with State Accountability Policies

State and, increasingly, federal data systems allow for comparisons between schools and school districts. These comparisons make many educators uncomfortable. Some argue that the measures being used are not reflective of the complexity of teaching and learning or of a school's or district's overall education program and goals. Some contend that economic or language differences between students are the real explanatory factor, and no comparison can fully take these differences into account.

Those constructing accountability systems are aware of these concerns, but these systems have been designed in line more with the needs of policy makers than with those of teachers. The ability and need to ascertain educational results and subsequently to compare schools are at the heart of much state education policy. Information, once discovered and organized, rarely goes away. In most cases, additional information is added, but few data systems, once constructed, are ever completely abandoned. This is particularly true when technology facilitates easy access to and manipulation of data.

These systems attract the attention of teachers and administrators, who then respond to the demands of such systems (Fuhrman & Elmore, 2001). External demands for accountability trigger requirements for internal accountability within schools and for fundamental changes in instruction, changes many teachers are reluctant to make. Rather than simply emphasizing what they do well currently, teachers will be expected to improve in relation to state goals. Teachers who view their school as being more accountable than they are individually will be challenged to conceive of accountability as both an individual and a collective phenomenon (Fuhrman & Elmore, 2001).

## Learning to Process Data and Adapt Practices Based on Data Profiles

How might educators see their current practices and perspectives altered to accommodate these new realities? Teachers can expect to have access to more data about educational conditions, practices, and results within their school and classroom. More important, they can anticipate that they will be expected to act upon these data in ways that lead to improved student learning.

Systems that track individual student learning over time have been in place in a number of states for close to a decade. Tennessee's is the best known, but Texas, New York, California, and other states have all been developing and implementing systems to track student performance (Miller-Whitehead, 1997; Sanders & Horn, 1998). When student achievement results are linked with the resources provided for student learning and tracked at the student level, the press to create new systems of accountability will become enormous (Picus, 2000).

Paradoxically, what these systems seem to be finding is that teachers have a much greater effect on student learning than previously assumed. They have the ability to bring about gains in student learning regardless of income, race, or other background factors (Orfield & DeBray, 1999).

In some schools, reporting scores publicly leads, predictably, to recrimination and finger pointing, particularly when data are tied to significant consequences or rewards. However, data just as easily can serve to redefine discussions of school improvement and to offer a perspective that can help all staff analyze problems objectively and pursue data-based solutions. As the sophistication of state and local data systems continues to increase, the information can be used to identify more targeted school improvement goals. This combination of data and tightly focused goals tends to concentrate and direct education practices within a school and within individual classrooms. A subtle or not-so-subtle accountability for student learning comes to pervade the school. Individual teacher discretion is bounded but not eliminated by the goals of the accountability system.

In the best case, this shared focus fosters a new sense of collective engagement and common purpose on the part of faculty members, who come to see themselves as working together to achieve common, mutually supportive goals. In the worst case, this new accountability and measurement capability leads to demoralized teachers who feel compelled to abandon previously effective or enjoyable activities in favor of prescribed methods directed at raising test scores. Isolation then remains even in the face of supposed common goals as each teacher works independently to improve student performance on state tests.

These seemingly paradoxical outcomes resulting from the same stimulus, namely, data on student performance, are a function of the policy environment, school leadership, and school culture. States that support school improvement as the primary goal of their data systems and that combine data with access to technical resources can create a climate within which schools can learn to utilize data to achieve collective goals. However, schools still must have leadership that does not abandon proven education practices in favor of narrowly conceived programs of test preparation. Furthermore, the culture of the school must allow communication and collaboration that support pursuit of common goals and attendant education practices. This complex set of prerequisites tends to limit the number of schools that have been able to employ data successfully for student improvement.

## Getting Each Student to Standard

Teachers face an additional challenge when confronted with data on student achievement and with a set of standards each student must meet: How can curriculum and instruction be organized to enable each student to meet the standard when students range from far below to far above the standard? Few teachers are able to develop curriculum individually or to customize instruction. In the emerging system of standards, data, goals, and accountability, teachers are challenged to adapt curriculum and instruction. To do so requires much greater collaboration among teachers within schools, among schools, and between schools and the state.

States have been reluctant to create curriculum geared to standards, favoring curriculum "frameworks" instead. Cohen and Hill (2001) describe how California created a mathematics curriculum framework in the mid-1980s, which led not to a state curriculum but to numerous vendors providing materials to schools and teachers without state quality control measures to ascertain the effectiveness of these "replacement units." Teachers working in standards-based systems need access to quality curriculum aligned with standards.

One alternative is the model developed in Australia that combines centralized guidance with local initiative. A broadly outlined federal curriculum frames high statewide standards that are measured by meaningful assessments. Teachers retain flexibility in instructional methodology and choice of curriculum, but individual states organize instruction into a series of courses, for which high-quality curriculum materials are provided (Fuhrman & Johnson, 1994; Watt, 1997). Teachers remain free to select the precise materials they use and to develop their own courses, but they have the state frameworks and curriculum available as common reference points.

Instruction has to be adapted to provide learners access to different learning methods and styles as they progress through common material. Some students need the support of social learning, while others function best working in relative isolation but in sync with their cohort. Some require individual tutoring, particularly to master key concepts or techniques. Some lessons are taught with a more applied emphasis and more concrete examples. Technology facilitates simulations and applications to illustrate key principles.

The necessary prerequisite is a set of standards that identifies what is most important to know and that limits the range of topics and subject matter that all students are expected to master. In mathematics, for example, if multiplication and division of fractions or uses of percentage and ratio are to be mastered by all students, students will need more than one option for learning these vexing topics. Because the content to be mastered is more clearly defined, teachers can develop the repertoire needed for all students to master the topics. Pairing a finite set of curriculum topics with a range of teaching techniques is how teachers reach more students in the new system envisioned by states, one in which requisite content knowledge and cognitive skills are clearly specified and delineated.

### Grading Practices vs. State Standards

Teachers grade on the criteria that they individually deem most appropriate. Particularly in secondary schools, teacher-generated grades have become an article of faith. These judgments of student performance are used to make many high-stakes decisions, such as college admission and scholarships, participation in extracurricular activities, enrollment in honors courses, and, of course, graduation. Evidence exists to suggest that grades represent a complex process of trade-offs by teachers among their personal philosophies, state goals, state tests, district grading practices, and parental pressure (Conley, 2000; McMillan, 2001). McMillan and Nash (2000) identified six themes influencing grades, including teacher beliefs and values, classroom realities, external factors, teacher decision-making rationale, assessment practices, and grading practices. The interplay of so many factors ensures that grading practices, standards, and results will be highly variable from teacher to teacher.

State testing and accountability policies compete with grades as legitimate measures of student performance. Terms like "proficient" or "highly proficient" are beginning to have meaning in many communities. This emerging competition between grades and state performance measures creates a problem for teachers. Which should they use, and, more important, how should they combine the two? Teachers rarely see natural connections between state assessments and grades. No mechanism exists to integrate the two into one comprehensive system combining teacher judgment and state standards in a harmonious fashion that provides students and parents deeper insight into a student's individual performance in comparison to classmates and to students statewide.

Elementary teachers have fewer difficulties incorporating state performance measures into their grading systems since at this level grades have few real consequences. Increasingly, elementary teachers are incorporating state measures of reading and mathematics as the basis of their grading systems. State writing assessments, in states where they are utilized, influence the criteria elementary teachers use to evaluate student writing, with state scoring rubrics often adopted wholesale on a school-wide basis, with unpredictable effects on writing instruction (Hillocks, 2002).

Secondary school teachers face a more significant challenge. How can they incorporate two modes of assessment in a way that motivates students to do well in class and on state tests? States have provided little or no guidance to teachers on how to create integrated grading systems. The result is that they have not connected the two. Students receive mixed messages about what is important and when it is important.

In some cases, teachers simply prepare students for state tests in ways that are separate from the rest of what they teach (Koretz, 1992; Wilson & Corbett, 1991). "Teaching to the test" (Smith, 2000) has become a slogan and a battle cry as teachers rebel against the idea that they must surrender their personal preferences in curriculum and evaluation in favor of state standards and assessments (Boser, 2000; Massachusetts Coalition for Authentic Reform in Education, 2002; Williams, 2000). These battle lines are firmly drawn and stubbornly defended (Ohanian, 2001). Stresses to teach to the test have become so great in some states that educators have been tempted to cheat to improve scores (Harrington-Lueker, 2000).

State policies will have to spell out the relationship between state test results and grading systems in order for state assessments to survive. North Carolina already requires that one-quarter of a student's grade, in subjects where state end-of-course examinations are given, be derived from the exam score (Olson, 2001b). If state assessment results are linked with college admission or placement, the connections between tests and grades will be further reinforced (Olson, 2001c). At the moment, teachers still have the opportunity to define the best ways to combine their judgments with data from state assessments in ways that motivate students and simultaneously maintain teacher discretion, but the window of opportunity will soon be closing as states begin to define the relationships between tests and grades.

### Teacher Evaluation

States have demonstrated a renewed interest in teacher evaluation policies. Most current policy was put in place or revised significantly in the 1980s. This first wave of policy often specified or standardized policies statewide for the first time (Conley, 1986). The current interest in teacher evaluation focuses on how to connect teacher evaluation and teacher professional development to enhance student learning (Danielson, 2001). The creation of state content standards has established common criteria against which to measure teacher knowledge and skill, something that was not possible to do when each district developed its curriculum expectations independently.

Teachers are markedly ambivalent and suspicious about attempts to link student learning to teacher evaluation, although studies are confirming the strength of the relationship between teacher effectiveness and student learning (Sanders & Horn, 1998). Potential resistance from teachers has not deterred states from delving into a range of performance-based evaluation schemes (Odden, 2000).

The desire to judge teacher performance is becoming a strong motivator for states to invest in and refine their student assessment and school accountability systems (Odden, 2000). Given the limitations of state data systems and the potential for resistance by educators, states have chosen at the moment to focus evaluation efforts on schools, not teachers. Credible data on student achievement against which to judge teaching performance are a key prerequisite to any eventual teacher performance evaluation system. This is the weak link that is limiting policy in this area. State testing systems, in many cases, need at least several more years before the credibility and stability of their data are accepted and adequate longitudinal results exist upon which teacher performance can be judged. Tennessee has led the way in creating data systems that link student test scores with individual teachers (Mathews, 2000).

The most promising option at the moment focuses evaluation on the degree to which teachers add new skills associated with effective teaching, rather than on judging teachers by student test scores. Known as "knowledge- and skills-based pay" (Odden, 2000), these strategies evaluate and compensate employees based on expertise instead of seniority. This type of system lays the foundation for a more professional model of teaching by clarifying the knowledge and skill base upon which teaching can be judged.

## Implications for Teacher Professionalism

It is easy to reach the impression that teacher professionalism would be the first victim of the state's increasing domination of educational goals and imposition of accountability measures. Such policies would seem to undercut teacher discretion and decision making and to reduce teachers to bureaucrats charged with following specific methods and procedures to achieve predictable results.

One of the findings from state testing programs is that teachers do make a tremendous difference in student learning (Darling-Hammond, 1997). This seemingly obvious conclusion was not necessarily universally accepted before large-scale studies confirmed it (Sanders & Horn, 1998). This finding forms the basis of any true system of teacher professionalism; if teachers don't affect student learning substantially, why allow them the discretion afforded professionals? Conversely, if their decisions do affect student learning, they must strive to make the best decisions possible, based on generally accepted professional practice, and should be held reasonably accountable for those decisions.

However, it is worth bearing in mind that teacher professionalism was and is a concept of somewhat vague and contradictory dimensions. Education is not necessarily a full-fledged profession. For example, the knowledge base needed to make informed decisions about what constitutes best practices is only now being developed (Darling-Hammond, Wise, & Klein, 1999; Weiss & Weiss, 1998). Generally accepted professional practice standards are not universal, which in turn makes it difficult to define outstanding teaching or to sanction substandard performance. Only recently have attempts been made to identify standards and construct tests around areas of teacher skill and responsibility that have been documented through empirical studies and theoretical research to promote improved student learning.

Major projects addressing this objective include the National Board for Professional Teaching Standards (NBPTS), founded in 1987 to certify teacher skill levels; the Interstate New Teacher Assessment and Support Consortium, which identified standards that defined the knowledge, skills, and performances essential for successful beginning teachers (Darling-Hammond, 1999; Darling-Hammond & Rustique-Forrester, 1997); and the Educational Testing Service's PRAXIS III: Classroom Performance Assessments, one of the first tests designed against research-based criteria of effective teaching (Danielson, 1996). The effects of these efforts are just now beginning to be seen among teachers who have taken the tests (Ladson-Billings & Darling-Hammond, 2000; Pool, Ellett, Schiavone, & Carey-Lewis, 2001).

Although evidence suggests that teachers who achieve the type of certification promoted by NBPTS are effective and that they are influencing practice within schools where they teach (Williams & Bearer, 2001), other studies still question the soundness of the constructs underlying NBPTS certification (Bond, Jaeger, Smith, & Hattie, 2001; Pool et al., 2001), suggesting additional study is required to solidify the validity of a professional knowledge-driven certification model.

The emphasis in much federal and state policy on effective practices, best practices, exemplary practices, continuous improvement, and data-driven systems conceivably could reinforce teacher professionalism (Olson & Viadero, 2002; U.S. Department of Education, 2001). However, professionalism by definition demands a zone of discretion in which the teacher draws upon professional knowledge to make decisions in ways that are consistent across the profession, yet uniquely adapted to and appropriate in the situation in which learning occurs and for the learners affected.

Federal policy requiring scientifically based methods may find itself in conflict with a nascent professional knowledge base not yet sufficiently robust to provide enough options for effective practice. Just as teachers are beginning to master a professional knowledge base, federal regulations may attempt to enshrine a limited number of techniques and programs that have been validated through research methods developed and used widely in the field of medical research. The effects on teacher professionalism of this notion of scientifically based effective practices are going to be felt in the ensuing years as federal legislation becomes fully implemented.

Professional teacher standards boards, in place in a number of states, including Oregon and Delaware (Sack, 2000), may be an arena where professionalism issues can be aired. These boards oversee licensing, deal with discipline, establish professional development requirements, and regulate preparation programs. While state education department personnel often manage these policies, professional standards boards, with their broader membership base, may be better equipped to define professional standards.

## Colleagueship in a Quasi-Competitive Environment

State direction of education policy has caused more interaction among teachers. It also has created the potential for competition—either among teachers or among schools. Accountability programs that offer either rewards or sanctions threaten well-established norms in most schools. If teachers are to achieve state goals, they generally have to rely on professional development programs to help them improve their skills and understand the reforms. These elements of accountability and professional development do not mix particularly well at the district or school level.

Professional development programs, the supposed key to systemic education reform, stumble badly when they encounter problems of localism. Corcoran, Fuhrman, and Belcher (2001) found in their study of the district role in reform implementation that staff trainers tended to be generalists unable to help teachers develop content knowledge. The desire to serve teacher and school needs led to the development of menus, which often contained sessions on the hot topics of the day. The need to use professional development sessions as a forum to communicate between central office and teachers fostered activities that were primarily informational in nature and aimed at creating awareness of current reform requirements and policies.

Professional development program decisions continued to be made at the district level, where little focus existed and where multiple initiatives competed for attention. "The net result of these preferences and beliefs was a potpourri of workshops and events rather than a coherent program of professional development" (Corcoran et al., 2001). While some evidence suggested that districts were moving the focus of staff development to content institutes to help teachers improve their knowledge base as a first step to ensuring that all students reach high standards, the primary delivery system for professional development had not changed.

As states increasingly implement accountability programs with rewards and sanctions for schools and individual teachers, long-held norms of teaching are being threatened. Researchers (Bird & Little, 1986; Little, 1982) have described the structure of workplace norms among schools and how these norms impede or contribute to collegiality. Little (1990) contends that schools have been collections of individuals operating as entrepreneurs with strong norms of privacy and noninterference and that the very organization of teaching sustains these norms and role perceptions. Collegiality is a fragile construct in this environment and must be carefully nurtured.

Rewards or sanctions for individual teachers threaten the egalitarian norms of teaching, which are based on collective, not individual, notions of performance. Public accountability systems create predictable tensions. Teachers who are rewarded individually have less incentive to help their peers, while peers are more likely to be resentful of those rewarded. Systems that award teachers collectively create more reason for teachers to be concerned about their less effective colleagues, although what they can do about this concern is still relatively unclear. Policy makers may not be concerned primarily about the tensions their policies create. These tensions can be minimized if reward or sanction systems are perceived as equitable and as being based on criteria teachers can actually achieve.

State policies in the area of accountability will lead to professional development that helps teachers develop requisite skills and work more collaboratively to improve student learning. An emphasis on common, shared goals may well lead to an increase in genuine and meaningful teacher collaboration. State accountability systems may then pull teachers in the opposite direction, creating in their minds a sense of a zero-sum game in which for someone to succeed, someone else must fail. In either event, the old norms of privacy and isolation will wither, which will be traumatic to teachers who have up until now been left alone in their classrooms for years on end.

## Role of Unions

Unions tend to be much maligned as an obstacle to education reform and improvement. Unions counter by pointing to evidence that student performance is better in states with higher levels of unionism (Nelson & Rosen, 1996) and that unions play a major role in advocating for and offering professional development and related activities designed to help teachers reach all students effectively (American Federation of Teachers, 1999b). At the same time, unions can be focused on the status quo and on work rules that inhibit organizational adaptability ("Hard bargaining," 2002). Unions have ventured tentatively into areas such as peer evaluation, but members have yet to perceive such activities to be as central to the role of unions as more traditional functions like collective bargaining (Murray, 2000).

Unions have shown a willingness to move beyond the trade union model based entirely on securing better compensation and work rules. The American Federation of Teachers (AFT) has adopted what some have described as the "new unionism" (Kerchner, Koppich, & Weeres, 1997, 1998a; Urban, 1991). For example, AFT affiliates in a number of cities have entered into agreements to participate in teacher evaluation and improvement programs (American Federation of Teachers, 1999a). A willingness to acknowledge and deal with poor-performing teachers would be an important step toward a more professional model of labor relations. The AFT also seeks involvement in teacher preparation and access to the profession as means to professionalize teaching.

Kerchner (Kerchner & Caufman, 1995; Kerchner, Koppich, & Weeres, 1997, 1998b) describes this new vision of unionism as one in which unions will be focused more on quality, individual schools, and career security. If unions do focus more on improved student learning as one of their goals, they will align more with state goals. Shedd and Bacharach (1991) present a model of how to replace existing formal structures that govern reporting relationships, decision making, and collective bargaining with more informal relationships to provide the necessary integration of management decision making at the district, school, and classroom levels. Governance structures of this nature could allow greater focus on reform objectives and more negotiation of work rules and conditions.

While conflict over compensation and benefits can be assumed to exist indefinitely, a shared sense of purpose by unions and state governors and legislatures regarding student achievement and school improvement could portend a new relationship on the policy level between these potential adversaries. The continuing press for privatization and competition also may serve to motivate unions to defend the status quo while simultaneously adapting in response to state goals of improved student achievement.

## Effects of State Policies on Unions

The net effect of the transfer of power from the local to the state level will be to consolidate the power of state unions. While unions will continue to seek a balance between the needs of their local constituents and the state-level organization, the state office will have greater influence and power as more policy is developed at the state level. This may lead unions to become much more involved in the negotiation of reform legislation or to drive union policy toward "lowest common denominator" issues, those where broad agreement among members exists. These generally favor the status quo over change.

The mismatch in power between individual local school districts and local teachers' unions will remain. Individual school boards will still have to contend with union locals that receive support from a state-level organization that can choose to target an individual district in hopes of winning agreement on an issue that will then set a pattern for bargaining in other districts. However, state government, with its greater resources, will be able to match up more equally against state unions. The likely outcome is that more policies will become consistent statewide, and unions will expend ever more resources on state elections and legislative lobbying. Over time, this new balance of power can be expected to lead to an increased capacity by state government to anticipate and respond to union priorities.

While unions will continue to fall into and out of political favor in state capitols, they will continue to be significant players, shaping major policy issues and the policy agenda. The only force on the horizon that can threaten the power of unions is the increasing emphasis on educational choices and options that do not require all teachers to be certified by the state. In some states, school choice policies and programs may be as much about challenging the power of teachers' unions as about offering parents more options.

## Teacher Role in Decision Making and School-Site Councils

What role should teachers play in decision making in this new landscape of policy and governance? Their voices have become much more central at the school level over the past 15 or more years as states have implemented site-based management and school-site councils. Connecting involvement in leadership to improvement in student learning has proved more elusive although by no means impossible (Education Commission of the States, 1996; Guskey & Peterson, 1995/1996; Johnson & Pajares, 1996; Johnson & Logan, 2000; Odden, 1995; Peterson, Marks, & Warren, 1996). Teachers are pivotal players in the success of state policy initiatives related to school-site decision making.

Local school councils will play an ever more important role in translating between the state and the school. These councils are composed of a mixture of parents, teachers, community members, school administrators, and students, and can serve as a different sort of lens for viewing state reform's potential effects on schools. The types of changes states are initiating require understanding of reform goals, not merely compliant implementation of procedures. School-site councils offer a vehicle and setting where state policies can be processed and understood, where meaning can be made and greater understanding reached about how the policies relate to the school's culture and goals. Fullan (1996) emphasizes the importance of meaning making and teacher networking as key elements for successful implementation of systemic reform, building upon the notion that all large-scale change is implemented locally (Fullan & Miles, 1992).

It is worth noting that school-site councils now are generally in place as a result of state law, marking these entities as new governance structures in a revised state–local system. The challenge faced by many schools is to define the proper and most effective use of these councils and their integration into existing governance components at the school and district level. Weiss (1993) found that councils often focused on the needs of adults more than those of children. Viewing school-site councils as tools to serve as a bridge between state goals and school programs is a new perspective for schools unaccustomed to linking with other governance levels. Site councils can be effective tools for governance integration if they function as a link between state policy and local adaptations and programs.

The current wave of policy initiatives at the state and federal levels is designed to achieve social goals or realize visions of schooling that may or may not be consistent with what teachers deem best for students and for themselves. Teacher professional judgment and self-interest can be in conflict with governmental goals and priorities. Teachers are expected to implement state policy at the same time that they are expected to take more ownership for achieving state goals locally and to be more involved in school-site decision making focused on improving education.

This unresolved tension and potential conflict of interest make teacher involvement in decision making a critical ingredient in reform implementation. The most effective means by which to maximize teachers' positive impact on school-site decision making are still being identified. The new relationship between schools and the state demands greater involvement at the local level for educators to process and respond to reforms generated externally.

The impetus for large-scale change is almost never generated locally. Schools and school districts have strong homeostatic tendencies, seeking to maintain equilibrium and to control the impact of external forces. State initiatives to bring about major change in schools serve a necessary purpose in this context. They serve to stimulate activity that would not occur otherwise. Teacher involvement in decision making creates a forum in which teachers can mediate between state intentions and school practices.

## THE RELUCTANT PARTNERS

Principals and teachers are among the most important of the reluctant partners the state must enlist for its reforms to be successful and for education to achieve excellence and equity goals simultaneously. State efforts to date have tended to run into strongly held beliefs about local autonomy that trigger resentment against state intrusion into the functioning of schools. People in schools don't like being told what to do. At the same time, when state policies result in changes that principals and teachers can see are benefiting students or when educators feel they have been consulted on policies, they are much more likely to take ownership of such policies.

Schools and individual classrooms within them will continue to be largely beyond the direct and immediate control of the state. Crafting policies that capitalize upon educator desires to be viewed as professionals and enlisting teachers and principals as partners in shaping and achieving state goals will be critical to the next generation of reforms. States continue to refine their policies, and new teachers are entering the profession who are not as accustomed to the broad autonomy their predecessors had throughout their careers. Nor are they automatically resentful of state guidance. The potential for a fruitful partnership exists. The obstacles to achieving it remain significant.

Chapter 10

# WHAT CHALLENGES AND POSSIBILITIES LIE AHEAD?

This book has presented the argument that states and the federal government are providing increasingly more leadership and direction in the generation of education policy along a range of dimensions and issues and that local control is being reduced and redefined. The key implication of these trends is that schools are being employed more directly to achieve state and federal education goals and policies. As a result, the role, purpose, and decision-making authority of local districts and boards of education must be reexamined and redefined.

The belief that local districts and individual schools will make significant improvements in performance if only left to their own devices has been largely overtaken by state policies that mandate and direct such expectations. While local districts continue to be important, even critical, players in educational improvement, they are not the drivers of improvement-related policies, nor do they or will they operate with broad discretion to determine which policies will be used to improve their schools. They may continue to regulate and dictate practices and organizational structures, but improvement is nowhere near as optional or locally defined as it once was. Local control now means the ability to make decisions consistent with broad state and federal goals for education and to align local programs in ways consistent with those goals. Most schools and districts are proceeding without a conscious acknowledgment that this sea change is occurring and will continue to occur.

## TAKING STOCK: WHERE ARE WE?
## WHERE ARE WE HEADING?

Many educators react to state initiatives with anger and frustration, waiting for things to return to "normal." While educators may be justified in criticizing some, many, or perhaps even all of the policy initiatives emanating from state capitals and the federal government, the idea that things will return to the way they were seems to reflect naiveté or wishful thinking in the current political context. What has been widely acknowledged at all levels of educational governance is the need for a true partnership between and among levels, with each level having clear responsibilities and duties. To achieve the partnership, new communication channels are needed to carry information both up and down the political structure to facilitate better comprehension of policy goals, appropriate modifications of policies, successful policy implementation, and, ultimately, school improvement.

## Is the "Loss" of Local Control a New Phenomenon?

It is important to note that the point is not simply that local control is being "lost." Fuhrman in 1974 presented a convincing argument that local control was already limited by state and federal activities in school finance and other areas, and had already been diminished to such an extent that increased state control over funding would do little to further erode local decision making.

For example, Fuhrman asserted, federal and state aid had already affected the right of local taxation because external funds were being taken into account when local budgets were developed. Districts were required to provide matching funds to receive some of this aid. In any event, local ability to raise revenue was constrained by the total amount of taxes residents had to pay for all local services.

Even in 1974, states legislated many areas of education policy in ways that restricted district options. Many had specific promotion or graduation requirements, courses that had to be taught at particular grade levels; teacher certification, tenure, and dismissal policies; limits on local taxation and bonded indebtedness; and even standard courses of study or textbook adoption lists (Fuhrman, 1974).

Local communities ceded control to professional administrators throughout the twentieth century. The power of teachers' unions has come to rival that of administrators, boards, and, in some cases, state legislatures. School boards remain collections of laypeople who are ever more dependent on administrative staff. The board's role in many districts has become *pro forma*, approving recommendations made by the educational bureaucracy. Local control exists in principle, but in practice boards tend to defer to administration, which in turn looks to other school districts or state-level professional organizations for guidance on what constitutes acceptable policy and program choices. In this fashion, districts tend to look more alike than different. Other sources of professional influence, including state education department staff, university professors, and even textbook publishers, contribute to a "striking uniformity" among districts throughout the nation despite local control. In this sense, the loss of local control is self-inflicted.

The actions of Congress and federal courts also limited significantly the broad discretion school boards previously had in determining local education practice. Civil rights legislation called greater attention to the effects of local board decisions on racial desegregation, stopping just short of unifying urban and suburban districts (Hudgins, 1975). The Supreme Court granted students broader rights of free speech and due process guarantees (Nolte, 1974; Zirkel, 1999). Special education legislation and subsequent litigation required schools to provide equal opportunities to categories of students previously ignored or neglected by schools, and created new fiscal obligations for schools (Verstegen, 1994a).

One significant effect of greater judicial involvement was that local districts deferred increasingly to lawyers when creating policy. This contributed to a tendency for boards to focus on what could not be done as much as or more than on what could be done. Local education practice tended to become standardized around real and imagined prohibitions and mandates. Local discretion was limited by both increased legal precedent and a growing psychological belief that it was dangerous to operate outside of known, familiar areas. Now districts are being called upon to develop new and creative ways to educate all students to high standards. This will require a reworking of the mind-set many districts have developed over the past 30 years wherein they perceive themselves as being hemmed in on all sides and reluctant to initiate anything significantly new or different.

### Top-Down, Bottom-Up: Will It Work?

The primary conceptual approach to marrying state activism with local authority has been the "top-down, bottom-up" partnership framework wherein the state sets general goals, establishes accountability, and provides adequate resources, while the local districts interpret policies and provide guidance and support for individual schools that are then free to innovate and adapt their programs and increase their flexibility so that they can achieve challenging state goals for all children. This is an appealing formula in many ways. It seems at once both to validate state action and to preserve existing governance relations, particularly local school districts as the primary organizational unit of the state educational system.

In practice, the formula may have serious limitations as a policy model or a vehicle for sustained educational improvement in relation to state goals. Goertz (2000) reviewed research on a series of studies conducted in states and districts operating under the top-down, bottom-up model to implement ambitious state-generated, standards-based education reforms that in many cases integrated and aligned with federal education policies. State-developed standards documents were fairly broad, going as far as to avoid advising local districts on the curriculum they might employ to achieve the state goals. However, teachers and local administrators often complained that the goals were too vague to guide local education practice, and that in any event local staff did not have the time or expertise necessary to translate the goals into education practices, programs, or structures.

Districts do continue to be important organizational units within the educational system, retaining considerable authority and control over schools. Larger districts translate external policies for schools, provide resources and support, and determine how the policies are to play out in schools. Support for curriculum development and staff training often emanates from the central level as well. Districts do respond to state mandates; however, the variability among district responses is generally greater than the similarities. District organization and culture vary from highly centralized to highly decentralized. Schools within districts vary from high need, low capacity to low need, high capacity. This variance challenges districts as they attempt to respond to state policy.

The "glue" that is supposed to bind the local districts and schools to state policy goals is a system of accountability keyed to incentives and sanctions for districts, schools, teachers, and students. This approach is working in one respect, but may be problematic in others. Assessment and accountability systems are getting the attention of teachers and administrators, who are changing their behaviors in response (Fuhrman & Elmore, 2001; Hoxby, 2001; Olson, 2002b). However, that attention is not necessarily being directed toward altering the basic routines of teaching and learning, redirecting resources to effective programs, or increasing the capacity of schools to adapt and improve on a continuing basis (Fuhrman & Elmore, 2001; Odden, 2001).

In the end, districts rarely sustain a policy direction long enough for an effective program or method to become thoroughly institutionalized. Reforms often are associated with a particular individual, usually the superintendent. When that individual leaves, generally as a result of being forced out after having offended too many political interests or groups as a result of reforms attempted, policy begins to drift, and eventually the reform focus is blunted and new initiatives emerge to compete. Schools return to many of their old routines, which they never entirely abandoned in the first place.

Kirp and Driver (1995) found that reform was a process that occurred in a single school, even a single classroom, at a time and that the broader policy conversation had a major impact at the site level. The state could set the context within which a local policy conversation took place. The state could stimulate interest in and reaction to its policies in ways that caused educators to examine but not necessarily change local practice.

Goertz (2001a) concluded that the tensions that exist among local, state, and federal governments have always existed and always will. These tensions are at the heart of the variation in policy and practices across states, districts, and schools. States and districts may all accept the goals of a standards-based educational system, but they interpret the rather broad goals of such a system in their own unique fashion and from their own perspectives. Merely setting standards is not enough. To achieve real improvement in student learning and achievement, Goertz (2001b) states, "policy makers must determine how much variability is acceptable and what the proper balance must be between compliance and flexibility."

These findings and others of a related nature suggest that local school cultures and structures continue to be strong and that the decentralization of decision making and authority to schools without a reshaping of these cultures is resulting in an accelerated version of responses to previous reforms, namely, a great deal of activity on the surface that does not result in deeper structural and functional changes. The difference is that this time the response is being justified under the banner of a top-down, bottom-up partnership.

## What Happens If or When Top-Down, Bottom-Up Fails?

This mismatch in expectations between states and schools seems certain to lead to tremendous disappointment, frustration, and eventually action at both the state and local levels. States believe they are supporting local decision making and governance, and that this support will lead to implementation and achievement of key state goals. Schools believe they have the right to select school goals and programs locally. The flexibility that states provide to achieve key state goals becomes an umbrella to justify a wide range of practices and decisions, some that undoubtedly benefit students and improve learning, but many others that function to preserve current practice and help ensure that demands on the adults who work in schools are not changed substantially.

If schools do not improve significantly, it seems likely that state policy leaders will blame educators for not taking advantage of the flexibility they theoretically were provided to redesign education and substantially improve schools. Educators could respond that they never received any real latitude to adapt, that the goals were either too vague or too unrealistic, that the resources provided were inadequate, and that the leadership they received did not enable them to react successfully to state policy mandates. These counterarguments may not be enough to assuage governors and legislators bent on educational improvement.

If this scenario comes to pass, it seems likely to fuel a new round of experimentation by the federal and state governments with governance, organization, and delivery methods for public education. These experiments continue to move control out of the hands of education professionals and local boards. School personnel, for their part, can be expected to become increasingly cynical and jaded in their responses to state policy initiatives. The fundamentally conservative core of schooling will reassert itself more forcefully, and education practice and adaptation will be confined to a relatively narrow range of activities. Schools will find ways to adapt to the demands of accountability systems, alter the systems to make them tolerable, or explain why schools should not be held to the specified standards. Communities and the populace at large will remain divided over the efficacy and appropriateness of large-scale testing and accountability, and public education will continue to meet the needs of some students while achieving only limited success with the portion of the student population most in need of a highly effective public education.

## WHAT ARE THE LONGER-TERM IMPLICATIONS OF CURRENT TRENDS?

The preceding scenario for the short-term implications of current trends is only one possibility and, in any event, the longer term may bring larger transformations within the educational system. If the fundamental relationship between local districts and other governance levels is changing, what are the implications over time? What will states do, for example, if school districts do not solve the problem of low-performing schools? What will happen if student test scores do not rise over time in relation to the standards states have established? Is there sufficient political will to sustain education reform or is this issue likely to fade over time and school districts resume their work in relative anonymity, out of the public eye once more? Will some of the recent experiments with new governance arrangements and structures be sustained and increased or will they be abandoned in favor of more traditional models?

### How the State–Local Equation Is Setting the Stage for More Choice and Competition

Standards can create the conditions under which school choice is more feasible, but cannot create competition. To create true competition, states must facilitate simple, convenient comparison of performance across different educational models and governance structures. As long as learning is entirely a locally defined phenomenon, it is difficult to determine who is doing a better job or how well the system as a whole is performing. Nationally normed standardized tests provide some evidence, but they are not particularly sophisticated nor do they provide much insight into how much value a school is adding to the education of its students. Furthermore, norm referencing doesn't establish with any certainty that the level of student or school performance is adequate. Cannell (1988; 1989) describes the "Lake Wobegon" effect, where every district is above average, for example. Schools and districts often define improvement in terms of two- or three-point improvement in average percentile scores. It is unclear what such gains mean for student skill and knowledge, workforce readiness, or international competitiveness.

State accountability systems, whatever their methodological weaknesses and limitations, have opened the door to more sophisticated means of comparisons. "Gain score" models that compare individual student performance at two points in time are increasing in popularity (Grissmer, Flanagan, Kawata, & Williamson, 2000; Rouk, 2000; U.S. Department of Education Planning and Evaluation Service, 2001). Multiple defined performance levels, such as "exceeds, meets, does not meet," have become more ubiquitous (Goertz & Duffy, 2001; Rothman, 1992a) and are now a federal requirement for all state assessment systems. Matching curriculum and assessments to create a new definition of "teaching to the test" has become increasingly acceptable as a way to align instruction across grades and school levels (Bushweller, 1997). States have developed various systems for rating and comparing schools, which find their way into newspapers and onto websites (Hoff, 2001b; Rouk, 2000).

These comparative systems can be made relatively easy to understand, even to the noneducator, and are becoming continually more user friendly. This information has spawned organizations devoted to sharing information and comparing school performance (Hoff, 2001a; National Center for Educational Accountability, 2002), one of the best examples of which is an organization named Just for the Kids (Hoff, 2001a; Just for the Kids, 2002; Keller, 2001).

As these systems become more commonplace, well understood, and widely accepted, they will set the stage for real competition. Comparative measurement systems previously have been based on standardized test scores, or measures such as SAT or ACT scores, all of which have correlated strongly with income. Parents will need access to a much broader set of indicators than one or two test scores. When and if they get that access, they will be capable of making better-informed decisions about the school they prefer for their children or about the ways in which their current school should improve.

Information is the prerequisite to improvement and choice. At first the demand for choice and improvement will most likely be within the public school system. Demand for additional options will be heard with greater frequency if schools do not provide the range of options and the quality that in theory local control was supposed to create in the first place.

## How Choice Might Change Current Organizational and Governance Structures

One conception of choice has the state becoming the organizer of competition and not the guarantor of the public school monopoly. For this approach to work, the state would have to assume a special obligation to ensure that students and parents in schools serving the poor and underprivileged have the same range of options as their more privileged counterparts. The system would evolve in time to accommodate a wide variety of structures that offer educational services, some entirely public, some entirely private, some a hybrid of the two. Educators themselves might become employees, contractors, and entrepreneurs simultaneously, working for a public school part of the time, contracting with a private management group at other times, and operating as an independent consultant in certain settings.

Properly organized and nurtured, educational choice could become an opportunity for teachers, individually and collectively, to exercise the creativity and flexibility that policy makers say they seek from local schools, if states can find ways to free teachers from bureaucratic oversight and still hold them accountable for results. Many variations on the traditional public school structure might then emerge. Currently, the only real options for teachers who want to engage in any sort of organization outside the traditional structure are external contractors, such as the Edison Corporation, or charter schools that separate themselves entirely from the existing school system. Neither of these are particularly attractive options for educators who have a strong allegiance to the public schools or, in any event, are required to surrender a certain amount of job security or to lose benefits if they choose to work in charter schools.

One possible option would be teacher collectives and collaboratives that operated within the structure and facilities of the public schools but had wide latitude, access to support services as needed, and accountability to the marketplace for students and to the state for results. These semiautonomous self-governing units could help sustain a form of local control while simultaneously addressing state goals for higher achievement and parent desires for greater choice. Parent allegiance is to their school, not their district, for the most part (Rose & Gallup, 1999). Governance arrangements that cultivated this sort of bonding between parents and groups of education service providers would be consistent with the original goals of local control. Such a model might resemble in some ways medical groups, with general practitioners and specialists, and patient choice. These collectives would be part of the school system, but would negotiate as a group, not as part of a bargaining unit. They would be free to create the organizational structures and arrangements they deemed most appropriate, although all teachers and administrators would be subject to state licensure requirements. This variation on the medical model helps retain a certain modicum of quality control over who teaches and administers, while fostering greater autonomy and collective action by educators to create new, more effective learning environments.

## Charters as Precursors of a New Governance Model: Back to the Future

Charter schools seem to be capable of achieving exactly the sort of tight relationship between school and community sought by choice advocates (Schwartz, 1996), although researchers point out that public schools are quite capable of creating and frequently do create exactly these types of relationships (Mintrom, 2000). Nevertheless, charters seem to be striking a chord with legislators and parents who perceive public schools as inflexible and unresponsive institutions.

Charter schools are an interesting phenomenon because they are public schools, the protestations of their opponents notwithstanding. They can be viewed in one light as an almost anachronistic attempt to leapfrog 100 years of educational governance system development to return to the time when each school was governed by its own individual board that ensured that the school was a reflection of community values. Rather than being a radical educational innovation, charter schools are perhaps the most conservative governance reform possible. Their existence in the current educational landscape is made possible in large measure by a philosophy that the state sets standards and measures performance, and consumers choose the service provider. The idea that charters sign a contract directly with the state is an expression of the new power and discretion states have in arranging and rearranging educational governance structures and bypassing local school districts.

## Choice Without State Standards and Control

Those who advocate a competing point of view toward choice, one that explicitly rejects the notion of state standards and assessments as the organizers and arbiters of the goals of publicly funded education, favor parental, not governmental, control over many, if not all, of the ideas to which their children are exposed via public education. This point of view rejects the state's role as the creator of a system of standards within which all education occurs.

Sizer (2000) states that it is a "fundamental American freedom" that parents have a right to determine the ideas to which their children are exposed and that they are taught in school: "Arrogation of this right by central governments is an abridgment of freedom." He argues that state curriculum frameworks, however valid from a scholarly point of view, are "attacks on intellectual freedom." Communities have a right to impose some common values, those that make freedom a practical reality, but also must be ready to compromise. When governments reach beyond these common values to define learning, they fail to trust or respect their citizens.

> Simply, the detailed contours of culture—and, willy-nilly, schools are crucibles of culture—are too important to be given to central authorities unilaterally to define and then to impose. Yes, there must be compromises between what I want and what the community wants. However, I personally want to be a party to the definition of those compromises. Yes, there is the matter of empirical evidence: I cannot simply walk away from such evidence when it suits my prejudices. However, I expect the government will never assume that it always knows best. . . .
>
> For my child, I would like a choice among schools that play out the necessary compromises between the values of the state and those to which I am thoughtfully committed. From among these I can elect a school that reflects my deepest and fairest sense of the culture in which I wish my child to grow up.
>
> This sort of parental authority and choice is well established for wealthy American families. . . . If such choices make sense for rich folks . . . why not make them available to everybody? (Sizer, 2000, pp. 73–74)

While not specifically advocating charter schools, Sizer calls for a form of choice with locally developed and approved standards that fall within the larger society's value system but that are arbitrated and assessed locally. This is not an explicit rejection of standards, but rather the acceptance of standards when the control of them remains local.

However problematic this point of view might be in practice, it represents a reaffirmation of local control within the context of a system that needs somehow to ensure that all students achieve to high levels. Sizer does not necessarily believe that each community should simply be left alone to allow its students to succeed or fail. He has faith that communities will always do what is best for their children. The state, however, is not the best or most legitimate source for determining the specific knowledge students learn.

Charter schools and other forms of radical decentralization are vehicles that potentially bridge the gap between state standards and assessment systems and Sizer's more community-based notions of involvement and ownership of standards. These new governance and organizational structures have serious potential drawbacks and numerous unanswered questions regarding their long-term effects on public education and the social structure of the nation. They do, however, give expression to the beliefs of many citizens that the state has overplayed its hand in removing control from the local level.

## The Challenge of Learning How to Govern in a Choice-Based System

The most significant stumbling block to increased parental choice is not necessarily lack of participation in the determination of standards but the historical lack of information about educational choices or experience making such choices. State standards and assessment systems can facilitate educational choices, among which would be the choice of a traditional public school, and fulfill parental needs for ownership and involvement (Mintrom, 2000; Nelson et al., 2000). As the expectation for options and the familiarity with choice increases, more consumer-responsive planning would generate a wider range of options that would displace the standardization of education that represents the current "local control" model.

A change to a flexible, consumer-responsive system will have effects on most aspects of educational administration, from the way in which students are assigned to schools to the contracts under which teaching and support staff work, the ways students are transported, the ways information on school effectiveness is collected and reported, the skills educational managers and leaders must possess, and even the focus and structure of local board meetings. In essence, power will be transferred from the professional staff to the parents and community in many important areas of system organization and operation. Educational governance structures organized on "command and control" models for over a century will be made responsive to market forces. This type of transition is extremely difficult for large organizations with long histories and strong cultures. It has proven a nearly impossible transition for organizations that have had monopoly status and then been required to operate in a competitive environment (Doyle, 1997; Reuter News Service, 1989; Rothman, 1990).

## ALIGNING GOVERNANCE WITH KEY VALUES, GOALS, AND PURPOSES

The American educational system has been characterized since its inception as one that accommodates a wide range of values and purposes. In contrast to countries with more centralized systems that espouse a consistent set of values, states and school boards in the United States have had the latitude, if they chose to exercise it, to conceptualize and pursue the educational aims they deemed most appropriate for their communities and constituents.

Le Métais (1997) examines the role of values in the national educational systems of 18 countries around the world. The American system is one in which national values have less influence on education because education policy is not controlled centrally. Instilling particular values is not as central to education in the United States as in many other nations. However, all educational systems reflect and transmit values, implicitly or explicitly. Any educational system is, at any given time, a combination of the past, the present, and the future in regard to the values it communicates and the aims it pursues.

The past is manifested via the values and teaching methods of teachers. These often are formed in the era when the teacher enters the profession. The present is represented by assessments and standards, which have a direct impact on practice. The future is laid out in curriculum documents that contain aspirations and visions of best practice. The system is a product of the interactions of these three convergent forces. Reform implementation takes place amid these three streams of activity and values.

## What Are the Purposes and Aims of American Education?

While American education has always been concerned with transmitting some values universally, these tend to be quite broad: characteristics like civic engagement, basic morality, and individual responsibility. School districts may adopt more explicit, even blatant, value positions. Some of this variation in values has been essentially harmless and did benefit local communities by reinforcing social bonds. Variation also resulted in the creation and perpetuation of inequities that were and are inconsistent with an equitable society. A number of national forces, including civil rights legislation, a new "national" economy where regional differences are less substantial, national media that highlight social and economic inequities, and a work environment that requires greater universal education and in which civil rights guarantees are more vigorously safeguarded, represent a set of common values that shape public education today. States have implemented finance systems consistent with greater equity. Local school districts are under increasing pressure to conform to this *de facto* set of core national educational values.

The lack of a strong federal role in education at the national level precluded the explicit statement of national educational goals until the 1990s. The enhanced federal education presence over the past 35 years has focused education on national equity by placing the rights of individuals, not the preservation of local school governance, at the center of federal policy. This has caused schools to attempt to meet the educational needs of all students in a more equitable fashion. This focus on equity, combined with economic competitiveness issues, has elevated universal educational excellence to the position of key educational goal, embodied in the phrase, "all students reaching high standards" (Robelen, 2002a).

Also implicit in national education policy is the very American notion that each individual is responsible for her or his own success or failure, and government is responsible mainly to ensure that everyone has an equal opportunity, more or less, to succeed. This value is being manifested in federal policy that aims to establish the expectations that all students can and eventually do succeed. Accountability for results, at an individual and organizational level, is becoming the criterion for judging education programs. Schools are now feeling the effects of policies that are struggling to find the right balance between holding students accountable and holding educators accountable.

These trends toward greater agreement on key goals for education will have significant long-term effects on education locally. Although vigorous and vehement exception will be taken to the "imposition" of state or national aims for education, the country seems headed in the direction of a redefined notion of educational purposes with a focus on instrumental uses of education for economic success and social equality. These values have always been important in some communities, but not necessarily all, as is the case now.

## Effects of Emergence of Broad National Educational Goals

The notion of the educational system as a tool to achieve social goals is not new. It has been seen as a means to socialize immigrants, teach vocational skills for a new industrial economy, and even prepare those raised in rural areas to live in cities. The difference is that these goals were accepted for the most part without explicit direction from the federal government. In the relative homogeneity that prevailed during the period when local school boards were "depoliticized," a surprising degree of commonalty in values and beliefs arose among board members (Tyack, 1974). The new landscape of educational governance is one in which local boards once again may be in broad agreement, but as a result of constraints imposed by federal and state laws and regulations that operationalize specific value positions.

For all the discussion about fear of a national curriculum or assessment, education policy continues to drift in the direction of greater consistency of values and purposes. Every indication is that this trend will continue if not accelerate. The increase in ethnic, linguistic, and economic class diversity that the society and schools have experienced the past 2 decades, and will continue to experience for the foreseeable future, suggests that the educational system will be called upon to serve as a vehicle for socialization and social mobility, although schools are likely to demonstrate greater sensitivity to issues of cultural diversity than they have in the past.

Local school districts and boards will have to mediate between the broad framework of federal and state values on one hand and local community needs and wishes on the other. The continuing tension between the two will lead to conflict and periodic adjustments in the balance between and among federal, state, and local demands and desires. Given that the broader national goals of equality and economic participation are well established, at least in principle, in most communities, they will serve as overall framers of local education programs. State standards and assessments will serve as the means by which equity is operationalized in schools. These state programs will be guided by federal legislation that establishes basic frameworks for education practice.

## What Organizational Structure Best Accommodates National Goals While Acknowledging Local Diversity?

American education faces a conundrum of sorts. The historical governance structure for education seems unlikely to enable the system to achieve the social goals laid out for it by current governments. The tortured implementation of school desegregation over more than 40 years illustrates that when national and local goals conflict, national goals win out in the end, but local action or inaction determines the speed and difficulty of policy implementation. State and federal governments, however, seem largely uninterested in fostering the evolution of the existing governance system, preferring instead to experiment with radical adaptations that initially affect the fringes of education primarily, such as charter schools and vouchers. Governments maintain a psychological and policy commitment to what increasingly appears to be an outdated and obsolete governance structure organized around myriad individual school districts, many of which are now historical curiosities or geographical oddities.

The problem is that the current structure contains some desirable elements among the many others that no longer function as intended. Chief among the desirable elements is the significant involvement in and ownership of local schools that come from the traditional school district, school board, and neighborhood schools when they are functioning as intended. The power and importance of this involvement has been demonstrated time and again. To lose this component of educational governance at a time when many other nations in the world are attempting to increase educational decentralization and build ownership of local schools seems foolhardy. However, a truly national educational system cannot permit each locality to choose its goals, standards, and accountability measures independently. It cannot even allow localities to select all aspects of their education programs in isolation, if such choices systematically exclude groups of students from participating successfully in the larger society.

## OUTLINES OF A NEW GOVERNANCE SYSTEM

What might a new governance system look like that attempted to address the multiple, conflicting goals of American education and simultaneously acknowledge the new realities of the local/state/federal relationship.

### The Emerging Outlines of the Federal Role

The federal role in a restructured and reconceptualized governance system is becoming clearer. A number of possibilities have been explored in previous chapters, including greater involvement in research and development, identification and endorsement of effective educational methods, ability to focus public opinion on the need for educational improvement, creation of pilot programs, and provision of resources to help targeted populations achieve equitable educational outcomes. The significance of the ESEA reauthorization of 2001 (No Child Left Behind) has been noted as well. Where will the federal government head now that it is becoming so much more of a central player in establishing the direction of education policy?

Equity issues will continue to be a central focal point for the federal agenda for at least two reasons. First, guaranteeing citizens equal protection under the law is a fundamental responsibility of the national government and is the legitimate basis for federal intervention into state and local education policy. A large body of law undergirds and supports policy in this area, which means lawsuits would be the result of any abandonment of this role. In essence, the federal government has little choice but to pursue and support educational equity.

Second, significant inequities remain in many areas of society despite sustained efforts to eliminate them. The achievement gap between African American and White students was cut in half over an 18-year period from 1970 and 1988, and the gap separating Latinos and Whites declined by one-third. Since that time, the gaps have begun to widen again (Haycock, 2001). Achievement rates remain lower for Hispanic, African American, Native American, and some Asian students than for White students, even after 30 years of programs such as Title I (Borman & D'Agostino, 1995). Closing this gap has become the centerpiece of federal policy and cannot be easily abandoned. For example, the No Child Left Behind legislation gives states until 2014 to close this achievement gap. Barring a dramatic change in national politics and sentiment, the federal government will remained focused on equity issues for the foreseeable future.

The most intriguing question is whether the federal government will extend notions of equity to fiscal matters and become engaged in equalizing funding across state lines. Per pupil spending in the lowest-spending states is currently half that of the highest-spending states. This results in situations where students in the highest-spending districts in some states receive fewer resources than students in the lowest-spending districts in other states (Rothstein, 2001). The past 30 years of school financing legislation and litigation have focused exclusively on within-state funding equity issues, which has resulted in a decrease in intrastate spending discrepancies. Interstate differences have remained relatively constant over the past 20 years. Per pupil funding, adjusted for regional cost differences, varied in 2001 from $9,362 per pupil in New Jersey to $4,579 per pupil in Utah (Education Week, 2002).

The 2000 presidential election saw calls for federal programs to provide funds for reducing class size and increasing teacher salaries, and for school construction (Steinberg, 2000). Any future movement by the federal government into the area of equalizing funding would only magnify federal influence on state and local education policies. As the experience with states has shown, greater involvement in funding leads to greater control over policy. If interstate funding equity ever comes to pass, the foundation for a federal education system will be well along the way to being laid. A national assessment system would then seem to be inevitable, as would national teacher licensing standards and national policy in a host of other similar areas.

## Creating Educational "Franchises"

Assuming that control over the organization and routine governance of schools would remain at the state level, how might states rethink governance such that equity goals and desires for local choice and control could be simultaneously addressed?

The first question to ask is: What are the responsibilities of governors and legislatures to provide the means by which local schools can successfully address state mandates, standards, and policies? The state would have to establish one set of governance mechanisms to oversee the entire educational system, rather than regulate one part, namely, school districts, and deregulate another, for example, charters.

One way to create a level playing field in the future is to empower state boards of education to grant "franchises" for the delivery of educational services. A franchise is defined as a right or privilege granted by a government to another agency. Although the word *franchise* conjures up images of hamburger or fried chicken outlets, the franchise has a long history and is one of the most well-established tools government has to oversee provision of services in areas where full competition is not feasible. Governments throughout the country currently manage a range of services via franchise arrangements.

Franchisees would be selected by the state board of education based on the quality and cost-effectiveness of their proposals. Franchises would be granted for a geographical area to a governmental agency or consortium of agencies and organizations. Within that area, the franchisee would be responsible for a portfolio of educational environments and opportunities adequate to meet local needs and ensure that all students reached high levels of achievement. Local school boards, for example, would be eligible to submit proposals to be granted franchises, as would counties and cities, or collaborations of all these governmental units. Other less traditional sponsors, such as universities, intermediate educational agencies, teachers' unions, or regional education labs, would be eligible to be granted franchises or to collaborate with other agencies in the operation of schools. Private entities would be equally eligible. Such entities might include for-profit companies with experience running schools, not-for-profit organizations, and other companies with expertise in one niche or aspect of service provision.

A franchisee might comprise a combination of public and private organizations that collectively possessed expertise in governance, finance, customer service, and effective educational techniques. Collectively, these organizations would bring expertise to ensure effective management of schools, high-performance teaching and learning models, and high-quality customer service. Education experts would be one, but only one, component of the management team.

Once a franchise was approved, the franchisee would receive the entire state per pupil funding and all applicable federal funds for each student it enrolled. A franchisee would be eligible to bid to occupy school buildings or access state funds specifically designed to assist franchises to develop physical space. State education departments would oversee franchisees to ensure they were meeting the service terms of their franchise. Franchisees would be judged ultimately by student performance and parental satisfaction. Information would be derived from a variety of sources.

It would be the goal of the franchisee to provide such exceptional service that its franchise would be renewed. Each franchisee would be required to have a governing board democratically elected by all eligible voters within its service area. It would always be in the interests of the franchisee to meet the needs of parents and students while remaining attentive to the terms of the franchise established by the state. However, if at any time dissatisfaction with a franchisee rose above a designated level, this would trigger a period of time during which competing proposals could be circulated. What amounts to a referendum on a franchise would then follow to determine if the franchise would be revoked early. If a franchisee could not meet the performance terms, the franchise would be put up for bid to other franchisees or entirely new proposals, which could result in the franchise being divided up or otherwise reorganized to best meet local conditions and expectations. Franchises would be reviewed more formally, perhaps every 5 years. Performance would be determined based on a number of indicators, but achievement of state goals and maintenance of local satisfaction would be co-equal.

In some respects this notion of franchises is only a small step off the path down which educational governance has already been heading. Numerous states grant charters to a range of sponsors, take over school districts or permit mayors to do so, authorize contractors to run districts, approve city–school district governance arrangements, reconstitute schools, and otherwise control and assign governance responsibilities. The franchise approach would, however, change one important aspect of the state–local relationship. School boards would not automatically be the sole legitimate sponsors of local education programs. Boards would be expected to compete for franchises along with everyone else. In practice, communities that were highly satisfied with their current schools would likely see little change. Those where significant dissatisfaction existed might well see additional options.

Given the magnitude of the state board of education's role in overseeing such a system, the state education department would have to be capable of providing the information necessary to make decisions to grant or renew franchises. Education departments would have to be transformed into agencies capable of collecting and analyzing data on the functioning of schools within a franchise. State education departments would no longer be in the position of defending local school districts or advocating specifically on their behalf with state legislatures. Education departments would be more concerned with generating appropriate policy recommendations for improving the overall functioning of the franchising system than with responding to specific issues raised by local school boards or superintendents, as they tend to do today.

Instead, the state would implement a series of single-purpose commissions to address key areas of state education policy, such as standards, assessment, and accountability. These commissions would be the forums within which franchisees would engage the state in negotiations around the terms and effects of specific policies. These commissions would be organized to facilitate two-way communication via well-developed websites, e-mail, and other electronic means that would disseminate new policies and capture reactions to policy as it was implemented.

This system would require coordination at the state level by a state board or a governor's office. While it is certainly possible that a more elaborated governance model such as this would be capable of sending contradictory messages to schools, it is equally likely that greater continuity would result from creating institutional centers at the state level for a series of important policy areas. If the state board and commissions were nonpartisan, with members serving overlapping terms, the likelihood increases that these bodies would provide some stability and continuity to state policy implementation. At the same time, they would provide the state with a greatly enhanced capacity to translate policy into practice and to communicate with the franchisees, all of whom should be interested in state policy and its potential effects on the renewal of their franchises.

### Schools as Members of Regional "Networks"

A less radical adaptation of governance would be for schools to be members of one or more education "networks" in addition to being part of a district. Schools would be free to utilize these networks to purchase goods and services collectively, to share materials and programs, and to develop close working connections among school staffs.

Networks would fulfill a number of needs. They would put school administrators and staff into contact with others whose schools had similar problems or needs. They would facilitate pooling and sharing of some resources as well as creating support for change, improvement, and professional development. They could engage in common curriculum development and program planning. They could help educators respond effectively to new state and federal policy demands.

They would be "governed" by one or more representatives from each member institution. Meetings would focus on ways in which the network might advance its needs and perspectives within the state policy system, gain more resources, marshal resources to help out a member facing an emergency, formulate common policies for relating to external agencies, and connect with other networks and organizations for mutually beneficial purposes. The governing board also would be a vehicle to nurture and develop leadership skills of individuals from member institutions.

In the current system, an individual school can find itself isolated because it may be quite different from other schools in its district or, in some districts, due to envy or rejection by colleagues who may resent a school's success or use of different instructional methods and programs. Districts do not have a particularly good track record of ensuring that effective education practices are disseminated within the district or that like-minded schools can share resources and solve problems.

The advent of sophisticated telecommunications systems and software opens the door for schools to be in regular contact and to collaborate on a number of fronts simultaneously with a range of educational service providers and other schools. Sharing personnel across long distances is still problematic, but utilizing itinerants who spend one or more weeks in a region working with schools on specific problems is one strategy that facilitates sharing expertise broadly across a region or state. In this way, schools could benefit from a common focus and a commitment to work collaboratively to solve common problems. The concept of learning community would have new meaning in such a network arrangement.

Schools often do affiliate around particular improvement programs or philosophical orientations toward reform, but rarely do they form confederations with high degrees of interdependence, coordinated resource allocation, and systematic sharing of improvement strategies, models, and techniques.

Nascent statewide school networks can be observed in some states as charter schools form organizations that have many of these characteristics. These networks often begin with a focus on purchasing, accounting, or other support services, but can grow to include conferences, audio and video links, and even shared curriculum. Each school retains its independence and unique focus as well as its responsiveness to local conditions and its particular governance structure. Within a framework of overall accountability to the state, the schools decide how best to affiliate and for what services.

This sort of need-driven organizational structure seems more consistent with current thinking about how best to enable institutions to be responsive to customers and markets and, in the case of education, to state values and goals simultaneously. Striking this balance between parents' very personal desires for their children and states' more general expectations for all students will require new governance methods that are like a double-hinged gate, capable of swinging in both directions.

## How States Can Nurture Educational Success

States can do more to support educational success than simply granting franchises and then sitting back to see who succeeds and who fails. Education departments can be reorganized to provide high-quality curriculum and specific courses of study, much as is done in some Australian states, while allowing teachers to continue to choose what precisely they want to teach. These state-developed programs would be designed specifically as models of how to get all students to reach high standards. One of the benefits of such efforts would be to break the stranglehold of textbook publishers and to stimulate more local curriculum development. Given advancements in publishing techniques and the more ubiquitous availability of online resources, the notion that states and even consortia of districts or schools could work together to produce sophisticated materials is nowhere near as far-fetched as it once may have seemed.

The state also must become serious about identifying effective education programs and practices and establishing the means to disseminate them.

If education is to remain a decentralized system, information on best practices has to be implemented much more quickly. Other nations take advantage of centralization to put new curricula or teaching practices into place rapidly, an idea that is anathema to American educators but that allows for more rapid educational improvement. Allowing ineffective practice to continue in the name of local control is not consistent with equity, excellence, or professionalization of education. Expecting all problems to be solved locally ignores the complexity of the challenge many schools face.

States will need to develop much more sophisticated systems for analyzing why a school is not succeeding or living up to its potential. The systems that states develop must surpass the "blunt instrument" approach of many current accountability schemes. To do so, they will need to enable schools or districts to diagnose how well a school has implemented and maintained organizational conditions that have a demonstrated link to student learning; the degree to which the school employs effective teaching practices and programs; the organizational culture and values under which the school operates; the relationship between the school and its external clients, including parents, community members, and central office staff; and the characteristics of the school's comprehensive profile of student learning. This combination of information on organizational variables and learning results enables schools to pinpoint problems, districts to identify how to assist schools, and states to paint a fuller picture of the conditions of education and the functioning of schools.

Although the state will need to work hard to provide schools with the information they need to improve, its primary responsibility will be to advocate for students and parents, not for professional educators. To fulfill this role, the state will publicize information about the current state of schools, and of districts' efforts to improve schools as well as their failure to do so. The state's goal will be to mobilize communities to take greater responsibility for local governance. This state–local connection helps strengthen one of the major benefits of local control, namely, community involvement in managing schools.

## THE PRESSING NEED TO CREATE
## NEW GOVERNANCE MODELS

This transformation is dependent on a recognition by all involved that relationships have changed fundamentally and irrevocably, and that such change is not necessarily and automatically a bad thing. Seeking the benefits of these new relationships and adjusting the structure of government and the perspectives and assumptions of all participants in the education policy and governance system are the sustained challenges that remain before American society. If these adjustments can be made in a conscious, rational, deliberate fashion, the potential to revamp, modernize, and improve educational governance and policy making is great. If participants are intent on denying or ignoring the changes that have occurred in favor of an almost sentimental attachment to a system that no longer functions as intended, governance and policy will become increasingly confusing, inconsistent, fractious, and nonrational.

The changes in American educational governance do not demand a moral response; they demand a practical response. That response is to design the most appropriate and effective governance and policy system possible. To do so will require all involved, but particularly board members and educators at the district and school levels, to re-examine long-held assumptions and beliefs about governmental relationships and responsibilities and to seek the means of governance that will be most effective in the long run, not just the means to solve the most immediate crisis facing education at the moment. This sort of rational planning is clearly the exception in a system that is inherently conservative, self-referential, and insular in nature.

However, it is not impossible to operate within a larger vision when making the daily decisions and solving the immediate problems that educational governance and policy systems confront. If the participants in the American political system can grasp the historical significance of the current situation and respond with a redesign that points toward a future in which local involvement can be preserved and state goals achieved, the chances that public education will remain a central and vibrant element of American society will be greatly increased.

If a deliberate plan to redesign policy and governance mechanisms is not undertaken, pressures to dismantle public education no doubt will continue to gain momentum and the ultimate result possibly will be an incremental dissolution of the current governance system. Given the long history and tradition of public education in America and its important role in local communities, a deliberate redesign seems preferable, however complex, conflict-laden, and difficult it might be. The next 10 years should tell the tale of the redesign of American educational governance, at least in terms of its institutional structures and organizational components. This book suggests some of the possible ramifications and implications for the participants in the system and the choices they have before them at this historic moment.

# REFERENCES

Abercrombie, K. L. (1999). Ky. changes school rating system. *Education Week*, *18*(40), 13.

Adams, J. E., Jr. (2000). *Taking charge of curriculum: Teacher networks and curriculum implementation*. New York: Teachers College Press.

Akers, J. (1990). Business must fill educational gap. *Computerworld*, 24(46), 25.

Allen, J. L., & Banchero, S. (2000, June 7). State to require college-bound exam. *Chicago Tribune*, p. 1.

Ambach, G. (1992). Connecting school and work. *Youth Policy*, *14*(1), 12–17.

American Federation of Teachers. (1999a). *Assuring teacher quality: It's union work*. Washington, DC: Author.

American Federation of Teachers. (1999b). *Improved reading achievement: It's union work*. Washington, DC: Author.

American Federation of Teachers. (1999c). *Making standards matter, 1999: An annual fifty-state report on efforts to raise academic standards*. Washington, DC: Author.

American Legislative Exchange Council. (1999). *Report card on American education*. Washington, DC: Author.

Amster, J. (1990). *Investing in our future: The imperatives of education reform and the role of business*. Queenstown, MD: Aspen Institute.

Angus, D. L., & Mirel, J. E. (1999). *The failed promise of the American high school*. New York: Teachers College Press.

Anthony, P. G., & Rossman, G. B. (1994). *The Massachusetts Education Reform Act: What is it and will it work?*

Archibald, D. A. (1990). *The Minnesota postsecondary options law: A case of choice*. Philadelphia, PA: The Consortium for Policy Research in Education.

Ayers, W. (1991). *Perestroika* in Chicago's schools. *Educational Leadership*, *48*(8), 69–71.

Bader, B. D. (1991, April). *"Abbott v. Burke" vs. New Jersey: Policy, politics and political economy*. Paper presented at the annual meeting of the American Educational Research Association, Chicago.

Ball, G. C. (1990). In search of educational excellence. Business leaders discuss school choice and accountability. *Policy Review*, *54*,54–59.

Balz, D., & Morin, R. (2000, July 2). Poll: Voters waffle over how to improve schools. *Register-Guard*, p. 3A.

Barth, P., Haycock, K., Jackson, H., Mora, K., Ruiz, P., Robinson, S., & Wilkins, A. (1999). *Dispelling the myth: High poverty schools exceeding expectations*. Washington, DC: Education Trust.

Bell, A. S. (1998, May). *California Academic Standards Commission develops standards for history–social science*. Perspectives Online. http://www.theaha.org/perspectives/issues/1998/9805/9805new1.CFM

Berends, M., Kirby, S. N., Naftel, S., & McKelvey, C. (2001). *Implementation and performance in new American schools: Three years into scale-up*. Santa Monica, CA: Rand Corporation.

Berman, P., & McLaughlin, M. W. (1976). Implementation of educational innovation. *Educational Forum, 40*(3), 344–370.

Berman, P., & McLaughlin, M. (1978). *Federal programs supporting educational change: Vol. 8. Implementing and sustaining innovations*. Santa Monica, CA: Rand Corporation.

Betts, J. R., & Danenberg, A. (2002). School accountability in California: An early evaluation. In D. Ravitch (Ed.), *Education policy 2002* (pp. 123–197). Washington, DC: Brookings Institution Press.

Bird, T., & Little, J. W. (1986). How schools organize the teaching occupation. *Elementary School Journal, 86*(4), 493–511.

Blair, J. (1999). Supreme court in S.C. sets stage for debate on school "adequacy." *Education Week, 18*(34), 19.

Blair, J. (2001a). Ed. schools strain to file report cards. *Education Week, 20*(28), 1, 30.

Blair, J. (2001b). University of Colo. at Boulder under fire for ed. school programs. *Education Week, 20*(39), 16.

Blair, J., & Archer, J. (2001). NEA members denounce high-stakes testing. *Education Week, 20*(42). (Web-based edition only)

Blair, J., & Hoff, D. (2001). Evolution restored to Kansas standards, but called "controversial" in Alabama's. *Education Week, 20*(23), 13.

Blank, R. K., Langesen, D., Bush, M., Pechman, E., & Goldstein, D. (1997). *Mathematics and science content standards and curriculum frameworks: States progress on development and implementation*. Washington, DC: Council of Chief State School Officers.

Blase, J. (1991). *The politics of life in schools*. Newbury Park, CA: Sage.

Block, A. W. (1983). *Effective schools: A summary of research* (ERS Research Brief). Arlington, VA: Educational Research Service.

Bond, L., Jaeger, R., Smith, T., & Hattie, J. (2001). Defrocking the National Board: The certification system of the National Board for Professional Teaching Standards. *Education Matters, 1*(2), 79–82.

Borman, G. D., & D'Agostino, J. V. (1995). *Title I and student achievement: A meta-analysis of 30 years of test results*. Paper presented at the annual meeting of the American Educational Research Association, San Francisco, CA.

Borsuk, A. J. (2000, March 9). Standardized testing not for everybody. *Journal Sentinel*.

Boser, U. (2000). Teaching to the test? *Education Week, 19*(39), 1, 10.

Boser, U. (2001). Pressure without support. *Education Week, 20*(17), 68.

Bridges, E. (1967). A model for shared decision making in the school principalship. *Educational Administration Quarterly, 20*(3), 11–40.

Bulkley, K. (1999). Charter school authorizers: A new governance mechanism? *Educational Policy, 13*(5), 674–697.

Burtless, G. (Ed.). (1996). *Does money matter? The effect of school resources on student achievement and adult success.* Washington, DC: Brookings Institution Press.

Bushweller, K. (1997). Teaching to the test. *American School Board Journal, 184*(9), 20–25.

Cain, G. G., & Watts, H. W. (1968). *Problems in making policy inferences from the Coleman report* (Discussion papers). Madison: University of Wisconsin, Institute for Research on Poverty.

California State Postsecondary Education Commission. (2001). *Assessment and change: The role of student testing in California education. Higher education update* (UP/01-2). Sacramento: Author.

Calvo, N. A., Picus, L. O., Smith, J. R., & Guthrie, J. W. (1999). *A review of the Oregon quality education model.* Sacramento, CA: Management Analysis and Planning.

Campbell, R. F., Cunningham, L. L., Nystrand, R. O., & Usdan, M. D. (Eds.). (1990). *The organization and control of American schools* (6th ed.). New York: Merrill.

Cannell, J. J. (1988). The lake wobegon effect revisited. *Educational Measurement: Issues and Practice, 7*(4), 12–15.

Cannell, J. J. (1989). *How public educators cheat on standardized achievement tests: The "lake wobegon" report.* Albuquerque, NM: Friends for Education.

Carter, S. C. (2000). *No excuses: Lessons from 21 high-performing, high-poverty schools.* Washington, DC: Heritage Foundation.

Center for Policy Research in Education. (1989a). State education reform in the 1980s. *CPRE Policy Briefs* RB-3.

Center for Policy Research in Education. (1989b). *The progress of reform: An appraisal of state education initiatives.* Rutgers University, Center for Policy Research, New Brunswick, NJ.

Center on Education Policy in Education. (2000). *A brief history of the federal role in education.* Washington, DC: Author.

Christenson, G., & Conley, D. T. (1993). *Postsecondary options programs for high school students in Colorado and Minnesota.* Eugene, OR: Oregon State System of Higher Education.

Clark, T. A., & Lacey, R. A. (1997). *Learning by doing: Panasonic partnerships and systemic school reform.* Boca Raton, FL: St. Lucie Press.

Clune, W. H. (1987). Institutional choice as a theoretical framework for research on educational policy. *Educational Evaluation and Policy Analysis, 9*(2), 117–132.

Clune, W. (1993a). The best path to systemic educational policy: Standard/centralized or differentiated/decentralized? *Educational Evaluation and Policy Analysis, 15*(3), 233–254.

Clune, W. H. (1993b). Systemic educational policy: A conceptual framework. In S. Fuhrman (Ed.), *Designing coherent policy: Improving the system* (pp. 125–140). San Francisco: Jossey-Bass.

Clune, W. (1998). *Toward a theory of systemic reform: The case of nine NSF state-wide systemic initiatives* (Research Monograph No. 16). Madison, WI: Wisconsin Center for Educational Research.

Cohen, D. K., & Hill, H. C. (2001). *Learning policy.* New Haven, CT: Yale University Press.

Cohen, D. K., & Spillane, J. P. (1993). Policy and practice: The relations between governance and instruction. In S. Fuhrman (Ed.), *Designing coherent policy: Improving the system.* San Francisco: Jossey-Bass.

Cohen, M. (1982). Effective schools: Accumulating research findings. *American Education*, pp. 13–16.

Coleman, J. S. (1966). *Equality of educational opportunity* (OE-38001). Washington, DC: National Center for Educational Statistics.

Commission on the Skills of the American Work Force. (1990). *America's choice: High skills or low wages!* Rochester, NY: National Center on Education and the Economy.

Committee for Economic Development. (1985). *Investing in our children.* New York: Author.

Committee for Economic Development. (1987). *Children in need.* New York: Author.

Conant, J. B. (1959). *The American high school today.* New York: McGraw-Hill.

Congress of the United States. (1998). *Higher education amendments of 1998* (PL-105-244). Washington, DC: Author.

Conley, D. T. (1986). *Certificated personnel evaluation in Colorado: A policy study of practices and perceptions at the time of the implementation of the Certificated Personnel Performance Evaluation Act* (*H.B. 1338*). Unpublished doctoral dissertation, University of Colorado, Boulder.

Conley, D. T. (1993). *A business view: Education reform in Oregon.* Oregon Business Council, Portland.

Conley, D. T. (1997a, March 25). *Questioning traditional admissions practices and conventional wisdom: Proficiency-based admissions standards system* (*PASS*) *research.* Paper presented at the annual meeting of the American Educational Research Association, Chicago.

Conley, D. T. (1997b). *Roadmap to restructuring: Charting the course of change in American education* (2nd ed.). ERIC Clearinghouse on Educational Management, Eugene, OR.

Conley, D. T. (1999). *Quality education model final report.* Salem: Oregon Department of Education.

Conley, D. T. (2000, April). *Who is proficient: The relationship between proficiency scores and grades.* Paper presented at the annual meeting of the American Educational Research Association, New Orleans.

Conley, D. T. (2001). Rethinking the senior year. *NASSP Bulletin, 85*(625), 17–25.

Conley, D. T. (2002a). *Higher education involvement in K–12 standard setting.* Eugene, OR: Center for Educational Policy Research.

Conley, D. T. (2002b). Preparing students for life after high school. *Educational Leadership, 59*(7), 60–63.

Conley, D. T., & Bodone, F. (2002, April). *University expectations for student success: Implications for system alignment and state standard and assessment policies.* Paper presented at the annual meeting of the American Educational Research Association, New Orleans.

Conley, D. T., & Goldman, P. (1994a). *Facilitative leadership: How principals lead without dominating.* Eugene, OR: School Study Council.

Conley, D. T., & Goldman, P. (1994b). Ten propositions for facilitative leadership. In J. Murphy & K. Seashore Louis (Eds.), *Reshaping the principalship: Insights from transformational reform efforts* (pp. 237–262). Newbury Park, CA: Corwin Press.

Conley, D. T., & Goldman, P. (1995). Reactions from the field to state restructuring legislation. *Educational Administration Quarterly, 31*(4), 512–538.

Conley, D. T., & Goldman, P. (1998, April). *How educators process and respond to state-level education reform policies: The case of Oregon.* Paper presented at the annual meeting of the American Educational Research Association, San Diego.

Conley, D. T., & Goldman, P. (2000). Half full, half empty? Educator response over time to state-level systemic reform initiatives. *International Journal of Educational Reform, 9*(3), 249–269.

Conley, D. T., & Stone, P. (1996). *Evaluation of the Oregon Business Council–David Douglas Model School District Partnership Program.* Portland: Oregon Business Council.

Conley, S. (1991). Review of research on teacher participation in school decision making. In G. Grant (Ed.), *Review of research in education* (pp. 225–268). Washington, DC: American Educational Research Association.

Corcoran, T., Fuhrman, S. H., & Belcher, C. L. (2001). The district role in instructional improvement. *Phi Delta Kappan, 83*(1), 78–84.

Cornett, L. M., & Gaines, G. F. (1994). *Reflecting on ten years of incentive programs: The 1993 SREB career ladder clearinghouse survey.* Atlanta: Southern Regional Education Board.

Cornett, L. M., Gaines, G. F. (1992). *Focusing on student outcomes: Roles for incentive programs. The 1991 national survey of incentive programs and teacher career ladders.* Atlanta: Southern Regional Education Board.

Cuban, L. (1984). School reform by remote control: SB 813 in California. *Phi Delta Kappan, 66*(3), 213–215.

Cuban, L. (1993). *How teachers taught: Constancy and change in American classrooms, 1890–1980* (2nd ed.). New York: Teachers College Press.

Cuban, L. (2001). How systemic reform harms urban schools. *Education Week, 20*(38), 48, 34, 35.

Daley, B. (2000, March 10). More money hasn't meant better scores, report says. *Boston Globe,* p. A01.

Danielson, C. (1996). *Enhancing professional practice: A framework for teaching.* Alexandria, VA: Association for Supervision and Curriculum Development.

Danielson, C. (2001). New trends in teacher evaluation. *Educational Leadership, 58*(5), 12–15.

Darling-Hammond, L. (1985). *Equality and excellence: The educational status of black Americans.* New York: College Entrance Examination Board.

Darling-Hammond, L. (1994). National standards and assessments: Will they improve education? *American Journal of Education, 102*(4), 478–510.

Darling-Hammond, L. (1997). *Doing what matters most: Investing in quality teaching.* New York: National Commission on Teaching & America's Future.

Darling-Hammond, L. (1999). *Reshaping teaching policy, preparation, and practice: Influences of the National Board for Professional Teaching Standards.* Washington, DC: American Association of Colleges for Teacher Education, National Partnership for Excellence and Accountability in Teaching.

Darling-Hammond, L. (2000, September 13). *Teacher quality and student achievement: A review of state policy evidence.* http://www.tcrecord.org.

Darling-Hammond, L., Bullmaster, M. L., & Cobb, V. L. (1995). Rethinking teacher leadership through professional development schools. *Elementary School Journal, 96*(1), 87–106.

Darling-Hammond, L., & Marks, E. L. (1983). *The new federalism in education: State responses to the 1981 Education Consolidation and Improvement Act.* Santa Monica, CA: Rand Corporation.

Darling-Hammond, L., & Rustique-Forrester, E. (1997). *Investing in quality teaching: State-level strategies.* Denver: Education Commission of the States.

Darling-Hammond, L., Wise, A. E., & Klein, S. P. (1999). *A license to teach: Raising standards for teaching.* San Francisco: Jossey-Bass.

David, J. L. (1989). *Restructuring in progress: Lessons from pioneering districts.* Washington, DC: National Governors' Association, Center for Policy Research.

David, J. (1994a). School-based decision making: Kentucky's test of decentralization. *Phi Delta Kappan, 75*(9), 706–712.

David, J. L. (1994b). *Transforming state education agencies to support education reform.* Washington, DC: National Governors' Association, Center for Policy Research.

David, J. (1995/1996). The who, what, and why of site-based management. *Educational Leadership, 53*(4), 4–9.

DiMaggio, P. J., & Powell, W. W. (1983). The iron cage revisited: Institutional isomorphism and collective rationality in organizational fields. *American Sociological Review, 48,* 147–160.

Doyle, D. P. (1997). Benchmarking—Real lessons from the real world. *School Business Affairs, 63*(9), 3–7.

DuFour, R., & Eaker, R. E. (1998). *Professional learning communities at work: Best practices for enhancing student achievement.* Bloomington, IN.: National Education Service; Alexandria, VA: Association for Supervision and Curriculum Development.

Edmonds, R. R. (1982, February). *Programs of school improvement: An overview.* Paper presented at the National Invitational Conference, "Research on Teaching: Implications for Practice," Warrenton, VA.

Edmonds, R. R., et al. (1977). *Search for effective schools: The identification and analysis of city schools that are instructionally effective for poor children.* Cambridge, MA: Harvard University Press.

Education Commission of the States. (1988). *Statewide restructuring of education: A handbook for business.* Denver: Author.

Education Commission of the States. (1996). *The progress of education reform: 1996.* Denver: Author.

Education Commission of the States. (1997). *America's public schools must change . . . But can they? Results from the ECS 1996 national post-election voter survey.* Denver: Author.

Education Week. (2001). *Quality counts: A better balance. Standards, tests, and the tools to succeed.* Washington, DC: Author.

Education Week. (2002). *Quality counts 2002: Building blocks for success.* Washington, DC: Author.

Educational Research Service. (1992). *Nationwide school reforms: Opinion data from the general public, school principals, and teachers.* Arlington, VA: Author.

Educational Testing Service. (2001, July 8). *What is ETS?* http://www.ets.org/aboutets/visitors.html

Elam, S. M., & Rose, L. C. (1995). The 27th annual Gallup poll of the public's attitudes toward the public schools. *Phi Delta Kappan, 77*(1), 41–56.

Elam, S., Rose, L., & Gallup, A. (1991). The 23rd annual Gallup poll of the public's attitudes toward the public schools. *Phi Delta Kappan, 73*(1), 41–56.

Elam, S. M., Rose, L. C., & Gallup, A. M. (1994). The 26th annual Gallup poll of the public's attitudes toward the public schools. *Phi Delta Kappan, 76*(1), 41–56.

Elmore, R. F. (1988). *Early experience in restructuring schools: Voices from the field* (Results in education series). Washington, DC: National Governors Association.

Elmore, R. (1990). On changing the structure of public schools. In R. Elmore & Associates (Eds.), *Restructuring schools: The next generation of educational reform* (pp. 1–29). San Francisco: Jossey-Bass.

Elmore, R. F. (1999). *Leadership of large-scale improvement in American education.* Unpublished manuscript.

Elmore, R. F., & Fuhrman, S. H. (1995). Opportunity-to-learn standards and the state role in education. *Teachers College Record, 96*(3), 432–457.

Elmore, R. F., & McLaughlin, M. W. (1988). *Steady work: Policy, practice, and the reform of American education.* Santa Monica, CA: Rand Corporation.

ERIC Clearinghouse on Educational Management. (1981). *School effectiveness. The best of ERIC on educational management* (No. 62). Eugene, OR: Author.

Evans, W., Murray, S., & Schwab, R. (1997). *State education finance policy after court mandated reform: The legacy of Serrano. 1996 proceedings of the eighty-ninth annual conference on taxation.* Washington, DC: National Tax Association–Tax Institute of America.

Fantini, M., & Gittell, M. (1973). *Decentralization: Achieving reform.* New York: Praeger.

Firestone, W., Fuhrman, S., & Kirst, M. (1991). State educational reform since 1983: Appraisal and the future. *Educational Policy, 5*(3), 233–250.

Firestone, W. A., Mayrowetz, D., & Fairman, J. (1998). Performance-based assessment and instructional change: The effects of testing in Maine and Maryland. *Educational Evaluation and Policy Analysis, 20*(2), 95.

Firestone, W. A., & Pennell, J. R. (1997). Designing state-sponsored teacher networks: A comparison of two cases. *American Educational Research Journal, 34*(2), 237–266.

Flanigan, J. (1992). Significant trends in educational finance 1980–85. *International Journal of Educational Reform, 1*(3), 248–254.

Fowler, F. C. (2000). *Policy studies for educational leaders.* Upper Saddle River, NJ: Prentice-Hall.

Freeman, D. J. (1985). *Public response to proposals for raising academic standards in secondary schools* (Research series No. 163). East Lansing: Michigan State University, Institute for Research on Teaching.

Fry, P. O. (1992). *Schools for the 21st century program in Washington state: A case study.* New Brunswick, NJ: Consortium for Policy Research in Education.

Fuhrman, S. (1974). *Local control: Fear or fantasy. A report of the New Jersey Education Reform Project.* Newark, NJ: Greater Newark Urban Coalition.

Fuhrman, S. (Ed.). (1993a). *Designing coherent education policy: Improving the system.* San Francisco: Jossey-Bass.

Fuhrman, S. (1993b). The politics of coherence. In S. Fuhrman (Ed.), *Designing coherent policy: Improving the system.* San Francisco: Jossey-Bass.

Fuhrman, S. (1994). *Politics and systemic education reform* (CPRE Policy Briefs): Consortium for Policy Research in Education, New Brunswick, NJ.

Fuhrman, S. (1999). *The new accountability* (CPRE Policy Brief RB-27). Consortium for Policy Research in Education, Philadelphia.

Fuhrman, S. (Ed.). (2001). *From the capitol to the classroom: Standards-based reform in the states.* Chicago: University of Chicago Press.

Fuhrman, S., Clune, W., & Elmore, R. (1991). Research on education reform: Lessons on the implementation of policy. In A. Odden (Ed.), *Education policy implementation* (pp. 197–218). Albany: State University of New York Press.

Fuhrman, S., & Elmore, R. (1992). *Takeover and deregulation: Working models of new state and local regulatory relationships* (RR-024). Philadelphia: Consortium for Policy Research in Education.

Fuhrman, S., & Elmore, R. (1995). Ruling out rules: The evolution of deregulation in state education policy. *Teachers College Record, 97*(2), 279–309.

Fuhrman, S., & Elmore, R. (2001). Holding schools accountable: Is it working? *Phi Delta Kappan, 83*(1), 67–72.

Fuhrman, S., & Johnson, S. M. (1994). Lessons from Victoria. *Phi Delta Kappan, 75*(10), 770–772, 774.

Fullan, M. G. (1996). Turning systemic thinking on its head. *Phi Delta Kappan, 77*(6), 420–423.

Fullan, M., & Miles, M. (1992). Getting reform right: What works and what doesn't. *Phi Delta Kappan, 73*(10), 745–752.

Fullan, M., & Stiegelbauer, S. (1991). *The new meaning of educational change* (2nd ed.). New York: Teachers College Press.

Gerstner, L. V., Jr. (1995). Reinventing education: Entrepreneurship in America's public schools, and the special role of business in catalyzing educational change. *Multimedia Today, 3*(4), 24–29.

Gewertz, C. (2001). A hard lesson for Kansas City's troubled schools. *Education Week, 19*(33), 1, 20–21.

Gewertz, C. (2002). It's official: State takes over Philadelphia schools. *Education Week, 21*(16), 1, 14, 15.

Glatthorn, A. A. (1981). Curriculum change in loosely coupled systems. *Educational Leadership, 39*(2), 110–113.

Glatthorn, A. A. (1999). Curriculum alignment revisited. *Journal of Curriculum and Supervision, 15*(1), 26–34.

Goertz, M. E. (2000, April). *Local accountability: The role of the district and school in monitoring policy, practice and achievement.* Paper presented at the annual meeting of the American Educational Research Association, New Orleans.

Goertz, M. E. (2001a). *The federal role in an era of standards-based reforms. In the future of the federal role in elementary and secondary education* (pp. 51–59). Washington, DC: Center on Education Policy.

Goertz, M. E. (2001b). Redefining government roles in an era of standards-based reform. *Phi Delta Kappan, 83*(1), 62–66.

Goertz, M. E., & Duffy, M. C. (2001). *Assessment and accountability across the 50 states* (RB-33). Philadelphia: Consortium for Policy Research in Education.

Goertz, M. E., & Pitcher, B. (1985). *The impact of NTE use by states on teacher selection* (ETS-RR-85–1). Princeton, NJ: Educational Testing Service.

Goldman, P., & Conley, D. T. (1997, March). *Persistence, disillusionment, and compliance in educator reactions to state school reform.* Paper presented at the annual meeting of the American Educational Research Association, Chicago.

Goodlad, J. (1984). *A place called school: Prospects for the future.* New York: McGraw-Hill.

Goodlad, J. (Ed.). (1987). *The ecology of school renewal.* Chicago: University of Chicago Press.

Goodlad, J. I. (1994). The National Network for Educational Renewal. *Phi Delta Kappan, 75*(8), 632–638.

Goodman, K. (1995). Forced choices in a non-crisis: A critique of the report of the California reading task force. *Education Week, 15*(11), 39, 42.

Goodman, R. H., & Zimmerman, William G., Jr. (2000). *Thinking differently: Recommendations for 21st century school board/superintendent leadership, governance, and teamwork for high student achievement.* Marlborough, MA: Educational Research Service and New England School Development Council.

Gordon, J. (1990). Can business save the schools? *Training, 27*(8), 19–27.

Grant, G. (1973). Shaping social policy: The politics of the Coleman report. *Teachers College Record, 75*(1), 17–54.

Grant, S. G. (1997). Appeasing the right, missing the point? Reading the New York State social studies framework. *Social Education, 61*(2), 102–106.

Grant, S. G. (2000). Teachers and tests: Exploring teachers' perceptions of changes in the New York State testing program. *Education Policy Analysis Archives, 8*(14). http://www.epaa.asu.edu/epaa/v8n14.html

Greenwald, R., Hedges, L. V., & Laine, R. D. (1996). The effect of school resources on student achievement. *Review of Educational Research, 66*(3), 361–396.

Grissmer, D., Flanagan, A., Kawata, J., & Williamson, S. (2000). *Improving student achievement: What state NAEP test scores tell us.* Santa Monica, CA: Rand Corporation.

Grossman, P., Kirst, M., & Schmidt-Posner, J. (1986). On the trail of the omnibeast: Evaluating omnibus education reforms in the 1980s. *Educational Evaluation and Policy Analysis, 8*(3), 253–266.

Guskey, T. R., & Peterson, K. D. (1995/1996). The road to classroom change. *Educational Leadership, 53*(4), 10–14.

Guthrie, J. (1986). School-based management: The next needed education reform. *Phi Delta Kappan. 68*(4), 305–309.

Hallinger, P., & Heck, R. H. (1998). Exploring the principal's contribution to school effectiveness: 1980–1995. *School Effectiveness and School Improvement, 9*(2), 157–191.

Halperin, S. (1994, November). *School-to-work: A larger vision.* Paper presented at the Statewide School-to-Work Conference, Newport, RI.

Hanks, D. B. (1997). *School choice programs: What's happening in the states, 1997.* Heritage Foundation, Washington, DC.

Hanushek, E. A. (1994). *Making schools work: Improving performance and controlling costs.* Washington, DC: Brookings Institution Press.

Hard bargaining. (2002). *Education Week, 21*(32), 28.

Harp, L. (1991). Schools urged to revamp instruction to stress workforce skills. *Education Week, 40*(10), 11.

Harp, L. (1993). Pa. parent becomes mother of "outcomes" revolt. *Education Week, 13*(3), 21.

Harrington, K. (1999). The sound and fury of teacher testing in Massachusetts. *Metropolitan Universities: An International Forum, 10*(2), 57–62.

Harrington-Lueker, D. (2000). When educators cheat. *School Administrator, 57*(11), 32–33, 35–39.

Haycock, K. (2001). Closing the achievement gap. *Educational Leadership, 58*(6), 6–11.

Henry, R. J., & Kettlewell, J. S. (1999). Georgia's P–16 partnerships. *Metropolitan Universities: An International Forum, 10*(2), 33–40.

Hess, A. (1999). Expectations, opportunity, capacity, and will: The four essential components of Chicago school reform. *Educational Policy, 13*(4), 494–517.

Hess, R. (1995, August–September). *Agendas, activity, and education reform: Policy diffusion and controversy in urban school districts, 1992–1995.* Paper presented at the annual meeting of the American Political Science Association, Chicago.

Hill, P. (2001). *Hero worship.* Palo Alto, CA: Hoover Institution.

Hillocks, G. Jr. (2002). *The testing trap: How state writing assessments control learning.* New York: Teachers College Press.

Hirth, M. (1996). Systemic reform, equity, and school finance reform: Essential policy linkages. *Educational Policy, 10*(4), 468–479.

Hoff, D. J. (1999). Kansas to revise standards without citing evolution. *Education Week, 19*(8), 16.

Hoff, D. J. (2000). Testing foes hope to stoke middle-class ire. *Education Week, 19*(28), 24, 31.

Hoff, D. J. (2001a). Group to take Texas reform tools nationwide. *Education Week, 21*(11), 5.

Hoff, D. J. (2001b). Panel reviews how states post education data online. *Education Week, 21*(10), 14.

Hoff, D. J. (2001c). Title I study: As teachers hone their craft, children gain. *Education Week, 21*(1), 44.

Hoff, D. J. (2001d). A world-class education eludes many in the U.S. *Education Week, 20*(30), 1, 14, 15.

Holayter, M. C. (1998). *Commission on Student Learning report.* Seattle: New Horizons for Learning.

Holmes Group. (1986). *Tomorrow's teachers.* East Lansing, MI: Author.

Hoxby, C. (2001). *Testing is about openness and openness works.* Hoover Institute. http://www.hoover.stanford.edu/pubaffairs/we/current/hoxby_0701.html

Hudgins, H. C., Jr. (1975). *Milliken v. Bradley: The Supreme Court draws a line.* Paper presented at the National Organization on Legal Problems of Education, Topeka, KS.

Jacobson, L. (1999). Outspoken state chief in Georgia still an "outsider" in second term. *Education Week, 18*(40), 1, 14–15.

Jacobson, L. (2000). Georgia governor's broad education plans stir debate. *Education Week, 19*(20), 15.

Jennings, N. E. (1996). *Interpreting policy in real classrooms: Case studies of state reform and teacher practice.* New York: Teachers College Press.

Johnson, J. (1995). *Assignment incomplete: The unfinished business of education reform. A report from Public Agenda.* Institute for Educational Leadership, Washington, DC, and Public Agenda Foundation, New York.

Johnson, J., & Immerwahr, J. (1995). First things first: What Americans expect from the public schools. A report from Public Agenda. *American Educator, 18*(4), 4–6, 8, 11–13, 44–45.

Johnson, M. J., & Pajares, F. (1996). When shared decision making works: A 3–year longitudinal study. *American Educational Research Journal, 33*(3), 599–627.

Johnson, P. E., & Logan, J. (2000). Efficacy and productivity: The future of school-based decision-making councils in Kentucky. *Journal of School Leadership, 10*(4), 311–331.

Johnston, R. C. (1996a). Calif. budget allows for smaller classes. *Education Week, 15*, 25.

Johnston, R. C. (1996b). In '96 sessions, charter laws keep spreading. *Education Week, 16*(14), 14, 19.

Johnston, R. C. (1999). Governors vie with chiefs on policy, politics. *Education Week, 18*(35), 1, 22.

Johnston, R. C. (2001). Fiscal ills persist in Philadelphia despite political shifts. *Education Week, 20*(25), 8.

Johnston, R. C., & Sandham, J. L. (1999). States increasingly flexing their policy muscle. *Education Week, 18*(31), 1, 19–20.

Joint Center for the Study of Educational Policy. (1996). *A review of research on the Kentucky education reform act 1995 (KERA).* Louisville: Kentucky University, Louisville University.

Jones, M. G., Jones, B. D., Hardin, B., Chapman, L., Yarbrough, T., & Davis, M. (1999). The impact of high-stakes testing on teachers and students in North Carolina. *Phi Delta Kappan, 81*(3), 199–203.

Joyner, C. C. (1999). *Ed-flex program: Increase in flexibility useful but limited by scope of waiver authority. Testimony before the Subcommittee on Early Childhood, Youth and Families, Committee on Education and the Workforce, House of Representatives* (GAO/T-HEHS-99–67). Washington, DC: U.S. General Accounting Office, Health, Education and Human Services Division.

Just for the Kids. (2002). http://www.just4kids.org/us/us_home.asp

Kannapel, P. J. (1995, April). *Opposition to outcome-based education in Kentucky.* Paper presented at the annual meeting of the American Educational Research Association, San Francisco.

Kearns, D., & Doyle, D. (1988). *Winning the brain race: A bold plan to make our schools competitive.* San Francisco: ICS Press.

Keller, B. (2001). Texas group makes news with data. *Education Week, 21*(13), 1, 21.

Keller, B. (2002). Rift over schools chief leads MD. to intervene. *Education Week, 21*(22), 5.

Kelley, C., Odden, A., Milanowski, A., & Heneman, H., III. (2000). *The motivational effects of school-based performance awards* (CPRE Policy Brief RB-29). Consortium for Policy Research in Education, Philadelphia.

Kerchner, C., & Caufman, K. D. (1995). Lurching toward professionalism: The saga of teacher unionism. *Elementary School Journal, 96*(1), 107–122.

Kerchner, C., Koppich, J., & Weeres, J. (1997). *United mind workers: Unions and teaching in the knowledge society.* San Francisco: Jossey-Bass.

Kerchner, C., Koppich, J., & Weeres, J. (1998a). "New and improved" teacher unionism: But will it wash? *Educational Leadership, 55*(5), 21–24.

Kerchner, C., Koppich, J. E., & Weeres, J. G. (1998b). *Taking charge of quality: How teachers and unions can revitalize schools. An introduction and companion to "United Mind Workers."* San Francisco, CA: Jossey-Bass.

Kimmelman, P., Kroeze, D., Schmidt, W., van der Ploeg, A., McNeely, M., & Tan, A. (1999). *A first look at what we can learn from high performing school districts: An analysis of TIMSS data from the First in the World Consortium* (SAI-1999–3011). Washington, DC: U. S. Department of Education, National Institute on Student Achievement Curriculum and Assessment.

King, R. A., & Mathers, J. K. (1997). Improving schools through performance-based accountability and financial rewards. *Journal of Education Finance, 23*(2), 147–176.

Kirp, D. L., & Driver, C. E. (1995). The aspirations of systemic reform meet the realities of localism. *Educational Administration Quarterly, 31*(4), 589–612.

Kirst, M. (1984). *Who controls our schools?* New York: Freeman.

Kirst, M. (2000). *Overcoming the high school senior slump: New education policies.* Palo Alto, CA: Stanford University.

Kirst, M., & Bulkley, K. (2000). "New, improved" mayors take over city schools. *Phi Delta Kappan, 81*(7), 538–540, 542–546.

Klecker, B., & Loadman, W. E. (1996, April). *A study of principals' openness to change in 168 restructuring schools.* Paper presented at the annual meeting of the American Educational Research Association, New York.

Koretz, D. (1991, April). *The effects of high-stakes testing on achievement: Preliminary findings about generalization across tests.* Paper presented at the annual meeting of the American Educational Research Association, Chicago.

Koretz, D. (1992). What happened to test scores, and why? *Educational Measurement, Issues and Practice, 11*(4), 7–11.

Kozol, J. (1991). *Savage inequalities: Children in America's schools.* New York: Harper Perennial.

Ladd, H. F. (Ed.). (1996). *Holding schools accountable: Performance-based reform in education.* Washington, DC: Brookings Institution Press.

Ladson-Billings, G., & Darling-Hammond, L. (2000). *The validity of national board for professional teaching standards (NBPTS)/interstate new teacher assessment and support consortium (INTASC) assessments for effective urban teachers: Findings and implications for assessments.* Washington, DC: National Partnership for Excellence and Accountability in Teaching.

Lashway, L. (2001). *The new standards and accountability: Will rewards and sanctions motivate America's schools to peak performance?* ERIC Clearinghouse on Educational Management, Eugene, OR.

Lawson, M. (1998). Calif. education officials approve back-to-basics standards in math. *Education Week, 17*(18), 6.

Lawton, M. (1995a). Close to deadline, Wilson signs bill to create assessment system. *Education Week, 15*(3), 25.

Lawton, M. (1995b). Students fall short in NAEP geography test. *Education Week, 15*(8), 1, 23.

Lawton, M. (1996). Calif. districts hit barriers on road to tests. *Education Week, 15*(34), 12.

Leithwood, K., Jantzi, D., & Steinbach, R. (1999). Do school councils matter? *Educational Policy, 13*(4), 467–493.

Lemann, N. (1995, August). The structure of success in America and the great sorting machine. *The Atlantic Monthly-Atlantic Unbound, 276*(2), 41.

Lemann, N. (1999). *The big test: The secret history of the American meritocracy.* New York: Farrar, Straus & Giroux.

Le Métais, J. (1997). *Values and aims in curriculum and assessment frameworks.* International Review of Curriculum and Assessment.

Levin, H. M. (1970). *A new model of school effectiveness.* Palo Alto, CA: Stanford Center for Research and Development in Teaching.

Levin, H. M. (1989). *Accelerated schools: A new strategy for at-risk students.* Bloomington, IN: Consortium on Educational Policy Studies.

Lieberman, A., & Grolnick, M. (1996). Networks and reform in American education. *Teachers College Record, 98*(1), 7–45.

Lieberman, M. C. (1960). *The future of public education.* Chicago: University of Chicago Press.

Lipsky, M. (1980). *Street-level bureaucracy: Dilemmas of the individual in public services.* New York: Sage.

Little, J. W. (1982). Norms of collegiality and experimentation: Workplace conditions of school success. *American Educational Research Journal*, 19(3), 325–340.

Little, J. W. (1990). The persistence of privacy: Autonomy and initiative in teachers' professional relations. *Teachers College Record*, 91(4), 509–536.

Little, J. W. (1993). Teachers' professional development in a climate of educational reform. *Educational Evaluation and Policy Analysis*, 15(2), 129–151.

Little, J. W., Erbstein, N., & Walker, L. (1996). *High school restructuring and vocational reform: The question of "fit" in two schools.* National Center for Research in Vocational Education, Berkeley.

Little, J. W., Erbstein, N., & Walker, L. (2001). High school restructuring and vocational reform: The question of "fit" in two schools. *NASSP Bulletin*, 85(635), 17–25.

Lowi, T. J. (1972). Four systems of policy, politics, and choice. *Public Administration Review*, 32, 298–310.

Lusi, S. F. (1997). *The role of state departments of education in complex school reform.* New York: Teachers College Press.

Madaus, G. F., Airasian, P. W., & Kellaghan, T. (1980). *School effectiveness: A reassessment of the evidence.* New York: McGraw-Hill.

Malen, B., & Ogawa, R. T. (1988). Professional–patron influence on site-based governance councils: A confounding case study. *Educational Evaluation and Policy Analysis*, 10(4), 251–270.

Malen, B., Ogawa, R., & Kranz, J. (1990). What do we know about school-based management? A case study of the literature—a call for research. In W. H. Clune & J. F. Witte (Eds.), *Choice and control in American education* (Vol. 2, pp. 289–342). Philadelphia: Falmer.

Malico, M. K. (1999, August 28). Clinton announces $95 million in support for charter schools. *U.S. Department of Education.* http://www.ed.gov/Press Releases/08-1999/support.html

Manno, B. V., Finn, C. E., Jr., & Vanourek, G. (2000). Charter school accountability: Problems and prospects. *Education Policy*, 14(4), 473–493.

Manzo, K. K. (2001). Protests over state testing widespread. *Education Week*, 20(36), 1, 26.

Marsh, D. D., & LeFever, K. (1997, March). *Educational leadership in a policy context: What happens when student performance standards are clear?* Paper presented at the annual meeting of the American Educational Research Association, Chicago.

Marzano, R. (2000). *A new era of school reform: Going where the research takes us* (#RJ96006101). Aurora, CO: Mid-Continent Research for Education and Learning.

Massachusetts Coalition for Authentic Reform in Education. (2002). *Statement on the MCAS and education reform by the Coalition for Authentic Reform in Education (CARE).* Author. http://www.caremass.org

Massell, D. (2000). *The district role in building capacity: Four strategies* (CPRE Policy Brief RB-32). Consortium for Policy Research in Education, Philadelphia.

Massell, D. (2001). The theory and practice of using data to build capacity: State and local strategies and their effects. In S. H. Fuhrman (Ed.), *From the capitol to the classroom*. Chicago: University of Chicago Press.

Massell, D., & Fuhrman, S. (1994). *Ten years of state education reform, 1983–1993: Overview with four case studies*. Philadelphia: Center for Policy Research in Education.

Massell, D., Kirst, M., & Hoppe, D. (1997). *Persistence and change: Standards-based systemic reform in nine states* (CPRE Policy Brief RB-21). Consortium for Policy Research in Education, Philadelphia.

Mathews, J. (2000, March 14). Tennessee system for gauging results angers some educators but gains acceptance elsewhere. *Washington Post,* p. A07.

McDermott, K. A. (2000). Barriers to large-scale success of models for urban school reform. *Educational Evaluation and Policy Analysis, 22*(1), 83–89.

McLaughlin, M. (1991). The RAND change agent study: Ten years later. In A. Odden (Ed.), *Education policy implementation* (pp. 143–156). Albany: State University of New York Press.

McMillan, J. H. (2001). Secondary teachers' classroom assessment and grading practices. *Educational Measurement: Issues and Practice, 20*(1), 20–32.

McMillan, J. H., & Nash, S. (2000, April). *Teacher classroom assessment and grading practices decision making*. Paper presented at the annual meeting of the National Council on Measurement in Education, New Orleans.

McQueen, A. (1998). Schools get first taste of new reform funds. *Education Week, 18*(10), 28, 34.

Meier, D. (1968). *The Coleman report.*

Meier, D. (Ed.). (2000). *Will standards save public education?* Boston: Beacon Press.

Mertens, S., & Yarger, S. (1988). Teaching as a profession: Leadership, empowerment, and involvement. *Journal of Teacher Education, 39*(1), 32–38.

Miller, S. K. (1983, April). *The history of effective schools research: A critical overview* (Working draft). Paper presented as part of the Symposium "Research on Effective Schools: State of the Art" at the annual meeting of the American Educational Research Association, Montreal.

Miller-Whitehead, M. (1997). *A longitudinal analysis of science scale scores grades 2–8 in Tennessee for 1992–1996*. ED414170.

*Milliken, governor of Michigan et al. v. Bradley et al. Certiorari to the United States Court of Appeals for the Sixth Circuit: Syllabus*. Washington, DC (1974).

Mintrom, M. (2000). *Leveraging local innovation: The case of Michigan's charter schools. Executive summary*. Lansing, MI: Institute for Public Policy and Social Research.

Murnane, R., & Levy, F. (1996a). Evidence from fifteen schools in Austin, Texas. In G. Burtless (Ed.), *Does money matter? The effects of school resources on student achievement and adult success* (pp. 93–96). Washington, DC: Brookings Institution Press.

Murnane, R., & Levy, F. (1996b). *Teaching the new basic skills. Principles for educating children to thrive in a changing economy*. New York: Free Press.

Murphy, J. (1990). *The educational reform movement of the 1980s: Perspectives and cases*. Berkeley: McCutchan.

Murphy, J. (1994, April). *Restructuring schools in Kentucky: Insights from super-intendents.* Paper presented at the annual meeting of the American Educational Research Association, New Orleans.

Murphy, J., & Beck, L. G. (1995). *School-based management as school reform: Taking stock.* Thousand Oaks, CA: Corwin Press.

Murray, C. E. (2000, April). *Exploring the "new" unionism: Perceptions of recently tenured teachers.* Paper presented at the annual meeting of the American Educational Research Association, New Orleans.

Myers, C. B. (1997, February–March). *Reconceptualizing learning, teaching, and schools as the next stage in teacher education reform and school renewal.* Paper presented at the annual meeting of the American Association of Colleges for Teacher Education, Phoenix, AZ.

Nasstrom, R. R. (1986, August). *A plan for academic excellence: Competition between secondary and post-secondary institutions.* Paper presented at the National Conference of Professors of Educational Administration, Flagstaff, AZ.

National Alliance of Business. (1989). *A blueprint for business on restructuring education: Corporate action package* (ED 312 486). Washington, DC: Author.

National Alliance of Business. (2001). *Emerging trends in contextual learning show positive results for students.* Washington, DC: Author.

National Center for Education Statistics. (1997). *High school course taking in the core subject areas: Indicator of the month* (extracted from "The Condition of Education, 1996"). Washington, DC: US. Department of Education.

National Center for Education Statistics. (2001). *Revenues and expenditures for public elementary and secondary education: School year 1998–99* (Statistics in Brief NCES 2001–321). Washington, DC: U.S. Department of Education, Office of Educational Research and Improvement.

National Center for Educational Accountability. (2002). http://www.measureto learn.org

National Commission on Excellence in Education. (1983). *A nation at risk: The imperative for educational reform.* Washington, DC: U.S. Government Printing Office.

Nelson, B., Berman, P., Ericson, J., Kamprath, N., Perry, R., Silverman, D., & Solomon, D. (2000). *The state of charter schools, 2000. National study of charter schools. Fourth-year report* (SAI-2000–3000). Emeryville, CA: RPP International.

Nelson, F. H., & Rosen, M. (1996). *Are teachers' unions hurting American education? A state-by-state analysis of the impact of collective bargaining among teachers on student performance.* Milwaukee: Institute for Wisconsin's Future.

Newmann, F. M., & Associates. (1996). *Authentic achievement: Restructuring schools for intellectual quality.* San Francisco: Jossey-Bass.

Nolte, M. C. (1974). Brush up in one short sitting: Ten years of tumult in school law, and their lessons. *American School Board Journal, 161*(1), 48–51.

Oakes, J. (1985). *Keeping track: How schools structure inequality.* New Haven, CT: Yale University Press.

Oakes, J. (1987). Tracking in secondary schools: A contextual perspective. *Educational Psychology, 22,* 129–153.

Oakes, J., & Lipton, M. (1992). Detracking schools: Early lessons from the field. *Phi Delta Kappan, 73*(6), 448–454.

Odden, A. (1991). The evolution of educational policy implementation. In A. Odden (Ed.), *Education policy implementation* (pp. 1–12). Albany: State University of New York Press.

Odden, A. (1992). *Rethinking school finance: An agenda for the 1990s.* San Francisco: Jossey-Bass.

Odden, A. (1995). Key issues in effective site-based management. *School Business Affairs, 61*(5), 4–12, 14, 16.

Odden, A. (1998). *Creating school finance policies that facilitate new goals* (CPRE Policy Brief RB-26). Philadelphia: Consortium for Policy Research in Education.

Odden, A. (2000). New and better forms of teacher compensation are possible. *Phi Delta Kappan, 81*(5), 361–366.

Odden, A. (2001). The new school finance. *Phi Delta Kappan, 83*(1), 85–91.

Odden, A., & Picus, L. (2000). *School finance: A policy perspective* (2nd ed.). New York: McGraw-Hill.

Odden, A., & Wohlstetter, P. (1992). The role of agenda setting in the politics of school finance: 1970–1990. *Educational Policy, 6*(4), 355–376.

Office of Educational Research and Improvement. (1999). *Effective leaders for today's schools: Synthesis of a policy forum on educational leadership.* Washington, DC: U.S. Department of Education.

Office of Elementary and Secondary Education. (1998). *Goals 2000: Reforming education to improve student achievement. Report to Congress.* Washington, DC: Author.

Office of Elementary and Secondary Education. (2001, October 29). *Reading excellence program.* U.S. Department of Education. http://www.ed.gov/offices/OESE/REA

Ohanian, S. (2001). News from the test resistance trail. *Phi Delta Kappan, 82*(5), 363–366.

Olson, L. (1990). Unexpectedly little interest found in state offers to waive key rules. *Education Week, 9*(29), 1, 19.

Olson, L. (1999). Following the plan. *Education Week, 18*(31), 28–30.

Olson, L. (2001a). Finding the right mix. *Education Week, 20*(17), 12–20.

Olson, L. (2001b). States turn to end-of-course tests to bolster high school curriculum. *Education Week, 20*(39), 1, 26, 17.

Olson, L. (2001c). Universities seek "seamless" link with K–12. *Education Week, 20*(21), 5.

Olson, L. (2002a). A "proficient" score depends on geography. *Education Week, 21*(23), 1, 14, 15.

Olson, L. (2002b). Survey shows state testing alters instructional practices. *Education Week, 21*(32), 14.

Olson, L. (2002c). Want to confirm state test scores? It's complex, but NAEP can do it. *Education Week, 21*(26), 1, 10, 11.

Olson, L., & Viadero, D. (2002). Law mandates scientific base for research. *Education Week, 21*(20), 1, 14, 15.

Oregon Business Council. (1996). *Restructuring K–12 education: An OBC action plan.* Portland: Oregon Business Council.

Orfield, G., & DeBray, E. H. (Eds.). (1999). *Hard work for good schools: Fact not fads in Title I reform.* Cambridge, MA: Harvard University Press.

Oxley, D. (1997, March). *Organizing schools into learning communities: Implications for a cultural change process.* Paper presented at the annual meeting of the American Educational Research Association, Chicago.

Pennell, J. R., & Firestone, W. A. (1996). Changing classroom practices through teacher networks: Matching program features with teacher characteristics and circumstances. *Teachers College Record, 98*(1), 46–76.

Peterson del Mar, D. (1994). *School-site councils.* ERIC Clearinghouse on Educational Management, Eugene, Or.

Peterson, K. D., Marks, H. M., & Warren, V. D. (1996). *SBDM in restructured schools: Organizational conditions, pedagogy and student learning.* Madison: Center on Organization and Restructuring of Schools, Wisconsin Center for Education Research.

Peterson, P., Rabe, B., & Wong, K. (1991). The maturation of redistributive programs. In A. Odden (Ed.), *Education policy implementation* (pp. 65–80). Albany: State University of New York Press.

Petrie, H. G. (Ed.). (1995). *Professionalization, partnership, and power: Building professional development schools.* Albany: State University of New York Press.

Picus, L. O. (2000). Student-level finance data: Wave of the future? *Clearing House, 74*(2), 75–80.

Pipho, C. (1998). The value-added side of standards. *Phi Delta Kappan, 79*(5), 341–342.

Pitsch, M. (1994, April 6). With students' aid, Clinton signs goals 2000. *Education Week,* pp. 1, 21.

Plank, D. N., & Boyd, W. L. (1994). Antipolitics, education, and institutional choice: The flight from democracy. *American Educational Research Journal, 31*(2), 263–281.

Pliska, A. M., & McQuaide, J. (1994). Pennsylvania's battle for student learning outcomes. *Educational Leadership, 75*(6), 66–69.

Pool, H. E., & Page, J. A. E. (1995). *Beyond tracking: Finding success in inclusive schools.* Phi Delta Kappa Educational Foundation, Bloomington, IN.

Pool, J. E., Ellett, C. D., Schiavone, S., & Carey-Lewis, C. (2001). How valid are the National Board of Professional Teaching standards assessments for predicting the quality of actual classroom teaching and learning? Results of six mini case studies. *Journal of Personnel Evaluation in Education, 15*(1), 31–48.

Popkewitz, T. S. (1991). *A political sociology of educational reform.* New York: Teachers College Press.

Prasch, J. (1984). Reversing the trend toward centralization. *Educational Leadership, 42*(2), 27–29.

Prestine, N. A., & McGreal, T. L. (1997). Fragile changes, sturdy lives: Implementing authentic assessment in schools. *Educational Administration Quarterly, 33*(3), 371–400.

Prichard Committee for Academic Excellence. (1985). *The path to a larger life: Creating Kentucky's educational future.* Lexington, KY: Author.

Prichard Committee for Academic Excellence. (1990). *The path to a larger life: Creating Kentucky's educational future.* (2nd ed.). Lexington, KY: Author.

Public Agenda. (2001a). *Reality check 2000* [Website]. http://www.publicagenda.org/specials/rc2000/reality.htm

Public Agenda. (2001b). *Reality check 2001* [Website]. http://www.publicagenda.org/specials/rc2001/reality.htm

Purkey, S., & Smith, M. (1983). Effective schools: A review. *Elementary School Journal, 83,* 427–452.

Rainwater, T. (2000). *ECS Statenotes: P–16 collaboration in the states.* Denver: Education Commission of the States.

Raywid, M. A. (1996). *Downsizing schools in big cities.* (ERIC Digest No. 112). ERIC Clearinghouse on Urban Education, New York.

Reckase, M. D. (2002, February). *Using NAEP to confirm state test results: An analysis of issues.* Paper presented at the Will No Child Truly Be Left Behind? The Challenge of Making this New Law Work conference, Washington, DC.

Reeves, D. B. (1998). Holding principals accountable. *School Administrator, 55*(9), 6–9, 4–12.

Reid, K. S. (2000). Governance report calls for overhaul. *Education Week, 20*(3), 1, 20.

Reid, K. S. (2001a). Chicago chief named amid urban turnover. *Education Week, 20*(42), 3.

Reid, K. S. (2001b). From worst to first. *Education Week, 20*(30), 32–37.

Resnick, L. B., & Wirt, J. G. (Eds.). (1996). *Linking school and work: Roles for standards and assessment* (Vol. 1). San Francisco: Jossey-Bass.

Rettig, M. D. (1992, April). *Policy adaptation and change: The case of the state takeover of the Jersey City Public Schools.* Paper presented at the annual meeting of the American Educational Research Association, San Francisco.

Reuter News Service. (1989, February 18). AT&T launches major restructuring. *Denver Post,* p. C-1.

Ribich, T. I. (1970). *Education and poverty revisited.* Paper presented at the staff conference of City University of New York, Sterling Forest, NY.

Richard, A. (2002). Florida breaking down walls between K–12, higher ed. *Education Week, 21*(22), 1, 26, 27.

Robelen, E. W. (2001). Off target? *Education Week, 21*(1), 1, 45–47.

Robelen, E. W. (2002a). An ESEA primer. *Education Week, 21*(16), 28, 29.

Robelen, E. W. (2002b). ESEA to boost federal role in education. *Education Week, 21*(16), 1, 28, 29, 31.

Robelen, E. W., & Walsh, M. (2002). Bush proposal: Give tax credit for K–12 tuition. *Education Week, 21*(22), 1, 37.

Rollow, S. G., & Yanguas, M. J. (1996). *The road to emergent restructuring and strong democracy: One Chicago school's experience of reform.* Wisconsin Center for Education Research and Center on Organization and Restructuring of Schools, Madison.

Rose, L. C., & Gallup, A. M. (1999). The 31st annual Phi Delta Kappa/Gallup poll of the public's attitudes toward the public schools. *Phi Delta Kappan, 81*(1), 41–58.

Rose, L. C., & Gallup, A. M. (2001). The 33rd annual Phi Delta Kappa/Gallup poll of the public's attitudes toward the public schools. *Phi Delta Kappan, 83*(1), 41–48.

Rothman, R. (1990, October 24). Choice insufficient to reform schools, RAND says. *Education Week, 10*(8), 6.

Rothman, R. (1992a). NAEP board mulls new standards for math performance. *Education Week, 11*(35), 5.

Rothman, R. (1992b). Pennsylvania board delays vote on "learning outcomes" plan. *Education Week, 12*(3), 19.

Rothstein, R. (2001). New federal roles in education. In Center on Education Policy (Ed.), *The future of the federal role in elementary and secondary education.* Washington, DC: Author.

Rouk, U. (2000). *"Tough love": State accountability policies push student achievement.* Austin, TX: Southwest Educational Development Laboratory.

Rutter, M., Maughan, B., Mortimore, P., Ouston, J., & Smith, A. (1979). *Fifteen thousand hours: Secondary schools and their effects on children.* Cambridge, MA: Harvard University Press.

Sack, J. L. (2000). Del. ties school job reviews to student tests. *Education Week, 19*(34), 24, 27.

Sack, J. L. (2002). Mich. may intervene in Inkster–Edison standoff. *Education Week, 21*(33), 3.

Sanders, W. L., & Horn, S. P. (1998). Research findings from the Tennessee value-added assessment system (TVAAS) database: Implications for educational evaluation and research. *Journal of Personnel Evaluation in Education, 12*(3), 247–256.

Sandham, J. L. (1999). Partisan politics lend new twist to state debates. *Education Week, 18*(39), 1, 16–17.

Sarason, S. (1971). *The culture of the school and the problem of change.* Boston: Allyn & Bacon.

Sarason, S. (1990). *The predictable failure of educational reform.* San Francisco: Jossey-Bass.

Schalock, D., & Cowart, B. (1993). *Oregon's design for 21st century schools and its implications for teachers: A paradigm shift.* Monmouth: Western Oregon State College.

Schmidt, P. (1995). Baltimore resists order to "reconstitute" 3 schools. *Education Week, 14*(3).

Schmidt, W. H., & Prawat, R. S. (1999). What does the third international mathematics and science study tell us about where to draw the line in the top-down versus bottom-up debate? *Educational Evaluation and Policy Analysis, 21*(1), 85–91.

Schwartz, W. (1996). *How well are charter schools serving urban and minority students?* (ERIC/CUE Digest No. 119). New York: ERIC Clearinghouse on Urban Education.

Scott, R. (1983). *Curriculum alignment as a model for school improvement.* Paper presented at the 1982 Regional Exchange Workshop, Los Angeles, CA.

Seattle Public Schools. (1997). *Weighted student formula: Budget allocations to schools for the 1997–98 school year.* Seattle: Author.

Secretary's Commission on Achieving Necessary Skills. (1991). *What work requires of schools: A SCANS report for America 2000.* Washington, DC: U.S. Department of Labor.

Sexton, R. F. (1995). *Building citizen and parent support for school reform: The Prichard Committee experience.* Lexington, KY: Prichard Committee for Academic Excellence.

Seymour, L. (2000, April 23). Innovative methods used to review facts. *Washington Post,* p. VD1.

Shapiro, N. S., & Haeger, J. (1999). The K–16 challenge: The Maryland case. *Metropolitan Universities: An International Forum, 10*(2), 25–32.

Shedd, J., & Bacharach, S. (1991). *Tangled hierarchies: Teachers as professionals and the management of schools.* San Francisco: Jossey-Bass.

Shields, C. M. (1996). Creating a learning community in a multicultural setting: Issues of leadership. *Journal of School Leadership, 6*(1), 47–74.

Siskin, L. S. (2001). *Daydreams and nightmares: Implementing the new regents exams in New York.* Unpublished manuscript.

Siskin, L. S., & Little, J. W. (Eds.). (1995). *The subjects in question: Departmental organization and the high school.* New York: Teachers College Press.

Sizer, T. (1992). A working design: The coalition of essential schools and re:Learning. *A leader's guide to school restructuring: A special report of the NASSP Commission on Restructuring.* Reston, VA: National Association of Secondary School Principals.

Sizer, T. (2000). A sense of place. In D. Meier (Ed.), *Will standards save public education?* Boston: Beacon Press.

Skrla, L. (2001). The influence of state accountability on teacher expectations and student performance. *The Review, 17*(2), 1–4.

Smith, A., & Wohlstetter, P. (2001). Reform through school networks: A new kind of authority and accountability. *Educational Policy, 15*(4), 499–519.

Smith, R. E. (2000, March 6). Research points to proficiency test stress. *Toledo Blade.*

Smith, W. F., & Fenstermacher, G. D. (Eds.). (1999). *Leadership for educational renewal: Developing a cadre of leaders.* San Francisco: Jossey-Bass.

Sommerfeld, M. (1995). Pioneering reform act under attack in Oregon. *Education Week, 14,* 13.

Souders, J., & Prescott, C. (1999). A case for contextual learning. *High School Magazine, 7*(3), 38–43.

Spillane, J. P. (1998). State policy and the non-monolithic nature of the local school district: Organizational and professional considerations. *American Educational Research Journal, 35*(1), 33–63.

Spillane, J. P. (2000a). Cognition and policy implementation: District policymakers and the reform of mathematics education. *Cognition and Instruction, 18*(2), 141–179.

Spillane, J. P. (2000b). A fifth-grade teacher's reconstruction of mathematics and literacy teaching: Exploring interactions among identity, learning, and subject matter. *Elementary School Journal, 100*(4), 307–330.

Spillane, J. P., & Callahan, K. A. (2000). Implementing state standards for science education: What district policy makers make of the hoopla. *Journal of Research in Science Teaching, 37*(5), 401–425.

Spillane, J. P., & Zeuli, J. S. (1999). Reform and teaching: Exploring patterns of practice in the context of national and state mathematics reforms. *Educational Evaluation and Policy Analysis, 21*(1), 1–28.

Spring, J. (1997). *Political agendas for education.* Mahwah, NJ: Erlbaum.

Steffy, B. E. (1992). Assault on the bureaucracy: Restructuring the Kentucky department of education. *International Journal of Educational Reform, 1*(1), 16–31.

Steffy, B. E. (1993). *The Kentucky Education Reform Act: Lessons for America.* Lancaster, PA: Technomics.

Stein, R. B. (1999). Seeking cooperation: Missouri's K–16 coalition. *Metropolitan Universities: An International Forum, 10*(2), 15–24.

Steinberg, A., Cushman, K., & Riordan, R. (1999). *Schooling for the real world: The essential guide to rigorous and relevant learning.* San Francisco: Jossey-Bass.

Steinberg, J. (2000, March 31). Under either Bush or Gore, new federal role in schools. *New York Times, 149*(51, 344), p. A1.

Steinberg, L. (1996). *Beyond the classroom: Why school reform has failed and what parents need to do.* New York: Simon & Schuster.

Stevenson, H., & Stigler, J. (1992). *The learning gap: Why our schools are failing and what we can learn from Japanese and Chinese education.* New York: Summit Books.

Stone, N. (1991). Does business have any business in education? *Harvard Business Review, 69*(2), 46–48, 52–55, 58–62.

Stout, K. E., & Stevens, B. (2000). The case of the failed diversity rule: A multiple streams analysis. *Educational Evaluation and Policy Analysis, 22*(4), 341–355.

Stricherz, M. (2001a). Governors seeking levers to improve education. *Education Week, 20*(28), 1, 16, 17.

Stricherz, M. (2001b). New York, Boston grant some schools more flexibility. *Education Week, 20*(42), 5.

Swanson, A. D. (1989). Restructuring educational governance: A challenge of the 1990s. *Educational Administration Quarterly, 25*(3), 268–293.

Taylor, D. L., & Bogotch, I. E. (1994). *School-level effects of teachers' participation in decision-making.* Baton Rouge: Louisiana State University Press.

Teddlie, C., & Stringfield, S. (1993). *Schools make a difference.* New York: Teachers College Press.

Texas Education Agency. (1993). *Public education waivers to improve student achievement, 1991–92* (TEA-GE3–200–01). Austin, TX: Author.

Third International Mathematics and Science Study. (1995). *U.S. TIMSS bulletin* (Vol. 43). Boston: TIMSS International Study Center.

Thompson, S. (2001). The authentic standards movement and its evil twin. *Phi Delta Kappan, 82*(5), 358–362.

Toch, T., Bennefield, R. M., & Bernstein, A. (1996). The case for tough standards. *U.S. News & World Report, 120*(13).

Tyack, D. (1974). *The one best system.* Cambridge, MA: Harvard University Press.

Tyack, D., & Cuban, L. (1995). *Tinkering toward utopia: A century of public school reform.* Cambridge, MA: Harvard University Press.

Tyack, D., & Tobin, W. (1994). The "grammar" of schooling: Why has it been so hard to change? *American Educational Research Journal, 31*(3), 453.

Tye, B. B. (1987). The deep structure of schooling. *Phi Delta Kappan, 69*(4), 281–284.

Urban, W. J. (1991). Is there a new teacher unionism? *Educational Theory, 41*(3), 331–338.

U.S. Department of Education. (2000, August 11). *Guidance on the Comprehensive School Reform Demonstration Program.* Washington, DC: Author. http://www.ed.gov/offices/OESE/compreform/csrdgui.html#B1

U.S. Department of Education. (2001). *No child left behind.* Washington, DC: Author.

U.S. Department of Education Planning and Evaluation Service. (2001). *The Longitudinal Evaluation of School Change and Performance* (LESCP) *in Title* I *schools.* Jessup, MD: U.S. Department of Education, Education Publications Center.

U.S. General Accounting Office. (1993). *Systemwide education reform: Federal leadership could facilitate district-level efforts* (GAO/HRD-93-97). Washington, DC: Author.

Valverde, G. A., & Schmidt, W. H. (1997). Refocusing U.S. math and science education: International comparisons of schooling hold important lessons for improving student achievement. *Issues in Science and Technology, 14*(2), 60.

Vergari, S. (2000). The regulatory styles of statewide charter school authorizers: Arizona, Massachusetts, and Michigan. *Educational Administration Quarterly, 36*(5), 730–757.

Vergon, C. B. (1988). The evolution of the school desegregation movement: Implications for equity and excellence. *Equity and Excellence, 24*(1), 26–35.

Verstegen, D. A. (1984, April). *The education block grant: How it measures up to meeting its stated and implied goals.* Paper presented at the annual meeting of the American Educational Research Association, New Orleans.

Verstegen, D. A. (1985, April). *The lawmakers respond: Texas education finance reform (Part* I): *Funding formulas—revisions and reviews.* Paper presented at the annual meeting of the American Educational Finance Association, Phoenix, AZ.

Verstegen, D. A. (1994a). *Historical overview: Fiscal provisions of the Individuals with Disabilities Education Act* (Policy Paper No. 2). Palo Alto, CA: American Institutes for Research in the Behavioral Sciences and Center for Special Education Finance.

Verstegen, D. A. (1994b). Reforming American education policy for the 21st century. *Educational Administration Quarterly, 30*(3), 365–390.

Verstegen, D. A. (1998). Judicial analysis during the new wave of school finance litigation: The new adequacy in education. *Journal of Education Finance, 24*(1), 51–68.

Viadero, D. (1991). Portland parents boycott schools over education for minorities. *Education Week, 10*(21), 5.

Viadero, D. (2000). High-stakes tests lead debate at researchers' gathering. *Education Week, 19*(34), 6.

Viadero, D. (2001). Memphis scraps redesign models in all its schools. *Education Week, 20*(42), 1, 19.

Washington State Board for Community and Technical Colleges. (1997). *Running start: 1995–96 annual progress report.* Olympia, WA: Author.

Watt, M. G. (1997, July). *National curriculum collaboration: The state of reform in the states and territories.* Paper presented at the biannual meeting of the Australian Curriculum Studies Association, Sydney.

Weick, K. (1976). Educational organizations as loosely coupled systems. *Administrative Science Quarterly, 21*(2), 1–19.

Weisman, J. (1991a). Business roundtable assessing state progress on reforms. *Education Week, 11*(12), 22.

Weisman, J. (1991b). Plan to pair business with government for reform is stymied in many states. *Education Week, 10*(21), 20–21.

Weisman, J. (1991c). Report cautiously optimistic on school–business ties. *Education Week, 10*(24), 19.

Weiss, C. H. (1993). Shared decision-making about what? A comparison of schools with and without teacher participation. *Teachers College Record, 95*(1), 69–92.

Weiss, E. M., & Weiss, S. G. (1998). *New directions in teacher evaluation* (ERIC Digest EDO-SP-97–9). Washington DC: ERIC Clearinghouse on Teaching and Teacher Education.

Weiss, S. (1999). *Americans' perceptions about public education* (Executive Summary). Denver: Education Commission of the States.

Wells, A. S., & Oakes, J. (1996). Potential pitfalls of systemic reform: Early lessons from research on detracking [Extra issue]. *Sociology of Education*, pp. 135–143.

Wenglinsky, H. H. (2000). *How teaching matters: Bringing the classroom back into discussions of teacher quality.* Princeton, NJ: Educational Testing Service.

Whitbread, N. (1974). How schools make a difference. *Forum for the Discussion of New Trends in Education, 16*(2), 40–44.

White, K. A. (1999). High-poverty schools score big on Ky. assessment. *Education Week, 18*(34), 18, 20.

White, P. A., Gamoran, A., Smithson, J., & Porter, A. C. (1996). Upgrading the high school math curriculum: Math coursetaking patterns in seven high schools in California and New York. *Educational Evaluation and Policy Analysis, 18*(4), 285–308.

Whitney, T. N., & Verstegen, D. A. (1997). *State school finance litigation: A summary and an analysis.* Denver: National Conference of State Legislatures.

Williams, A. (2000, March 26). Teaching to the test: Some say a growing focus on assessment is squeezing life out of classrooms. *The Register-Guard*, 1A, 14A.

Williams, B., & Bearer, K. (2001). *NBPTS-parallel certification and its impact on the public schools: A qualitative approach.*

Wilson, A. (1980). Landmarks in the literature: How powerful is schooling? *New York University Education Quarterly, 11*(3), 28–31.

Wilson, B. L., & Corbett, H. D. (1991). *Two state minimum competency testing programs and their effects on curriculum and instruction*. Philadelphia: Research for Better Schools.

Wirt, F. M., & Kirst, M. W. (1989). *Schools in conflict: The politics of education* (2nd ed.). Berkeley: McCutchan.

Wirt, F. M., & Kirst, M. W. (2001). *The political dynamics of American education* (2nd ed.). Richmond, CA: McCutchan.

Wise, A. E., & Leibbrand, J. A. (2000). Standards and teacher quality: Entering the new millennium. *Phi Delta Kappan, 81*(3), 612–616, 621.

Wohlstetter, P., & Mohrman, S. A. (1994). *School-based management: Promise and process* (CPRE Finance Briefs FB-05–12/94). Philadelphia: Consortium For Policy Research.

Wohlstetter, P., & Odden, A. (1992). Rethinking school-based management policy and research. *Educational Administration Quarterly, 18*(4), 529–549.

Wohlstetter, P., & Smith, A. K. (2000). A different approach to systemic reform: Network structures in Los Angeles. *Phi Delta Kappan, 81*(7), 508–510, 512–515.

Wohlstetter, P., Van Kirk, A. N., Robertson, P. J., & Mohrman, S. A. (1997). *Organizing for successful school-based management*. Alexandria, VA: Association for Supervision and Curriculum Development; Los Angeles: University of Southern California, Center on Educational Governance.

Xu, M. (1996). *Will raising standards improve student achievement? A review of the literature*. Albany: State University of New York, New York State Department of Education, Office of Elementary, Middle, Secondary and Continuing Education Research and Evaluation Team.

Yee, G., & Cuban, L. (1996). When is tenure long enough? A historical analysis of superintendent turnover and tenure in urban school districts. *Educational Administration Quarterly, 32*, 615–641.

Young, S. (1971, December). *Accountability and evaluation in the 70's: An overview*. Paper presented at the annual meeting of the Speech Communication Association.

Zernike, K. (2000, April 14). Teachers union to propose tougher standards for profession. *New York Times,* p. A11.

Ziebarth, T. (1999). *The changing landscape of education governance* (SI-99–4). Denver: Education Commission of the States.

Ziebarth, T. (2000). *Models of state education governance*. Denver: Education Commission of the States.

Ziebarth, T., & Rainwater, T. (2000). P–16 collaboration paves the way for achievement. *State Education Leader, 18*(3), 1.

Zimmerman, J., Norris, D., Kirkpatrick, J., Mann, A., & Herndon, R. (1990). *Partners for success: Business and education*. Portland, OR: National Association for Schools of Excellence.

Zirkel, P. A. (1999). The 30th anniversary of "Tinker." *Phi Delta Kappan, 81*(1), 34–40, 58.

# Index

*Abbott v. Burke*, 54
Abercrombie, K. L., 109
Ability grouping, 67–68, 87, 93
Academic Standards Commission
  (California), 141–142
Accelerated Schools, 86
Accountability systems
  local, 145–147, 160, 161, 163
  state, 1, 5, 10, 13, 46, 47, 50, 53,
    58–60, 68–70, 85, 113–114,
    146, 155, 165–166, 169, 181
Achievement gap, 44, 58, 69–70, 192
Adams, J. E., Jr., 113
Adequacy standards, 40–41, 60–63
Aims of education, 189–190
Airasian, P. W., 55
Akers, J., 80
Alabama, 40
Alignment. *See* Policy alignment
Allen, J. L., 123
Ambach, G., 66
American Association of School
  Administrators, 76
American College Testing (ACT), 77–
  79, 118, 184
American Federation of Teachers
  (AFT), 76, 104, 106–107, 174
*American High School Today, The*
  (Conant), 67
American Legislative Exchange
  Council, 60
*America's Choice*, 128
Amster, J., 81
Angus, D. L., 120

Annenberg Challenge, 82
Anthony, P. G., 40
Archer, J., 164
Archibald, D. A., 119
Arizona, 51, 81
Assessment systems
  local school district, 29
  state, 1, 2, 10, 13, 28–29, 35, 47,
    69, 85, 111, 146, 181
Association of American Universities,
  124
Australia, 168
Ayers, W., 50

Bacharach, S., 174
Bader, B. D., 54
Ball, G. C., 81
Baltimore, Maryland, 150
Balz, D., 8, 71
Banchero, S., 123
Barnes, Roy, 127
Barth, P., 57
Basic skills, 44, 66, 76
Bearer, K., 172
Beck, L. G., 49
Belcher, C. L., 154–155, 173
Bell, A. S., 142
Bennefield, R. M., 80, 81
Bennett, William, 2, 43
Berends, M., 89
Berman, P., 84, 128, 188
Bernstein, A., 80, 81
Betts, J. R., 108
Bird, T., 173

Blair, J., 41, 75, 106, 116, 164
Blank, R. K., 46
Blase, J., 105
Block, A. W., 55
Bodone, F., 118
Bogotch, I. E., 49
Bond, L., 172
Bonuses, 14
Borman, G. D., 192
Borsuk, A. J., 107
Boser, U., 73, 107, 169
Boyd, W. L., 52, 64
Bridges, E., 49
Bulkley, K., 51–52, 64, 72, 149
Bullmaster, M. L., 116
Bully pulpit, 26
Burtless, G., 60
Bush, George H. W., 23, 33–34
Bush, George W., 34
Bush, Jeb, 127
Bush, M., 46
Bushweller, K., 184
Business community, 6–7, 20–21, 34, 79–81

Cain, G. G., 55
California, 14, 40, 43, 44, 46, 81–82, 108–109, 113, 127, 131, 141–142, 150, 166, 167
California Learning Assessment System (CLES), 108–109
Callahan, K. A., 94–95, 164
Calvo, N. A., 60
Campbell, R. F., 37
Cannell, J. J., 184
Carey-Lewis, C., 171, 172
Carnegie Corporation, 82
Carnegie Forum for the Advancement of Teaching, 116
Carter, S. C., 57
Caufman, K. D., 174
Center for Policy Research in Education, 85, 91
Center on Education Policy, 20
Central administrative offices, 153–158, 179–180

Certification of teachers, 29, 105, 115–117
Chapman, L., 1
Charter schools, 31, 51–52, 71–72, 82, 87–88, 106, 128, 135–136, 185, 186, 187
Charter Schools Expansion Act (1998), 31
Chicago, Illinois, 58, 72, 81
Christenson, G., 119
Civil rights legislation, 180, 189
Clark, T. A., 80
Clinton, Bill, 24, 31, 34, 35
Clune, W. H., 64, 73, 91, 104, 113, 130
Coalition of Essential Schools, 86
Cobb, V. L., 116
Cognitive lag, 11
Cohen, D. K., 1, 14, 44, 79, 113, 164, 167
Cohen, M., 55
Coherent policy (Fuhrman), 5
Coleman, J. S., 55, 59
Coleman Report, 55
College education, 44, 77, 119–122
College Entrance Examination Board (CEEB; College Board), 77–79, 118
Colorado, 119
Commission on Student Learning (Washington State), 139–140, 141
Commission on the Skills of the American Work Force, 23, 66, 80, 128
Commissions, 138–143
  examples of, 139–142
  governance implications of, 142–143
  national, 23, 66, 80, 128, 138
  state, 139–143, 149
Committee for Economic Development, 23
Common Schools, 18
Comparator bands, 161
Compliance-oriented implementation, 91–92
Comprehensive School Reform Demonstration Program, 24

Conant, James Bryant, 67–68
Conley, D. T., 1, 11, 14, 45, 49, 60, 81, 85–87, 91, 94–96, 110, 118–122, 140, 161, 164, 168, 170
Connecticut, 111, 150, 152, 163
Consolidation, of school districts, 9–10, 150
Content standards, 43–44, 106, 111, 117
Continuous improvement, 75
Corbett, H. D., 169
Corcoran, T., 154–155, 173
Core technologies of schools, 92
Cornett, L. M., 114–115
Council of Chief State School Officers, 46, 76
Counseling programs, 98
Cowart, B., 117
Cuban, L., 40, 72, 89, 90, 96, 115
Cunningham, L. L., 37
Curriculum
 influence of educational policies on, 1, 2–3
 international comparisons of, 2, 58
 local school board and, 148–149
Cushman, K., 120

D'Agostino, J. V., 192
Daley, B., 94
Dallas, Texas, 114
Danielson, C., 170, 171
Darling-Hammond, L., 25, 106, 116, 117, 164, 171
David, J. L., 49, 50, 134
Davis, Gray, 127
Davis, M., 1
DeBray, E. H., 166
Decentralization, 16, 25, 49–51, 73, 75, 77, 105, 154–155
Delaware, 172
Democrats, 8–9
Denenberg, A., 108
Desegregation, 3, 21–22
Discrimination, 19
*Dispelling the Myth* (Barth et al.), 57
Doyle, D. P., 80, 188

Driver, C. E., 11, 88, 181–182
Duffy, M. C., 1, 26, 69–70, 184
DuFour, R., 163

Eaker, R. E., 163
Economic development, 66–67, 80–81, 129
Economic productivity goals, 23
Edison Corporation, 150, 185
Edmonds, R. R., 55
Educational Testing Service (ETS), 77–79, 118, 171
Education Commission of the States, 5, 43, 70, 76, 80, 176
Education Consolidation and Improvement Act (ECIA), 25
Education Flexibility Partnership Demonstration Program (Ed-Flex), 25, 30
Education for All Handicapped Children Act (1975), 22
Education Trust, 57
*Education Week*, 1, 111, 193
Effective principals, 160, 161
Effective schools research, 56–58, 145, 197–198
Elam, S. M., 6, 71
Elementary and Secondary Education Act (ESEA; 1965), 21, 133
 reauthorization of 2001, 2, 24, 27–31, 35, 70, 75, 76, 81, 192
Ellett, C. D., 171, 172
Elmore, R. F., 14, 43, 48, 73, 84–85, 91, 92, 164, 166, 181
Equalization, 147–148
Equal protection clause, 38–39
Equity issues, 19–20, 21, 32–33, 39, 43, 54, 68, 192
Erbstein, N., 86, 95, 163
ERIC Clearinghouse on Educational Management, 55
Ericson, J., 128, 188
Evans, W., 40

Fairman, J., 1, 27, 111–112
Family role in education, 17

Fantini, M., 49
Federal role in educational policy
  equity issues and, 19–20, 21, 32–33,
    39, 43, 54, 68, 192
  finance systems and, 27, 28, 192–
    193
  future decline in, 36–37
  impact on local practices, 24–26,
    73–75
  impact on states, 26–27, 34–36
  national educational goals, 54
  need for new governance systems,
    198–199
  new relationship with states, 34–36
  new role, 192–193
  social goals and, 19–26
  sustainability of, 33–34
  trend toward, 1, 2–3, 26–33, 73–75
Fenstermacher, G. D., 113
Finn, C. E., Jr., 31
Firestone, W. A., 1, 27, 93, 111–113
First International Mathematics and
  Science Study, 2
First in the World Consortium, 58
Flanagan, A., 184
Flanigan, J., 56
Florida, 48, 100, 127
Ford Foundation, 82
Foundations, 82–83, 113, 124
Fowler, F. C., 76
Franchises, educational, 193–196
Freeman, D. J., 70
Fry, P. O., 48
Fuhrman, S. H., 1, 5, 14, 40, 43–45,
  48, 69, 73, 91, 93, 103, 104, 114,
  154–155, 166, 168, 173, 179, 181
Fullan, M. G., 88, 176

Gaines, G. F., 114–115
"Gain score" models, 184
Gallup, A. M., 6, 71, 185
Gamoran, A., 105
Gates Foundation, 82
Gender equity, 21–22
Georgia, 123, 127–128, 129, 163–164
Gerstner, Louis V., Jr., 80

Gewertz, C., 52, 68, 149
Gittell, M., 49
Glatthorn, A. A., 104
Goals 2000, 35
Goals of public education, 19–26, 54,
  66–68, 91–92, 190–191
Goertz, M. E., 1, 26, 27, 30–31, 34–
  35, 50, 69–70, 112, 117, 180–
  182, 184
Goldman, P., 14, 45, 85–87, 91, 94,
  110, 161, 164
Goldstein, D., 46
Goodlad, J. I., 86, 105
Goodman, K., 9
Goodman, R. H., 144
Gordon, J., 80
Governors
  partisan nature of, 8–9, 23–24
  role in educational reform, 126–129,
    131–132, 140, 146–147
Grading, 105, 168–170
Grant, G., 55
Grant, S. G., 9, 134
Greenwald, R., 60
Grissmer, D., 184
Grolnick, M., 113
Grossman, P., 4, 121
Grouping strategies, 67–68, 87, 93
Guskey, T. R., 176
Guthrie, J. W., 4, 49, 60

Haeger, J., 123
Hallinger, P., 159–160
Halperin, S., 35
Hanks, D. B., 128
Hanushek, E. A., 60
Hardin, B., 1
Harp, L., 66, 81
Harrington, K., 117
Harrington-Leuker, D., 114, 169
Hartford, Connecticut, 150
Hattie, J., 172
Haycock, K., 57, 192
Heck, R. H., 159–160
Hedges, L. V., 60
Heneman, H., III, 114

Henry, R. J., 123
Herndon, R., 80
Hess, A., 50
Hess, R., 87, 91
Higher Education Amendments
    (1998), 30–31, 116
High-performing schools, 56–58
High-school college connections, 77,
    119–122
High-stakes testing, 46, 73, 77–79,
    164, 184
Hill, H. C., 1, 14, 44, 113, 164, 167
Hill, P., 149
Hillocks, G., Jr., 169
Hirth, M., 1
Hoff, D. J., 58, 81, 91, 106, 129, 184
Holayter, M. C., 139
Holmes Group, 116
Hoppe, D., 46, 85–86, 96, 97
Horn, S. P., 114, 166, 170, 171
Hoxby, C., 181
Hudgins, H. C., Jr., 32–33, 180

Illinois, 58, 72, 81, 123
Immerwahr, J., 66, 70
Incentive systems, 14, 87–88, 114–
    115, 170–171, 172–173
Individuals with Disabilities Education
    Act (IDEA), 2–3
Integration, 3, 21–22
Intensification model, 4, 42–45, 93–
    94, 121
Interest groups in education, 7, 106
International achievement standards,
    2, 58
Interstate New Teacher Assessment
    and Support Consortium, 171
Iowa, 104
Iron triangle, 8–9

Jackson, H., 57
Jacobson, L., 128, 129
Jaeger, R., 172
Jantzi, D., 50
Jennings, N. E., 86, 87, 110, 112
Job training goals, 20–21

Johnson, J., 66, 70
Johnson, M. J., 176
Johnson, P. E., 176
Johnson, S. M., 168
Johnston, R. C., 10, 14, 72, 73, 81–
    82, 126, 127, 131, 132
Joint Center for the Study of
    Educational Policy, 97
Jones, B. D., 1
Jones, M. G., 1
Joyner, C. C., 25
Just for the Kids, 10, 184

Kamprath, N., 128, 188
Kannapel, P. J., 9, 97
Kansas, 106
Kawata, J., 184
Kearns, David, 80
Kelleghan, T., 55
Keller, B., 42, 146–147, 184
Kelley, C., 114
Kellogg Foundation, 82
Kentucky, 12–13, 14, 40, 46, 49, 54,
    81, 93, 109, 123, 128, 139, 141,
    157
Kerchner, C., 174
Kettlewell, J. S., 123
Kimmelman, P., 58
King, R. A., 114
Kirby, S. N., 89
Kirkpatrick, J., 80
Kirp, D. L., 11, 88, 181–182
Kirst, M. W., 4, 7, 9, 46, 52, 64, 71,
    72, 85–86, 93, 95–97, 118, 121,
    149
Kitzhaber, John, 127
Klecker, B., 11
Klein, S. P., 171
Koppoch, J., 174
Koretz, D., 107, 169
Kozol, J., 68
Kranz, J., 50
Kroeze, D., 58

Lacey, R. A., 80
Ladd, H. F., 14

Ladson-Billings, G., 171
Laine, R. D., 60
"Lake Wobegon" effect, 184
Langesen, D., 46
Lashway, L., 113–114
Lawson, M., 142
Lawton, M., 44, 108
LeFever, K., 73
Legislatures, state, 128–129, 131–132
Leibbrand, J. A., 115
Leithwood, K., 50
Lemann, N., 55, 117
Le Métais, J., 189
Levin, H. M., 55, 86
Levy, F., 60, 95
Licensing standards, 76–77
Lieberman, A., 113
Lipsky, M., 110
Lipton, M., 67
Little, J. W., 86, 90, 95, 163, 173
Loadman, W. E., 11
Local school boards, 144–153. *See
    also* Local school districts
  accountability and, 145–147
  as boards of directors, 152–153
  curriculum changes, 148–149
  "loss" of local control and, 179–180
  relationship with state, 74–75
  school improvement and, 145–148
  urban districts, 52–53, 72–73, 149–
    150
  viability as democratic institutions,
    150–152
Local school districts, 144–158. *See
    also* Local school boards
  accountability systems, 145–147,
    160, 161, 163
  assessment systems, 29
  central administrative offices, 153–
    158, 179–180
  changes in roles, 144–158
  consolidation trend, 9–10, 150
  federal educational policies and, 24–
    26, 73–75
  local control and, 12–13, 16–17, 18
  local superintendents, 13, 153–158

need for new governance systems,
    198–199
  school boards in, 74–75, 144–153
  site-based management, 49–51, 55
  state educational policies and, 4–5,
    11–14, 18–19, 45, 49–51, 58–
    59, 84–102
  trend away from policy role, 1
Local superintendents, 153–158
  impact of state educational policies
    on, 13
  multiple demands on, 153–155
  new skills for, 155–157
  reshaping of system by, 157–158
Logan, J., 176
Los Angeles Unified School District,
    150
Lowi, T. J., 91, 93, 97
Lusi, S. F., 45, 132–134

Madaus, G. F., 55
Malen, B., 49, 50
Malico, M. K., 31
Mann, A., 80
Mann, Horace, 18
Manno, B. V., 31
Manzo, K. K., 81
Marks, E. L., 25
Marks, H. M., 176
Marsh, D. D., 73
Maryland, 123–124, 146–147, 150
Marzano, R., 55–56
Massachusetts, 17, 18, 40, 81, 93–94,
    111, 169
Massell, D., 44, 46, 85–86, 96, 97, 155
Mathematics
  annual statewide assessments in, 28
  international comparisons, 2, 58
Mathers, J. K., 114
Mathews, J., 170
Maughan, B., 55
Mayors, 153
Mayrowetz, D., 1, 27, 111–112
McDermott, K. A., 109
McGreal, T. L., 86
McKelvey, C., 89

McLaughlin, M. W., 73, 84–85
McMillan, J. H., 168
McNeely, M., 58
McQuaide, J., 9
McQueen, A., 24
Meier, D., 55, 115
Memphis, Tennessee, 89
Mertens, S., 116
Michigan, 51, 131–132
Milanowski, A., 114
Miles, M., 176
Miller, S. K., 56
Miller-Whitehead, M., 166
*Milliken v. Bradley*, 32–33
Millkin Foundation, 82
Minimum competency, 67
Minnesota, 119
Mintrom, M., 186, 188
Mirel, J. E., 120
Mississippi, 129
Missouri, 123
Mohrman, S. A., 50, 95
Montana, 104
Mora, K., 57
Morin, R., 8, 71
Mortimore, P., 55
Murnane, R., 60, 95
Murphy, J., 49, 53, 157
Murray, C. E., 174
Murray, S., 40
Myers, C. B., 116

Naftel, S., 89
Nash, S., 168
Nasstrom, R. R., 119
National Alliance of Business, 80–81, 120
National Assessment of Educational Progress (NAEP), 2, 28, 44, 70
National Association of Secondary School Principals, 76
National Board for Professional Teaching Standards (NBPTS), 76, 171–172
National Center for Educational Accountability, 184

National Center for Education Statistics, 40, 120
National Center on Education and the Economy, 23
National Commission on Excellence in Education, 138
National Conference of State Legislatures, 76
National Defense Education Act (1957), 21
National Education Association (NEA), 33–34, 76
National Governors Association, 76
National Network for Educational Renewal, 86
National School Boards Association, 76
National Science Foundation, 82–83, 113
National security goals, 21
*Nation at Risk, A*, 6, 22–23, 26, 70, 138
Nelson, F. H., 128, 174, 188
Networks
    of educators, 112–113, 161
    of schools, 196–197
New American Schools, 89
Newark, New Jersey, 52
New educational equity, 54
New Haven, Connecticut, 52
New Jersey, 41, 52, 54, 193
Newmann, F. M., 95
New York City, 53, 82, 124, 150
New York state, 81, 131, 166
"No Child Left Behind" Act (2001), 2, 24, 27–31, 70, 75, 76, 81, 192
*No Excuses* (Carter), 57
Nolte, M. C., 180
Nongovernmental influences on educational policy, 75–83
    business community, 6–7, 20–21, 34, 79–81
    foundations, 82–83, 113, 124
    parents, 57, 81–82, 187
    quasi-governmental and nongovernmental agencies, 76–77
    testing organizations, 77–79, 118, 171

Norris, D., 80
North Carolina, 14, 93, 163, 169
North Dakota, 104
Nystrand, R. O., 37

Oakes, J., 67, 105
Obey-Porter bill, 24
Odden, A., 3, 4, 33, 40, 41, 50, 73,
    91, 95, 114, 170, 176, 181
Office of Educational Research and
    Improvement, 160
Office of Elementary and Secondary
    Education, 24, 25
Ogawa, R. T., 49, 50
Ohanian, S., 106, 115, 164, 169
Olson, L., 1, 47, 48, 70, 111–112,
    121, 124, 164, 169–170, 172, 181
Opportunity to learn standards, 43–44
Oregon, 48, 49, 60–63, 66–67, 80, 81,
    117, 122–123, 127, 128, 140–
    141, 172
    Oregon Proficiency-based Admission
        Standards System (PASS), 122–
        123
    Oregon Quality Education Model
        (OQEM), 60–63, 140–141
Orfield, G., 166
Organizational structure, 191
Ouston, J., 55
Oxley, D., 163

Page, J. A. E., 67
Pajares, F., 176
Parental involvement, 57, 81–82, 187
Path dependence, 109
Patronage, 18
Pechman, M., 46
Pennell, J. R., 113
Pennsylvania, 17, 52, 81, 82, 149
Performance pay, 87–88
Perot, Ross, 80, 81
Perry, R., 128, 188
Peterson, K. D., 176
Peterson, P., 91
Peterson del Mar, D., 49
Petrie, H. G., 116

Pew Charitable Trusts, 82, 124
Philadelphia, Pennsylvania, 52, 82,
    149
Picus, L. O., 4, 60, 166
Pipho, C., 10
Pitcher, B., 117
Pitsch, M., 35
Plank, D. N., 52, 64
Pliska, A. M., 9
Policy alignment, 103–125
    advantages of, 104–105
    challenges of, 125
    defining, 103
    disadvantages of, 105–107
    implementing, 110
    K-16 programs, 117–122
    levers for, 111–117
    limitations of, 107–110
    national projects in, 124
    P-16 programs, 122–124
Politicization of education, 8–9, 18–
    19, 23–24, 70–72, 129
Pool, H. E., 67
Pool, J. E., 171, 172
Popkewitz, T. S., 19, 50
Porter, A. C., 105
Poverty, 6, 21
Power shifts, 11
Prasch, J., 4, 49
Prawat, R. S., 16
Prescott, C., 120
Prestine, N. A., 86
Prichard Committee (Kentucky), 128,
    139, 141
Principals, 159–163
    accountability systems and, 160,
        161, 163
    impact of state educational policies
        on, 13
    as information managers, 162–163
    as networkers, 161
    as policy adapters, 162
    as policy processors and interpreters,
        160–161
    as reluctant partners with states, 177
    shared responsibility and, 163

as site innovators, 162
state expectations for, 59
Professional development, 29–30, 86–87, 89, 172–174
Professionalism, 171–172
Progressive Era, 18–19
Property taxes, 19–20
Public Agenda, 164
Purkey, S., 55
Purposes of public education, 66–68, 189–190

Quality standards, 43–44, 60–63, 75, 80
Quasi-governmental agencies, 76–77

Rabe, B., 91
Racial integration goals, 21–22
Rainwater, T., 118, 122, 123
Raywid, M. A., 120
Reading
    annual statewide assessments in, 28
    scientific, research-based approach to, 29
Reading Excellence Program, 24
Reagan, Ronald, 68
Reckase, M. D., 70
Reeves, D. B., 112
Reid, K. S., 72, 95, 144
Remedial courses, 44
Republicans, 8–9, 23–24
Research and development, 29, 32–33
Resnick, L. B., 66
Rettig, M. D., 72
Reward systems, 14, 87–88, 114–115, 170–171, 172–173
Rhode Island, 40
Ribich, T. I., 55
Richard, A., 127
Riley, Richard, 35
Riordan, R., 120
Robelen, E. W., 28, 31, 35, 75, 189–190
Robertson, P. J., 50, 95
Robinson, S., 57
Rollow, S. G., 163

Rose, L. C., 6, 71, 185
Rosen, M., 174
Rossman, G. B., 40
Rothman, R., 9, 81, 184, 188
Rothstein, R., 36–37, 193
Rouk, U., 184
Ruiz, P., 57
Rustique-Forrester, E., 171
Rutter, M., 55

Sack, J. L., 150, 161, 172
*San Antonio Independent School District v. Rodriguez*, 38
Sanders, W. L., 114, 166, 170, 171
Sandham, J. L., 8–9, 10, 72, 87, 127, 132
Sarason, S., 11, 92
SAT, 44, 77–79, 184
Schalock, D., 117
Schiavone, S., 171, 172
Schmidt, H. W., 16
Schmidt, P., 85
Schmidt, W. H., 44, 58
Schmidt-Posner, J., 4, 121
School choice, 183–188
    charter schools, 31, 51–52, 71–72, 82, 87–88, 106, 128, 135–136, 185, 186, 187
    external contractors, 150, 185
    impact on organizational and governance structures, 185–186
    learning how to govern, 188
    without standards and control, 186–188
    state-local equation and, 183–185
School-level roles, 159–177. *See also* Teachers
    collegiality, 172–174
    principals, 159–163
    regional networks of schools, 196–197
    school-site councils, 49–51, 175–177
    unions, 76, 104, 106–107, 174–175, 179–180
School lunch programs, 97–98

School-site councils, 49–51, 175–177
School to Work Opportunities Act, 35
Schrontz, Frank, 80
Schwab, R., 40
Schwartz, W., 186
Science, international comparisons, 2, 58
Scott, R., 104
Second International Mathematics and Science Study, 2
Secretary's Commission on Achieving Necessary Skills (SCANS), 23, 66, 80, 95
Serrano, 38–39
Serrano II, 38–39
Sexton, R. F., 81, 139
Seymour, L., 95
Shapiro, N. S., 123
Shared responsibility, 163, 166–167
Shedd, J., 174
Shields, C. M., 163
Silverman, D., 128, 188
Siskin, L. S., 90, 164
Site-based management, 49–51, 155
Sizer, T., 86, 187
Skrla, L., 114
Smith, A., 55, 112–113
Smith, A. K., 161
Smith, J. R., 60
Smith, M., 55
Smith, R. E., 107, 169
Smith, T., 172
Smith, W. F., 113
Smith-Hughes Act (1917), 20
Smithson, J., 105
Social capital, 113
Solomon, D., 128, 188
Sommerfeld, M., 127
Souders, J., 120
South Carolina, 129, 163–164
Spillane, J. P., 46, 79, 91–92, 94–95, 110, 164
Spring, J., 96
Standards
  adequacy, 40–41, 60–63
  content, 43–44, 106, 111, 117

for data collection by states, 10–11
grass-roots opposition to, 9
international, 2, 58
licensing, 76–77
opportunity to learn, 43–44
quality, 43–44, 60–63, 75, 80
statewide, 1, 2, 35, 41–44, 46–47, 67
Standards for Success, 124
State boards of education, 128–137
  contradictory goals of, 132–134
  new role of, 130–132
  policy-making at state level, 128–130
  transforming, 134–137
State-local partnerships, 98–102, 183–185
State role in educational policy, 38–63
  accountability systems, 1, 5, 10, 13, 46, 47, 50, 53, 58–60, 68–70, 85, 113–114, 146, 155, 165–166, 169, 181
  assessment systems, 1, 2, 10, 13, 28–29, 35, 47, 69, 85, 111, 146, 181
  changes in roles, 126–143
  charter schools, 51–52
  commissions and, 128, 138–143
  contradictory goals, 132–138
  definition of academic proficiency, 28
  education reform in the 1970s, 38–42
  education reform in the 1980s, 42–45, 121
  education reform in the 1990s, 45–53, 121
  enumeration clause and, 17
  expectations for educational leaders, 58–59
  federal government role and, 26–27, 34–36
  finance systems, 3–4, 5, 19–20, 38–42, 59–63
  forces behind state reforms, 65–75
  governors and, 8–9, 23–24, 126–129, 131–132, 140, 146–147

legislatures and, 128–129, 131–132
local districts and, 4–5, 11–14, 18–19, 45, 49–51, 58–59, 73–75, 84–102
need for new governance systems, 198–199
new roles, 193–198
noneducators and, 7, 71
partisan nature of, 8–9, 18–19, 23–24, 70–72
public pressure to improve schools, 6–7
small-district consolidation, 9–10, 150
standardized data collection systems, 10–11
state board of education and, 128–132
state-district relationships, 11–14, 39–42
state education agencies and, 132–138
state policy implementation, 84–102, 126–130
state superintendent and, 8–9, 128–130, 131, 146–147
statewide academic standards, 1, 2, 35, 41–44, 46–47, 67
term limits and, 7
top-down, bottom-up partnership, 46, 180–183
trend toward, 1, 3–11, 41–42, 53–58, 73–75
urban school districts, 52–53, 72–73, 149–150
waivers and deregulation, 47–49
State superintendents, 8–9, 128–130, 131, 146–147
Steffy, B. E., 11, 13, 40
Stein, R. B., 123
Steinbach, R., 50
Steinberg, A., 120
Steinberg, J., 193
Steinberg, L., 105
Stevens, B., 96, 130
Stevenson, H., 44, 58

Stiegelbauer, S., 88
Stigler, J., 44, 58
Stone, N., 80
Stone, P., 81
Stout, K. E., 96, 130
Stricherz, M., 126–127, 131, 164
Stringfield, S., 55
Swanson, A. D., 49
Systemic reform (Fuhrman), 5

Tan, A., 58
Taylor, D. L., 49
Teachers, 163–177
attitudes toward reform programs, 74, 91–92, 94, 178–179
autonomy of, 159
certification of, 29, 105, 115–117
culture of schools, 90, 159, 172–174
data profiles and, 166–167
evaluation of, 117, 170–171
grading practices, 105, 168–170
impact of state educational policies on, 14, 163–166
incentive systems, 14, 87–88, 114–115, 170–171, 172–173
licensing standards, 76–77
networks of, 112–113, 161
policy alignment and, 111–112
professional development and, 29–30, 86–87, 89, 172–174
professionalism of, 171–172
as reluctant partners with states, 177
role in decision making, 175–177
standards for students, 167–170
teacher education programs, 30–31, 115–117
unions and, 76, 104, 106–107, 174–175, 179–180
Technical assistance, 28, 146
Teddlie, C., 55
Tennessee, 89, 166
Term limits, 7
Texas, 41, 42, 48, 76, 81, 111, 114, 131, 166
Third International Mathematics and Science Study (TIMSS), 2, 58

Thompson, S., 105, 107, 164
Time, as limited resource, 94–95
Title I requirements, 24, 28–31, 69, 75, 88–89, 98, 153–154
Title IX, 2–3
Tobin, W., 147
Toch, T., 80, 81
Top-down, bottom-up partnership, 46, 180–183
Tracking, 67–68, 87, 93
Transformational education policy, 96–98
Tyack, D., 52, 96, 98, 147, 190
Tye, B. B., 92

Unfunded mandate, education reform as, 94
Unions, 76, 104, 106–107, 174–175, 179–180
U.S. Congress, 75
U.S. Constitution, 17, 38–39
U.S. Department of Education, 24, 25, 30, 32, 35, 76, 88–89, 105, 133, 172, 184
U.S. General Accounting Office, 54
U.S. Supreme Court, 38, 180
Urban, W. J., 174
Urban school districts, 52–53, 72–73, 149–150
Usdan, M. D., 37
Utah, 193

Values of education, 19, 180, 189
Valverde, G. A., 44
van der Ploeg, A., 58
Van Kirk, A. N., 50, 95
Vanourek, G., 31
Vergari, S., 135
Vergon, C. B., 32
Vermont, 113
Verstegen, D. A., 25, 39, 40, 42, 54, 180
Viadero, D., 82, 87, 89, 111–112, 172
Virginia, 81
Vocational Education Act (1963), 20–21
Vouchers, 31–32, 71–72

Walker, L., 86, 95, 163
Warren, V. D., 176
Washington State, 12, 119, 124, 139–140, 141
Watt, M. G., 168
Watts, H. W., 55
Weeres, J., 174
Weick, K., 12, 164
Weisman, J., 80
Weiss, C. H., 176
Weiss, E. M., 171
Weiss, S. G., 66, 70–72, 171
Wells, A. S., 105
Wenglinsky, H. H., 116
West Virginia, 40
Whitbread, N., 55
White, K. A., 112
White, P. A., 105
Whitney, T. N., 39
Wilkins, A., 57
Williams, A., 107, 169
Williams, B., 172
Williamson, S., 184
Wilson, A., 55
Wilson, B. L., 169
Wirt, F. M., 7, 9, 52, 71, 95–96
Wirt, J. G., 66
Wise, A. E., 115, 171
Wohlstetter, P., 3, 50, 95, 112–113, 161
Wong, K., 91
Wyoming, 40

Xu, M., 106

Yanguas, M. J., 163
Yarbrough, T., 1
Yarger, S., 116
Yee, G., 72
Young, S., 68

Zernike, K., 117
Zeuli, J. S., 46, 91–92, 110
Ziebarth, T., 118, 122, 128, 149
Zimmerman, J., 80
Zimmerman, William G. Jr., 144
Zirkel, P. A., 180

# ABOUT THE AUTHOR

**David T. Conley** is an Associate Professor in the area of Educational leadership and Policy at the University of Oregon. He is the founder and director of the Center for Educational Policy Research. He received his bachelor's degree from the University of California, Berkeley, and his master's and doctoral degrees from the University of Colorado, Boulder. His research interests include educational standards and assessments, high school-college alignment and articulation, high school restructuring, adequacy-based funding models, and educational governance structures. His family includes his wife, Judy, and his three daughters, Robyn, Laurel, and Genevieve.